Gender in World History

'A comparative history of immense ambition . . . [It] will be profitably consulted by gender historians. It successfully demonstrates that gender is a historical construct that is rebuilt by each generation and varies from culture to culture.' *Journal of Contemporary History*

Covering societies from classical times to the twenty-first century, *Gender in World History* is a fascinating exploration of what happens to established ideas about men and women, and their roles, when different cultural systems come into contact. This book breaks new ground to facilitate a consistent approach to gender in a world history context.

This second edition is completely updated, including:

- expanded introductions to each chronological section
- extensive discussion of the contemporary era bringing it right up to date
- new chapters on international influences in the first half of the twentieth century and globalization in the latter part of the twentieth century
- engagement with the recent work done on gender history and theory.

Coming right up to the present day, *Gender in World History* is essential reading for students of world history.

Peter N. Stearns is Provost and Professor of History at George Mason University. His books include *The Other Side of Western Civilization* (5th edition, 1999), *Childhood in World History* (Routledge, 2005) and *Consumerism in World History* (2nd edition, Routlege, 2006).

Themes in World History
Series editor: Peter N. Stearns

The *Themes in World History* series offers focused treatment of a range of human experiences and institutions in the world history context. The purpose is to provide serious, if brief, discussions of important topics as additions to textbook coverage and document collections. The treatments will allow students to probe particular facets of the human story in greater depth than textbook coverage allows, and to gain a fuller sense of historians' analytical methods and debates in the process. Each topic is handled over time – allowing discussions of changes and continuities. Each topic is assessed in terms of a range of different societies and religions – allowing comparisons of relevant similarities and differences. Each book in the series helps readers deal with world history in action, evaluating global contexts as they work through some of the key components of human society and human life.

Gender in World History

2nd Edition

Peter N. Stearns

Routledge
Taylor & Francis Group

NEW YORK AND LONDON

First published in 2000
by Routledge
270 Madison Avenue, New York, NY 10016

Simultaneously published in the UK
by Routledge
2 Park Square, Milton Park, Abingdon, Oxon OX14 4RN

Reprinted 2002, 2005

2nd Edition 2006

Transferred to Digital Printing 2006

Routledge is an imprint of the Taylor & Francis Group, an informa business

@ 2000, 2006 Peter N. Stearns

Typeset in Garamond by
Keystroke, Jacaranda Lodge, Wolverhampton
Printed and bound in Great Britain by
CPI Antony Rowe, Chippenham, Wiltshire

British Library Cataloguing in Publication Data
A catalogue record for this book is available from the British Library

Library of Congress Cataloging in Publication Data
Stearns, Peter N.
  Gender in world history / Peter N. Stearns. – 2nd ed.
    p. cm. – (Themes in world history)
I. Sex role–History. 2. Man-woman relationships–History. 3. Sex
differences–History. I. Title. II. Series.
  HQ1075.S73 2006
  305.309–dc22

                                        2005026249

ISBN10: 0–415–39588–7 (hbk)
ISBN10: 0–415–39589–5 (pbk)
ISBN10: 0–203–969898 (ebk)

ISBN13: 978–0–415–39588–5 (hbk)
ISBN13: 978–0–415–39589–2 (pbk)
ISBN13: 978–0–203–96989–2 (ebk)

For Deborah, Clio, Cordelia and Mary with love and thanks

Contents

Acknowledgements

My thanks to Tom Sweterlitsch and Veronica Fletcher, for splendid work as research assistants on this book, and to Joanne Ursenbach, Debbie Williams and Crescent Bennett for help with the manuscript. Thanks also to the many world history students and colleagues at George Mason University for contributing to new ideas about teaching this subject. I am grateful to several anonymous readers for good suggestions toward the revised edition, and to the Routledge editors for encouragement and support.

P.N.S.

Introduction

France invaded Vietnam in the later nineteenth century. Its motivations were economic and strategic, though there were wider, romantic fascinations with the Pacific in the minds of many leaders. Consequences of France's colonial administration would include the spread of plantations producing rubber, a wealthy class of colonial owners and administrators and, ultimately, fierce and successful Vietnamese anti-colonialism.

Consequences also included new visions of gender. French officials in Vietnam became quickly confused by how the Vietnamese seemed to look, and their confusion was enhanced by a sense of superiority rooted in conquest. The men, first of all, seemed effeminate. They were small-boned and slender. Their faces seemed hairless: as a French military doctor noted, "The absence of beards and the general appearance hardly permit us to distinguish the sexes". Vietnamese soldiers, with colorful and unfamiliar costumes, looked like "women costumed for circus pantomime". It was easy to ridicule the vanquished in gender terms. The French were also fascinated by eunuchs in the Vietnamese royal court – officials who had been castrated so they could not trouble women in the royal family, a widespread tradition in various parts of Asia that was actually being phased out in Vietnam. Eunuchs were described as "human monsters", with the vices of both sexes. Add to this a standard conqueror fear that Vietnamese men were dangerously oversexed – even though this did not at all comport with the idea of effeminacy – and the sense of weirdness could be overwhelming, though also easily justifying the belief that superior French people should rule.

Women were also scrutinized. First impressions, by upper-class French officials, emphasized how ugly Vietnamese women were – thick bodied, devoted to physical labor (as were French peasant women, but the officials rarely saw them). "A man or a woman?" one French intellectual asked: "In this country, one never knows: same costume, same ugliness." But women – again, the contradictions, held together only by the belief in superiority – were also sexually immoral, libertines, easily induced into affairs with the colonialists. There was a widespread belief that many Vietnamese families indulged in incest, so few young girls could avoid molestation.

By 1900, with French administration fully established, another voice was heard: French women resident in the colonies. They viewed themselves as representing French civilization, eager to set up households that looked just like those back home (though with more local servants, of course, since they were cheap). They disliked Vietnamese women who formed relationships with French men – as an observer (male) put it, "Some of them display a ferocious jealousy in this regard". They were eager to promote efforts to teach Vietnamese women European-style respectability and domesticity, even though this often involved more emphasis on subservience to fathers and husbands than the Vietnamese themselves had urged.

Here, then, was massive gender contact. Europeans had firm gender standards at this point, emphasizing how different men and women were. This fact, plus their status as nervous conquerors, made it easy to find another gender system strange and reprehensible, though also sometimes exciting. Weirdness and exaggeration are common features when one society encounters the gender standards of another. So, when conquest is involved, are efforts to run down local masculinity. Habits of colonial administration, from underrating the local military to assuming that local women want sexual relationships, are powerful results of these kinds of contacts.

What about the other part of the exchange? Some Vietnamese would deeply resent French attitudes. Others might seek to adjust gender behavior, including styles of dress, to appear more respectable, and this could have frivolous, or demeaning, or liberating results, depending on the situation. Some would be eager to reassert older standards, including a sense of proud masculinity; this would factor into later anti-colonial violence, when a colonial tendency to discount military prowess might also make resistance easier. It was unlikely that gender standards, either for those in occupation or for those being occupied, could ever return to their pre-contact levels.

Contact possibilities have many faces. A society that stresses women's deference may encounter one that believes women are more moral than men. A society that values masculinity but in which men are relatively short may meet another society that thinks masculinity is only truly possible when men are tall. A society tolerant of homosexuality may meet one rigorously repressive. The permutations are numerous, intriguing, and often extremely important in defining relationships between societies and in stimulating change in gender standards when contact occurs.

This book deals with the interactions between definitions of male and female, and the roles assigned to men and women, on the one hand, and encounters between different cultures, on the other. In focusing on these interactions, it emphasizes two of the liveliest topics in historical research in recent decades, and brings them to bear on the field of world history.

The rise of contemporary feminism in Western society, from the 1960s onward, plus the huge changes in women's work and home roles have spurred a massive, exciting inquiry into women's conditions in the past and into how past patterns have conditioned current responses. Increasingly, this inquiry has also spilled over into men's roles – in the history of both genders – if only because neither gender can be understood without comparison to the other. Historians have shown the great variety of definitions of femininity and masculinity, and how these relate to the ways societies function not only in family life, but also in political institutions and economic activities. They have examined how recommended gender standards influence actual behavior, though also how, in many societies, many individual men and women insist on different patterns. And they have explored how gender standards can change – as in the revolution in women's work roles, in Western Europe and the United States, during the past half century.

Many scholars have also shown how gender affects far more than the standards of masculinity and femininity or male–female relations. Larger social systems both reflect and implement gender norms. This means that political institutions, even military organizations, are shaped in part by gender assumptions. We shall see that inter-regional contacts, like Western colonialism, often reached deeply into the societies involved through their gender assumptions. Or, to take an example vital to American social life, how much does the nation's strong valuation of guns follow from larger assumptions (and, some would argue, insecurities) about what it takes to be a man?

Historical research on gender and its impact has explored a wide variety of societies, besides the West, bringing gender history and world history into increasing contact with each other. Various gender patterns have been compared as a means of testing important differences and similarities in the ways men and women define themselves and their functions in life. General trends have been explored. For example, it is usually agreed that inequality between men and women increases when societies shift their economic activities from hunting and gathering to agriculture. Further, as agricultural civilizations become more prosperous, with stronger governments, gender inequalities, particularly in the upper classes, tend to increase still more, as men try to press women to become more purely domestic in function, more dependent on the family and more decorative. Dynamics of this sort have helped merge gender history and world history, even though most world histories until recently have downplayed gender issues in their focus on the activities of largely male political elites and intellectuals. It remains true, however, that gender issues are usually considered within particular societies, rather than across boundaries, which is one of the reasons it has sometimes proved difficult to merge gender and world history. This book opens the topic up to see how elements of gender formulations, the definitions of what men and women are and do, respond to international forces.

Growing attention to world history has not matched the outpouring of historical research on gender, but it has produced important developments in its own right. One key area of inquiry has focused on the range and variety of contacts among major societies, through migration, trade, missionary activity and other means. Instead of consisting mainly of the separate histories of one civilization after another, world history is increasingly seen in terms of shared processes and contacts. Important studies have shown the range of early trade routes and the impact of the diffusion of ideas. While the intensity and scope of international contacts have increased in modern centuries, making this approach still more important in defining world history, the themes of exchange and interaction help define earlier periods as well. Thus historians have explored the cultural implications of Alexander the Great's conquests in the Middle East and northwestern India: what impact did Greek styles and ideas have on Persia and India, and vice versa? They have probed the interactions between Islam and sub-Saharan Africa, noting that while Islam clearly found an audience in various parts of Africa it did not necessarily win full conversion to the social and cultural standards of the Middle East.

In general, contact among two or more different societies is seen as potentially fruitful, in opening possibilities for imitation and innovation, but also tense and complex. Few societies ever convert quickly or fully to the patterns of another, even amid extensive contact or outright conquest. Much more common is a set of compromises, called syncretism, in which local beliefs are merged with some of the ideas brought in through contact, even when the fusion unites seemingly incompatible elements. Thus Indians in Central America converted sincerely to Catholicism, under Spanish pressure in the sixteenth and seventeenth centuries, but also preserved rituals and gods from more traditional religion that were explicitly attacked by their missionary tutors.

Clearly, both gender roles and cultural contacts form vital parts of world history. Equally clearly, thanks to the expansion of historical knowledge in recent decades, we know quite a bit about each topic area. This book unites the topics, as a means of relating gender history more fully to common world history themes. The goal is to show how international contacts affected some of the more deeply rooted aspects of the societies involved – the aspects embraced by standards of masculinity and femininity, and their relationship.

Gender values are deeply personal, part of individual and social identity. People may be particularly reluctant to surrender the standards defining femininity and masculinity, even when pressed by a society that seems exceptionally powerful and successful, or they may seek ways to compensate for any concessions that must be made. At the same time, representatives of an active trading or missionary society may form strong judgments about a region if they disapprove of the way women are treated or allowed to behave. Thus Arab travelers in Africa frequently lamented the way women acted, in societies they otherwise esteemed. Japanese visitors to the United States in the nineteenth century particularly singled out women's independence as a feature they found questionable (in a period when, by contemporary American standards, women are often regarded as repressed). Frequently, in fact, not only judgments but also myths about outlandish gender patterns are a crucial product of international contact – like the stories about Amazon tribes of women warriors that circulated in ancient Greece or some of the impressions of freewheeling sexuality retailed by Western anthropologists visiting Pacific islands even in our own century. Gender values are so important that they serve as something of a touchstone in figuring out what international contacts are all about.

Comparison of international interactions affecting gender reveals much about the values of all the societies involved – whether the society is being influenced by, forming judgments about, or even resisting outright an alternative set of standards. This book tells a set of stories about ways in which gender values and cultural contacts have interacted, as part of the stuff of world history ever since records became sufficiently abundant for the topic to be explored. The result is a more human face on otherwise somewhat abstract episodes about when Greece and India encountered each other, or when Christian missionaries moved into nineteenth-century Korea – where the meaning of outside religious pressures can be measured in part by their complex consequences in the lives of Korean men and women.

Ultimately, however, the book seeks to do more than unite key topics in world history. It also asks questions about change over time. Have societies become more or less open to outside influences on gender patterns, as international contacts have increased? Has tolerance for diversity in gender relations increased or decreased over time? What can we learn from past episodes in our own age, when a host of international agencies (including feminist groups) now deliberately try to alter gender standards in particular societies judged as harsh or backward? Are gender relations in fact becoming more uniform, as global interactions proliferate – or is insistence on distinctive gender values, distinctive definitions of masculinity and femininity, one of the ways particular societies seek to preserve a sense of identity, precisely because outside influences become steadily more visible? These questions require careful historical analysis, after the data are presented in individual case studies.

Whether in particular historical episodes or in higher-level analysis of patterns over time, the inherent drama of the interaction must be preserved. Many societies are quite sure they know what manhood and womanhood are all about. What happens when they encounter influential or persistent strangers who tell them they are wrong? This is an old drama, which continues in the liveliest fashion today. Some societies prove open to influence. Others divide, with certain groups responding, others pulling back. Still others try to resist entirely. And, finally, some societies, seeking to resist outside influence on matters so personal, actually change in trying to highlight traditional emphases. The options are complex, precisely because the problems slice so deeply into individual and collective identities.

Initial chapters of the book set the stage, in terms of gender traditions and cultural contacts alike. To understand the impact of contacts on beliefs about femininity and masculinity, we begin, in Chapter 1, by setting out some well-established civilization patterns concerning gender. Classical China, India and the Mediterranean all maintained systems of male dominance or patriarchalism, but they emphasized different specifics and detailed mechanisms, in relation to dominant cultural values. These gender systems suggest some clues as to how outside influences might be received – and also how the classical civilizations themselves might influence other regions.

Part I turns to interactions involving major civilizations during the classical and postclassical periods. Chapters 2 and 3 look at some relatively early contacts among civilizations, and how these could affect artistic representations of men or women, or generate a mixture of myth and fancy about how other people operated in this vital area. Early travelers' accounts, for example, highlighed shocking tales about outlandish women, an indication of how gender could be used to shape opinions about strangeness more generally. During the classical period itself (1000 BCE–450 CE), contacts between the eastern and western Mediterranean suggested how certain influences might affect women, when well-established cultures greeted those in a more formative stage. And the spread of Buddhism from India to China marked the first time two major statements of gender interacted directly, with intriguing results.

The next chapters examine developments during the postclassical period (450–1450). Here, three kinds of contact predominated and sometimes interacted. Most obviously, the further spread of missionary religions raised vital issues in places like Africa, India, Central Asia, or Russia. How would local ideas about men and women interact with solemn statements from major religious systems, often backed up by religious laws? The outreach of Islam, the most dynamic religion in the period, is particularly revealing here, and it continued into succeeding centuries, particularly with Turkish expansion into southeastern Europe. Relatedly, many societies in the postclassical period imitated more powerful neighbors. The impact of imitation can be particularly explored by looking at China's effect on the less rigid hierarchy between men and women that had characterized Japan. Finally, interactions between nomadic peoples and settled agricultural societies created some interesting tensions and mutual judgments, particularly during the momentous centuries of Mongol expansion.

Chapters in Part II turn to the influences emanating from Western Europe, which were crucial to a new set of contacts and imitations that opened up in the centuries after 1450. Russia began borrowing from Western culture, with interesting implications where ideas about men and women were concerned. Western influence also affected certain parts of Asia, as with the Spanish conquest of the Philippines and, later, British activities in India. Finally, of course, the colonization of the Americas brought important if implicit debates among colonizers, native Americans and imported slaves about what gender should mean. The growing outreach from Western Europe should be compared with the results of more varied contacts in the previous period. Did the West make a consistent difference in the societies it influenced? Was there indeed a clear Western gender model?

Later chapters in this section turn to the nineteenth century, where the story remains focused on Western influence but with three differences from the early modern centuries. First, the influence was far more wide-ranging, as Western intervention began to affect Pacific Oceania and New Zealand, China, Korea and Japan, and Africa. More societies had to make decisions about what to do concerning Western standards and Western criticisms. Second, Western gender patterns themselves were changing rapidly, raising interesting questions about what models to imitate. On the whole, challenges to the traditions of agricultural civilizations increased precisely because Europeans were building new ideas about what it was proper for men and for women to do. Finally, Western judgments about other societies in terms of how they dealt with issues of masculinity and femininity became more confident and patronizing, which put significant pressure on some of the societies involved. It was harder to escape some awareness of Western judgments, at least in urban areas throughout the world. While some of the most obvious tensions related to disagreements about female respectability, there were important repercussions concerning masculinity as well, sometimes with some unexpected consequences as societies tried to outdo the West in masculine assertiveness. Never had gender standards been subjected to such sweeping outside influences.

The interactions between gender traditions and international influence continued of course in the twentieth century, heightened by the development of larger feminist movements, and the impact of international organizations such as the United Nations (with its sponsorship of global conferences on the status of women, a first in world history), but also the new capacity of various societies to reassert their own identities in an age of decolonization. These developments form the themes of Part III. Larger strands of immigration across cultural lines – for example from Asia to the United States, or from North Africa to Europe – raised a special set of conflicts over gender values. The chapters in Part III deal with immigration, with the Middle East as a complex specific case, with new kinds of influences flowing from formal global movements including communism, and with the rise of an international popular culture and the broader process of globalization. Collectively, they provide a chance to discuss whether a characteristic "modern" pattern of interaction between contact and gender was emerging, in contrast to the kinds of episodes discussed in Parts I and II. Does international now mean liberating, or is this formula becoming too simplistic? Has tolerance for outside example increased or decreased over time? And is there a pattern emerging that suggests future directions, as the world continues to shrink but debates over men's and women's roles still rage?

The cases selected for this book are hardly exhaustive. Other instances of contact have been important. The cases are, however, significant and in many ways representative. They also feed the crucial larger focus – on change over time, or the lack thereof. The contacts discussed in Part I involve agricultural civilizations, sometimes in interaction with nomadic societies. With some exceptions, interactions in this context tended to heighten gender inequalities. Chapters in Parts II and III involve interactions between commercial, often industrializing, societies with agricultural or economically "developing" civilizations. Against the backdrop of Part I, has the dynamic become different, with new opportunities for liberation rather than rigidification – or are the patterns more complex than this formula would allow? Looking at gender in world history through exchanges among societies provides the basis for fundamental analysis about the directions of change.

Three final points. The book focuses on gender, which involves roles and definitions of men as well as of women. More attention goes to women, because more direct information is available about how women have defined themselves or been defined; but men and masculinity are involved as well. It is the balance between women and men, rather than either sex separately, that ultimately counts. As historians have moved from initial interests in women's history, to the more encompassing gender history, this interaction is exactly what they have sought.

Evaluations in the book assume that relative equality between the sexes is a "good" thing, which is a modern and not uncontested value. It is in this sense that some chapters use words like "improvement" or "deterioration". People who believe that one sex or the other ought to be superior can still read the book with profit, simply agreeing to disagree about some of the assessments. The book does not assume, however, that it is easy to figure out what gender system best promotes women's status. Current Western feminist definitions are important but they are not the only measure. Some systems that seem strange by modern Western standards may have worked very well. In this more important sense, the book does not intend to impose easy judgments, which would greatly oversimplify comparisons among societies involved in contact or the analysis of change over time.

The final point, in obvious tension with point two, involves men's characteristic superiority in power throughout world history, at least in terms of cultural standards, laws and economic position, and very often in personal life as well. Bases for this superiority involve physical assertion and the special constraints placed on women by childbearing and at least early care. In some cases, to be sure, women have been able to carve out some authority through force of personality or by using age and social rank as alternative criteria – but their success could actually confirm the larger system, by inhibiting active protest. Historical processes have frequently deepened the system of inequality – certainly agricultural and most nomadic societies have far greater gender gaps than hunting and gathering societies did. Changes in masculinity as well as in femininity are directly involved in shifts of this sort. A key question is how much more modern conditions have improved relationships, as agricultural economies have declined, and how much accelerated international contacts have promoted change. Here, active historical perspective is essential.

Further reading

On France and Vietnam, see Matt Matsuda, *Empire of Love: Histories of France and the Pacific* (New York: Oxford University Press, 2005), and Frank Proschan, "Eunuch Mandarins, Soldats, Effeminate Boys, and Graceless Women: French colonial constructions of Vietnamese genders", *GLO: A Journal of Lesbian and Gay Studies*, 8 (2004): 435–67.

Chapter 1

The traditional base

Civilizations and patriarchy

By the fourth millennium BCE, a number of societies were beginning to move toward that phase of organization called "civilization". While contacts among different groups were virtually as old as the existence of the human species, most early civilizations formed somewhat separately. Mesopotamian civilization, arising after 3500 BCE, thus differed from Egyptian civilization, which emerged soon after in North Africa, not too far to the south. By the fourth millennium BCE also, most agricultural societies had developed new forms of inequality between men and women, in a system often termed patriarchal – with husbands and fathers dominant. Civilizations would usually deepen patriarchy, and at the same time they would define its details in distinctive ways that fitted the wider beliefs and institutions of each individual civilization. In this sense, in putting a particular stamp on patriarchy, each civilization linked gender issues to aspects of their cultural and institutional structure. This chapter, setting the stage for the study of the impact of societal contacts on gender systems, takes up these several developments: civilizations, contacts, patriarchy, and particular patriarchies and exceptions.

Human society began on the basis of small groups of people, in bands of hunters and gatherers. With this structure, people had fanned out into most habitable areas of the world by 12,000 BCE. Then, around 10,000 BCE, in the northern Middle East, agriculture was introduced, radically changing the economic framework for human life in those regions that accepted it. As agriculture spread, many societies formed more stable residential patterns, though there were important groups that continued a hunting and gathering existence or relied on the nomadic herding of animals, as in large stretches of Central Asia. Agriculture also allowed the generation of some surplus production over immediate needs. On the strength of surplus, small numbers of people could specialize in non-agricultural activities, such as craft manufacturing, religion or government. Improvements in agricultural production were gradual, but around 4000 BCE, again initially in and around the Middle East, an important series of inventions ushered in further change, of which the introduction of the wheel and the use of metals, particularly bronze, headed the list. Resulting from this in turn, around 3500 BCE, the first civilization formed in Sumeria, in the Tigris–Euphrates valley. This was soon followed by the establishment of other river-valley civilization centers, along the Nile in Africa, the Indus in northwestern India and the Yellow River in China.

Civilizations differed from other kinds of agricultural societies in that they had formal governments, rather than less explicit and distinct leadership. They relied more on cities, though only a minority of people lived there. They encouraged higher levels of trade. Most of them, also, had writing, which facilitated bureaucratic and commercial activities.

There are two important problems in highlighting civilizations as key units in world history. The first involves recognizing that neither agriculture nor civilization captured all major groups of people, even thousands of years after the form was first established. Nomadic herding groups, in regions like Central Asia, provided a key alternative. So did groups, like many Indian tribes in North America, that combined hunting with transitory, slash-and-burn agriculture. Some of these societies avoided the kind of patriarchy that dominated civilizations. While most nomadic groups also played up the inferiority of women – for women's economic functions declined when gathering was displaced by herding – there were exceptions, with some nomadic societies avoiding full patriarchy; and many hunting groups maintained strong economic roles for women. They might emphasize sharp distinctions between men and women – for example, in assuming that men had special responsibilities for warfare or for prowess as horsemen – but they often did not set up the kind of systematic inequality characteristic of major civilizations. The existence of alternatives to full patriarchy obviously created the possibility for a host of complex encounters – when, for example, the gender assumptions of a nomadic or hunting group came into direct contact with those of a patriarchal civilization.

The second problem involves the concept of civilization itself. World historians often debate this term. Civilization as a form of human organization involving cities and organized states, among other things, is hardly superior to other societies in gender terms. Civilizations often extend and formalize inequalities; but they are different from the other forms, and they are important to study because they have embraced the largest concentrations of people since their origins. Different civilizations – Chinese, for example, or Indian – develop distinctive characteristics. This is the second use of the term. A good bit of the world history of gender involves tracing the particular values and institutions individual civilizations developed, and what happened when they encountered other civilizations. Even here there is some danger of oversimplifying or stereotyping a particular civilization, or of ignoring similarities underneath surface distinctions.

It remains true that leaders of civilizations delighted in claiming special qualities, as part of promoting unity within and separation from the outside world. Almost all civilizations thus developed a pronounced sense of how different they were from "others" – whom the Greeks would call "barbarians".

While not all civilizations expanded greatly, there was some expansionist tendency in order to add resources and relieve population pressure. With expansion came an obvious need to identify some common features – whether in language, religion or political style – that would hold the territory and its often diverse populations together. Each civilization developed something of its own flavor. Egypt emphasized a strong monarchy, pronounced concern for the afterlife and a rather cheerful, colorful art. Mesopotamia, more prone both to natural disasters and to political instability, placed less stress on a single, central government; its religion was more pessimistic, looking to punishments in the afterlife. On the other hand, Mesopotamia introduced a more extensive interest in science.

The early civilization period, in the four Afro-Eurasian centers, lasted until about 1000 BCE, by which point several had collapsed or weakened, often in the face of a new set of invasions from nomadic groups, such as the Indo-European tribes, from Central Asia. There followed a classical period in the history of civilizations. In the Mediterranean (involving North Africa, West Asia and southern Europe), in India and in China, larger civilization complexes began to emerge from 800 onward. Classical civilizations expanded their cultural, political and commercial apparatus. Internal trade increased, allowing different regions within the civilization to specialize. More ambitious governments formed empires. China promoted the most durable imperial tradition, but empires were recurrently important in India and in Greece and particularly in Rome as well. Key statements of cultural values – Hinduism and Buddhism in India, Confucianism and Daoism in China, civic religion but also secular philosophy in Greece and Rome – helped provide a cultural cement. These cultures offered some unity, at least in the upper classes, throughout the society: Chinese gentry could speak and write the same language and participate in a common philosophical system. The shared cultures and institutions also helped extend the sense of identity, of separateness from other societies.

As agricultural economies and then civilizations formed, cultural contacts of various sorts continued. Because the human species has so often been migratory, contacts and exchanges were virtually endemic. Through them, well before the classical period, various areas had gained access to new food stuffs, originally not natural to the region, and to new technologies – including agriculture and metalworking. Migrations and periodic nomadic invasions provided one source of contact. Trade was another. Well before the classical period, trade routes extended from China through India and Central Asia to the Middle East and the Mediterranean; collectively, these are sometimes called the Silk Road, for the principal item of exchange. At the same time, the impact of many contacts was fairly limited. Very rich people in the Mediterranean liked Chinese silk – a favorite fabric in the Roman Empire, for example – but they knew almost nothing about China, as there was no direct travel. Trade occurred in stages.

Most developments within a civilization remained internal, just as the bulk of commerce did. Constraints included not only the considerable suspicion of outsiders, but also the fact that long-distance travel was slow and risky, which limited the extent and impact of exchange. The great classical civilizations rarely had immediate contact with each other. Most were buffered by zones inhabited by nomads or less organized agricultural peoples. Contacts extended out, without usually reaching the next major civilization. Thus both the Middle East and Egypt, and then the classical Mediterranean, established links with the developing center along the upper Nile River in sub-Saharan Africa, initially called Kush. China, under the Han dynasty, had some influence in Korea and Vietnam. India, the most active trading society, exchanged with various parts of Southeast Asia including present-day Indonesia.

The most striking example of direct contact between the largest classical civilizations, prior to the final centuries of the classical era after 300 CE, involved Alexander the Great's conquests in the fourth century BCE, through the Middle East and Persia and into northwestern India. A Greek-influenced kingdom, Bactria, was established in this part of South Asia (parts of present-day Pakistan and Afghanistan) for over a century. From this unusual exchange, parts of South Asia for a time imitated Hellenistic artistic styles, with statues of Buddha draped in Mediterranean-style clothing. India also utilized some mathematical concepts developed in Greece. Further, the exchange encouraged later Indian rulers to think about sending Buddhist emissaries to the Middle East. There they won no real converts, but did possibly introduce ethical concepts that would influence philosophical systems like those of the Stoics and, through them, Christianity. This was an important result, but overall the contact, exceptional in the first place, had few durable consequences. Civilizations themselves gained greater coherence from internal exchanges – like the spread of Confucianism from north China to the south or the increasing impact of northern Indian institutions, including Hinduism and the caste system, on south India. But the most characteristic political and cultural forms of each civilization were rather separate: Confucianism was Chinese, Hinduism (except for a bit of outreach to Southeast Asia) was Indian, and so on.

While civilizations developed, amid contacts but also the limitations of exchange, gender systems – relations between men and women, assignment of roles and definitions of the attributes of each sex – had been taking shape as well. Indeed, the biggest change affecting gender – the rise of agriculture – predated civilization itself. Ultimately this evolution would intertwine with that of the civilizations.

The shift from hunting and gathering to agriculture had gradually ended a system of considerable equality between men and women. In hunting and gathering, both sexes, working separately, contributed important economic goods. Birth rates were relatively low, kept that way in part by prolonged lactation. The result facilitated women's work in gathering grains and nuts, for too-frequent childbirth and infant care would have been a burden. Women's work in turn often contributed more caloric value to the society than hunters did – though hunters always claimed greater prestige. Settled agriculture, where it spread, changed this in favor of more pronounced male dominance. While cultural systems, including polytheistic religion, might refer to the importance of goddesses, held to be the generators of creative forces associated with fertility and therefore vital for agriculture, the new economy promoted greater gender hierarchy. Men were now usually responsible for growing grain; women's assistance was vital, but men supplied most of the food. The birth rate went up, partly because food supplies became a bit more reliable, partly because there was more use for children as laborers. This was probably the key reason why men took over most agricultural functions, as motherhood became more time-consuming. This meant that women's lives became defined more in terms of pregnancy and childcare. This was the setting for a new, pervasive patriarchalism.

In patriarchal societies, men were held to be superior creatures. They had legal rights lacking to women (though law codes protected women from some abuse, at least in principle). Thus king Hammurabi's laws in Mesopotamia, from the second millennium BCE, decreed that a woman who has "not been a careful housewife, has gadded about, has neglected her house and has belittled her husband" should be "thrown into the water". There were no equivalent provisions for men, though the code did establish that a wife could leave her husband if he did not furnish her upkeep.

Many agricultural societies prevented women from owning property independently. Many allowed men to take multiple wives (if they could provide for them). Most punished women's sexual offenses – for example, committing adultery – far more severely than they punished men's. Indeed, some historians have argued that a key motive for patriarchy rested in the felt need to make as sure as possible that a wife's children were sired by the husband. Given the importance of property in agricultural societies (in contrast to hunting and gathering), men came to feel an urge to control their heritage to later generations, and that began with regulating wives' sexuality. Other symptoms were equally important. Sons were preferred over daughters. Many families used infanticide to help control their birth rate, and infant daughters were more often put to death. Culturally, the patriarchal systems emphasized women's frailty and inferiority. They urged largely domestic duties, and sometimes restricted women's rights to appear in public. Patriarchy's reach was powerful and extensive. Many women were so intimidated and isolated by the system that protest was unlikely – though it was also true that individual women could achieve some satisfaction by manipulating husbands and sons or by lording it over inferior women in the household.

The advent of civilizations – always initially within the framework of an agricultural economy – served mainly to consolidate patriarchy, not to introduce fundamental innovations. Yet civilization did have two kinds of impact: further inequality and some interesting differentials in style and emphasis.

On the first point, within agricultural civilizations, women's inequality tended to increase over time, as the civilizations became more successful. Jewish law, arising a little later than the Hammurabic Code, was more severe in its treatment of women's sexuality or public roles. In other parts of the Middle East, a custom arose of insisting on veiling women in public, as a sign of their inferiority and the fact that they belonged to their fathers or husbands. Deterioration of women's roles in China, over time, showed in the appearance of the custom of footbinding under the Tang dynasty, after the classical period had ended; small bones in a girl's foot were broken to prevent easy walking, and the resulting shuffling gait was taken as a sign of beauty and respectable modesty. Pressures of this sort bore particularly on upper-class women, where families had enough wealth to bypass women's productive work; they tended to spread, however, and had symbolic impact even more widely. Chinese footbinding ended only in the early twentieth century.

The reasons for the trend of deterioration in established civilizations involved the growing power of male-dominated governments, which tended to reduce some of women's informal political role within families. The key factor, though, was the increase of prosperity, particularly for the upper classes, which permitted the emphasis on women's ornamental rather than practical roles.

The power of patriarchy bore most heavily on women, but obviously it affected definitions of masculinity as well. Men, whatever their private personalities, were supposed to live up to their dominant roles. They should avoid coddling women, especially in public. Often, they were supposed to be ready to assume military or other leadership duties, and of course they were in principle responsible for the economic survival of the family. In many cases, oldest sons were particularly privileged, even among males, for patriarchy could provide a pecking order based on capacities to assume full power within families. Some societies allowed certain categories of men somewhat different definitions, to indulge in more woman-like behavior or attire or to emphasize homosexual orientations. Other groups of men might be singled out: in a number of religions priests were supposed to avoid sex, while men who watched over wives and concubines in a ruler's court (and who sometimes gained considerable political power in part because they could not sire children to rival those of the king or emperor) might be castrated, as eunuchs – a backhanded testimony to the emphasis on male sexuality.

Patriarchy also shaped the development of boys, encouraging complex relationships with mothers and fathers alike. At least in the upper classes, fathers appeared as remote, authoritarian figures in their sons' lives. Emotional ties to mothers, often lifelong, could be intense.

While agriculture and then civilization progressively deepened inequalities between men and women, one final point is crucial, and it was well established during the early civilization period of world history: particular patriarchal systems varied greatly, and the systems were not universal in any event. The same emphasis on distinctive definitions of overall culture or political institutions that civilizations forged in their gestation periods applied also to ideas about men and women and their roles.

It is not always clear why civilizations' gender systems differed – just as it is hard to explain why classical Indian society ended up emphasizing religion more than China did, or why Greece and China differed in their definitions of science. Once the differences were launched, in gender as in other matters, they tended to persist. Comparisons here are subtle: all the river-valley and classical civilizations were patriarchal, even as they enforced distinctive specific roles and cultures. The similarities and the differences could be equally important.

Among the early river-valley civilizations, neighboring Egypt and Mesopotamia clearly illustrated the potential for patriarchal emphases to differ. Whereas Mesopotamia stressed women's inferiority and subjection to male control, Egyptian civilization gave women more credit, at least in the upper classes, and experienced the rule of several powerful queens. The beautiful Nefertiti, as wife of the pharaoh Akhenaton, was influential in religious disputes during his reign. Later, Cleopatra played a powerful though ultimately abortive role as Egyptian queen, struggling to modify the controls of the Roman Empire. Women were also portrayed elaborately in Egyptian art, and provisions for their burial could be elaborate (though never rivaling those for powerful men). Both women and men could become stars on the body of the sky goddess Nut, one way in which afterlife was envisaged. There was no doubt about Egyptian patriarchy. An Egyptian writer, Ptah Hotep, made this clear in around 2000 BCE as he wrote: "If you are a man of note, found for yourself a household, and love your wife at home, as it beseems. Fill her belly, clothe her back. . . . But hold her back from getting the mastery." Still, in daily life and in social impact, the Egyptian system was distinctive.

Not all agricultural societies allowed polygamy; India differed here from China and the Middle East. Some societies traced the descent of children from the mother – this was and is true in Jewish law – rather than the father. This did not prevent inequality, but it gave motherhood more cultural and legal importance. Legal codes could vary greatly with regard to women's property rights or their ability to leave an unhappy marriage. Cultural representations varied widely. In some religions, goddesses played a vital, powerful role, while in other cultural systems male principles dominated more fully. China, with less religious emphasis, thus offered less symbolic outlet for women than did India, with its strong interest in goddess figures, or the Mediterranean, with its gender-diverse polytheism.

Variations affected men as well. Societies with strong religions, like India, might give top billing to men as priests and holy figures, in contrast to societies like the classical Mediterranean that tended to stress military and athletic qualities for ideal men. Approaches to homosexuality or bisexuality varied. In Greece and Rome, upper-class men often took boys as protégés and lovers. This was not seen as conflicting with normal family roles or with a strong emphasis on masculine prowess.

The differences possible in patriarchal systems showed clearly in the three main classical civilizations. China instituted the most thoroughgoing patriarchy, as part of the Confucian emphasis on hierarchy and order. Man in the family was in principle like the emperor in society: he ruled. Women were urged to be subservient, proficient in domestic skills. Ban Zhao was an influential woman who, despite her position or perhaps because of it, wrote a classical patriarchal manual for her sex (some time in the first century CE; it became China's most durable women's manual, republished into the nineteenth century). Her advice: "Humility means yielding and acting respectful, putting others first . . . enduring insults and bearing with mistreatment. . . . Continuing the sacrifices means serving one's husband-master with appropriate demeanor." Industrious pursuit of household duties and conceiving sons rounded out the lives of successful women, according to the Chinese system.

India's system contrasted. Women were held to be inferior; Indian thinkers debated (without agreement) whether a woman would have to be reincarnated as a man in order to advance spiritually if she had led a worthy life, or whether she could proceed directly to a higher realm. Marriages were carefully arranged by parents to assure larger family goals, often when girls and boys were quite young. Women were supposed to serve fathers and then husbands faithfully. In contrast to China, however, Indian culture paid considerable and approving attention to women's cleverness and beauty. Love and affection gained greater credit, which could link women and men informally, despite basic inequality; mothers-to-be were surrounded by solicitude. Emphasis on confining women domestically was also lower in classical India.

Classical civilization in the Mediterranean presented yet a third case. Strong emphasis on rationality in philosophy and science helped launch a tradition of distinguishing between male intellectual traits and the more emotional, inferior mental powers of women. Greek thinkers urged that women be treated well, while stressing their inferiority and their largely domestic roles. Not only public roles, but also athletics were confined to men. Raping a free woman was a crime, but carried a lesser penalty than seducing a wife – for the latter involved winning affections and loyalty away from the husband. But some women held property; their public presence was greater than in China. And conditions improved in the Hellenistic era, at least in the upper classes, as women participated in cultural pursuits and in commerce (though under male guardianship).

Furthermore, in Rome, women's conditions again improved with time – another exception to the general pattern (though there was a subsequent downturn after the first century CE, under the Empire). Early Roman society imposed harsh penalties on women, for example for sexual offenses. "The husband is the judge of the wife. If she commits a fault, he punishes her; if she has drunk wine, he condemns her; if she has been guilty of adultery, he kills her." Later Roman interest in the rule of law, however, plus a desire to encourage stable family life, brought some improvements. The powers of the husband were curbed by the establishment of family courts, composed of members of the wife's as well as the husband's family of origin, in cases of dispute or accusation. Women freely appeared in public and attended major entertainments. While they were punished for adultery through the loss of a third of their property, these provisions were relatively mild compared with other patriarchal civilizations. Finally, Roman literature, like Greek, was filled with stories of active, whimsical goddesses as well as of gods.

In sum: variation coexisted with patriarchy, before and during the classical period, even as some important societies escaped full patriarchy altogether. Differences affected male roles and definitions as well as those for women. Trends over time differed, too.

Here was a fertile context for the complex impact of cultural contacts, when different societies gained some mutual knowledge. Precisely because patriarchy generated tensions in relationships between men and women, with men anxious to preserve dominance but sometimes uncertain about how this should play out in family settings, and with women usually avoiding protest but not necessarily being overjoyed with their lot, knowledge or assumed knowledge about how another society handled gender issues could have powerful results. It would be easy, particularly for men who were most likely to experience the results of exchanges through trade or war, to use contacts to try to confirm the correctness of their own arrangements, and thereby to exaggerate or distort gender patterns in the other society. The importance and solidity of patriarchy might suggest the need for prolonged, unusual contact in order to break through to new patterns. But contacts could unsettle; they could suggest options and alternatives. Patriarchal standards differed enough from one society to the next to make the contact potentially disruptive, and the potential expanded when confrontations between nomadic societies and established civilizations occurred.

Neither the river-valley civilization period nor the more richly evidenced classical period emphasized the importance of contact with differing standards; the focus was on building separate systems, including patriarchal systems, and integrating diverse peoples through this process. Most people were usually unaware that other societies might do things differently, but exchanges among societies, though rare, did exist, including occasional travels beyond the familiar range. Through these exchanges, in turn, we can gain a first glimpse into possible reactions: how would cultures that had struggled to define gender roles as a key component of the social order deal with occasional evidence that other arrangements were possible?

For by the end of the classical period the possibility of interchange was heating up. Troubles with the political system, particularly in Rome and China, opened new possibilities for contacts, both through outside invasions and through religious missions. Various nomadic peoples pressed into the established civilization territories – Huns from Central Asia into China and later India, Germanic tribes into southern Europe. Buddhist and Christian missionaries were poised to seek converts outside their home base, both in other civilizations and among the less politically organized regions such as Central Asia or northern Europe. What had been a periodic experience during the early civilization and classical period, through invasions, wars and limited trade, now became commonplace, as various peoples gained some sense of other ways in which gender standards could be organized.

Part I

From classical civilizations through the postclassical period

Chapters in this section deal with a number of kinds of contact between civilizations or between civilizations and other types of societies, particularly nomadic groups, during the classical and postclassical periods. The focus is on the centuries from about 500 BCE to about 1500 CE. These are the first periods for which we have extensive information about the kinds of contacts that might have affected constructions of gender – that is, the way men and women and male and female roles were defined. Earlier exchanges had unquestionably influenced gender roles, for example when agriculture was copied from an established center and a new emphasis on patriarchy resulted. But the specifics, including the ways womanhood and manhood were explicitly discussed, are shrouded in considerable mystery.

As discussed in Chapter 1, classical civilizations, centered particularly in China, India and the Middle East/Mediterranean regions, had emphasized expansion and internal integration. Great efforts went into constructing political and cultural systems, together with trade specializations, that would draw the civilization area together. Contacts existed, mainly through inter-regional trade, but they did not usually have deep impact. Where gender was concerned, the emphasis was on consolidating patriarchy through linkage to each society's culture and institutions.

Overall, the classical period, which ran from about 1000 BCE until about 500 CE, was a time of expansion and integration for the major centers. A Persian empire blossomed in the Middle East, far larger than its river-valley predecessors in the region. Chinese culture and institutions spread from north to south, establishing the fabled Middle Kingdom. Hindu religion and social institutions took shape in India, though the rise of Buddhism complicated the picture. Greek and then Roman societies fanned out in the Mediterranean and parts of the Middle East.

Clarifying gender standards was part of shaping the classical civilizations. In China, manuals were written about how women and men should behave – a clear sign of the need to define roles, and a market, at least among the literate upper classes, for this definition. Greek philosophers like Aristotle discussed gender as part of basic political and social theory. Hindu and Roman jurists paid attention to gender specifications. Setting gender standards was part of defining society itself.

Contacts did exist in the classical period, and we take them up in the next two chapters. Mostly, they were either limited or sporadic. Trade in luxury goods was important. The Roman Empire sent regular expeditions to India, and at one point a Chinese emperor dispatched a special mission to pick up an Indian rhinoceros for his zoo. These exchanges were interesting, but they were not at a level where gender was heavily involved. And since the major societies were busy establishing their own gender standards, and because they were all patriarchal in any event, they may not have been particularly open to impact in this area. A few exceptions developed in the complex societies of the Mediterranean and the Middle East, and the Buddhist link with China proved unusually interesting in what was, otherwise, a rather limited menu of interactions.

The next, postclassical period – 500–1450 – was quite a different matter, for several reasons. The surge of missionary religions guaranteed a wider set of episodes with implications for gender – as the Buddhist entry into China had already suggested. Inter-regional trade, joining Asia, Africa, and Europe, became more regular and substantial – another set of contacts. A variety of societies began deliberately to imitate their neighbors, seeking to advance culturally and economically – thus Russia and the Byzantines, Japan and China. Finally, military encounters – Arab armies with Indians or Chinese, Europeans and Arabs, and, later on, the wave of Mongol invasions – brought another set of interactions. Not all of these episodes had implications for gender, but many did. The pace of exchange was accelerating, and aspects of gender were reconsidered in the process. The Arab world and China wielded the greatest influence during the postclassical period as a whole, but the Mongol invasions redefined power relationships and the nature of international contacts toward the period's end.

At the end of the classical period, as internal decline and outside invasions cut into the great empires such as that of China's Han dynasty, India's Gupta Empire and the Roman Empire, key religions began to spread beyond the rough boundaries of individual civilizations. Buddhism had a massive if contested impact on China, while Christianity spread into Europe, ultimately beyond Rome's furthest borders. Then the rise of Islam ushered in yet another force. Along with Arab conquests and extensive international trade, the spread of world religions helped establish an unprecedented series of regular exchanges among the civilizations of Asia, Africa and Europe. At the same time, the geographical area covered by civilizations expanded. Regions that had been on the fringe of civilizations actively copied more established centers, particularly in cultural matters such as religion, artistic styles, even writing. Thus Japan interacted with China, Europe with the Mediterranean world, Russia with the Byzantine Empire, and sub-Saharan West Africa with the Muslim lands.

Gender relations during the postclassical period tended to emphasize growing inequality, in the pattern familiar in agricultural societies. This was when footbinding spread in China, while in India a new practice called *sati* urged widows to hurl themselves on their husbands' funeral pyres on the grounds that they had nothing left to live for. Use of *sati* was rare, but symbolically revealing. While Islam reduced some drawbacks for women in Arab society, subsequent developments, including veiling, emphasized further gender distinctions. But postclassical civilizations were also marked by the growth of cultural interactions, which increased the instances when gender values might be reassessed in light of knowledge of what other societies were doing. The expanding world religions emphasized spiritual equality between the genders, which could contradict traditional views while complicating – or sometimes unwittingly abetting – the real-life trends toward greater inequality. The postclassical period involves fascinating currents and countercurrents concerning women, and contacts played a vital role in the redefinition process.

Contacts had other gender implications as well. Homosexuality was reconsidered in some instances, with varying results. Religious conversions and new merchant roles both might affect the criteria for masculinity, though not necessarily in similar directions.

Several themes shine through the kinds of contacts discussed in the following chapters, relevant to gender in both classical and postclassical centuries. First, recurrent interactions with nomadic groups had important implications for all parties involved, right through the Mongol period. Second, travelers' accounts were often interesting, in what they revealed about myths and assumptions concerning gender practices of "other" people – and, while the frequency of the accounts increased in the postclassical centuries, important statements issued from the classical period as well. Third, the major episodes of contact involved clear if varied systems of patriarchy, as at least part of the interactions, though nomadic groups or societies in an early, imitative phase of civilization might be involved as well.

Finally, many key contacts, from the late classical period onward, involved new religious elements, thanks to intense missionary activity and the fact that religion often accompanied trade and war. Contact with unfamiliar religions could provide a crucial gender test. The major world religions – Buddhism, Christianity and Islam – all insisted on fundamental spiritual equality; women had souls along with men. So in principle they could disrupt patriarchy considerably. But the religions also made their peace with male dominance in various ways, and because they emphasized the afterlife, rather than changes in conditions in this world, they might implicitly accept patriarchy. Religious interactions, in other words, had unpredictable effects, though they almost always challenged existing gender relationships in some respects. These issues are explored in Chapters 3 and 4, and they also apply to situations discussed later, in Part II, when Christianity became a clearer world force.

Contacts launched in the late classical and particularly the postclassical periods continued their work even in subsequent centuries. This duration, explored in Chapters 3 and 4, testifies to the importance of new interactions but also to the time required to modify established gender habits.

Further reading

On contacts and civilization: Jerry Bentley, *Old World Encounters: Cross-Cultural Contacts and Exchanges in Pre-modern Times* (New York: Oxford University Press, 1993). On gender: Dale Walde and Noreen Willows (eds), *Archaeology of Gender* (Calgary: Archaeological Association of the University of Calgary, 1991); Margaret Ehrenburg, *Women in Prehistory* (London: British Museum Press and Norman, Okla.: University of Oklahoma Press, 1989); Barbara Lesko (ed.), *Women's Earliest Records from Ancient Egypt and Western Asia* (Atlanta, Ga: Scholars Press, 1987).

Chapter 2

Early contacts
Influences from cultural diversity

Developments during the classical period allow some insights into the ways that exchanges with alternative value systems might affect gender – and particularly the evaluation and roles of women. The Middle East and Mediterranean regions (West Asia, North Africa and southern Europe) provide an important test case, for two reasons. First, enough documentation is available to offer some sense of how divergent ideas about women might influence groups that encountered them. Second, the region was unquestionably diverse, and several waves of conquest and invasion provided opportunities for contact and exchange.

At the same time, the patterns that emerged during the late centuries BCE and early centuries CE suggest somewhat tentative impacts. While very diverse cultures coexisted in the region, they were all highly patriarchal, which could easily limit the results of any encounter. Romans might notice few differences between their ideas about women and those they discerned when they traded with and then conquered the Greeks. At the same time, while ideas about women were well developed, and an important part of classical philosophies, they were not clearly articulated in widely popular cultural systems such as religions. Religious exchanges played a role in gender shifts during the period, as we shall see, but they had a far less sweeping quality than the missionary world religions that would begin to spread a few centuries later. Contact, in other words, did not necessarily bring religious conversion; and, without this, specific ideas about women might not be deeply affected.

Thus major contact, like that which arose in the fourth century BCE between Greek and northwestern Indian cultures, did not cause noticeable results where gender was concerned, despite measurable impact on other aspects of art and thought. Clearly, this was a rather preliminary period in the history of civilization contacts, where exchanges were complex and sometimes surprisingly limited.

There was one other feature during a time in which key societies, like Greece and Rome, were establishing their ideas about men and women: this was that it was possible to develop outlandish notions about what gender was like outside the familiar boundaries of one's own civilization. Early travelers reflect a fascinating sense of strangeness, even anxiety, which denotes the characteristic ignorance about more remote peoples but also some nervousness about the solidity of one's own conventions, back home.

Greece and Hellenism

As a civilization took shape in Greece after about 800 BCE (earlier societies had been disrupted by invasions), many standard features of patriarchy quickly surfaced. Whether Greece borrowed ideas about men and women from Mesopotamia or Egypt (from which it definitely derived some other characteristics) is simply unknown. Most likely the system resulted from the standard implications of settled agriculture and an increasingly explicit political system.

Greek patriarchy did generate a few distinctive twists, along with standard beliefs in women's inferiority and their primary domestic obligations. Many Greek city-states were quite militaristic, which may have supported a more aggressive version of masculinity. In Sparta, where military organization was particularly pronounced, boys were kept separate from girls for key periods of training. While women engaged in physical exercise, their main functions were motherhood – to create more boys – and support of male valor. One Spartan summed up the advice to women: "Marry a good man, and bear good children."

Many upper-class Greek men were bisexual, taking boys as protégés and lovers. This did nor preclude marriage, but it may have reduced social contacts with women. Greek politics, which often involved extensive participation in voting and government service, emphasized the male-headed household. Control of property was vital to voting rights, which may have explained this orientation in part. Certainly women were not seen as fit for political activities, and this exacerbated the standard gulf between the two genders. Greek philosophical focus on rationality created another gap, for women were judged closer to nature and incapable of reason. A writer drove the point home:

> In the beginning god made the female mind separately. One he made from a long-bristled sow. In her house everything lies in disorder, smeared with mud . . . and she herself unwashed, in clothes unlaundered, sits by the dungheap and grows fat. Another he made from a wicked vixen: a woman who knows everything. No bad thing and no better kind of thing is lost on her; for she often calls a good thing bad and a bad thing good. Her attitude is never the same.

At an extreme, women were seen as punishments visited on men by angry gods.

While women could be honored as mothers and as participants in religious festivals, their daily status was low. They were not viewed as legally competent

– first their fathers and then their husbands served as guardians. Even widows returned to the guardianship of their original family. The Greek word for marriage meant loan: women were passed on loan from father to husband. This was the context in which adultery and seduction were much more heavily punished than rape, for the former involved taking women from their husband; the punishment reflected the offense to him. Overall, the Greek version of patriarchy, while less systematic than the Chinese, shared many elements in the emphasis on women's ineptitude and servile status.

Greek travelers: Herodotus

The Greek system inevitably encountered alternative views. Even within Greece there was variety. Athenian leaders often criticized Spartans for giving women too much leeway. Greeks also traded widely in the Mediterranean and Black Sea areas, which exposed them to many different cultural systems. In general, alternative ways of doing things were greeted with a mixture of scorn – the Greek labeled other people "barbarians" – and tolerance. There was no sense that there was much to learn that might usefully amend customs back home. At the same time, considerable ignorance of the outside world and complacency about Greek patterns, along with some tensions where women were concerned, could combine to produce interesting exaggerations of male-female relationships in other societies.

Herodotus, the first great Greek historian and writer of a travel account, was born around 484 BCE. Trained in Athens, he traveled through much of the Persian Empire, that is, through most of the Middle East, as well as Egypt and neighboring parts of North Africa including Libya. He also journeyed to Europe north of the Danube and the Black Sea. Through his travels, unusually extensive for the time, he picked up stories about societies even beyond his ken. He wrote about the world he had discovered in a *History*, loosely focused on the great Greek wars with Persia that had occurred between 499 and 479 BCE.

Herodotus was a careful observer, eager to sort out fact from fiction. He was also tolerantly interested in customs that differed from those of his native Greece. Thus he reported with some amazement that Egyptians did not practice female infanticide, but with no sense of any relevance for Greece. Yet Herodotus also accepted or repeated a number of distortions. He was quite gullible where bizarre animals were concerned and readily accepted stories of societies where people routinely ate their aging parents. Moreover, he was open to dramatic variations in the treatment of women.

In his description of the Lydian people, for example, he claimed that:

> the daughters of every lower-class Lydian family work as prostitutes so that they can accumulate enough of a dowry to enable them to get married, and they arrange their own marriages. . . . Apart from this practice of

having their female children work as prostitutes, Lydian customs are not very different from Greek ones.

Again a tolerant observer, delighting in the variety of human life, Herodotus nevertheless accepts a highly implausible generalization, interestingly focused on extreme sexual habits. In the case of another group, the Agathyrsians, from north of the Black Sea, he claims, "any woman is available to any man for sex, to ensure that the men are all brothers and that they are on amicable and good terms with one another, since they are all relatives. In other respects their way of life is similar to that of the Thracians [a group in northern Greece}." In describing the Libyans, from North Africa, he says: "Another unique custom of theirs is that when their young women are about to get married they parade them in front of their king, and whichever one of them pleases him the most is deflowered by him." Of another Libyan group, he says:

> It is their custom for each man to have a number of wives, but . . . any woman is available to any man for sex; a staff set up in front of a house indicates that sexual intercourse is taking place inside. When a Nasmonian man gets married, first it is the custom for the bride to have sex with all the guests one after another on her wedding night; every man she has sex with gives her something he has brought with him from his house as a gift.

Other stories emphasized violence rather than sex. A tribe influenced by Greeks living in Egypt, the Ausees,

> celebrate a festival to Athena [a Greek goddess} once a year at which the unmarried young women of the tribe divide into two groups and fight one another with sticks and stones; the women say that this is how they fulfil their ancestral duties to [the} goddess. . . . They say that any women who die of their wounds were not true virgins. Before they let them fight, they join together to dress up the prettiest of the current generation of young women in a Corinthian helmet and a set of Greek armor.

Here, if true, was a fascinating case of syncretism, with Greek paraphernalia borrowed for a ritual that was not Greek at all. Herodotus ends this vignette again with sex:

> They have intercourse with women promiscuously; rather than living in couples, their sex life is that of herd animals. When a woman's baby is grown, in the course of the third month the men all convene and the child is taken to be the son or daughter of whichever of the men it resembles.

Herodotus devoted considerable attention to the Amazons, a group of warrior women, often operating without men, who presumably lived in Central Asia.

Here, he elaborated a belief already widespread in Greece. Greeks claimed to have fought Amazons, who viciously killed every man they could. In one account, where Amazons did mix with other folk at least to marry and reproduce, an Amazon girl had to kill a man before she could wed. Another story saw the Amazons mix with another tribe, called Scythians, whose men managed to have intercourse with the warriors. The Scythians invited the Amazons to their homeland, but the Amazons replied:

> We would find it impossible to live with your women, because our practices are completely different from theirs. We haven't learnt women's work. We shoot arrows, wield javelins, ride horses – things which your women never have anything to do with. They just stay in their wagons and do women's work; they never go out hunting or anywhere else either.

And the young men agreed, and from then onward the women warred and hunted with their husbands, "wearing the same clothes as the men do".

Several points emerge from the gender elements of this travel account. First, Herodotus often finds behaviors of women far stranger than anything else he encounters, probably a natural result of coming from a tightly organized patriarchal background which made it easy to label and exaggerate differences. Second, he rarely condemns – in this, he is like other observers later in world history, eager to embrace and embellish human variety. By the same token, though, he finds nothing admirable: there is no suggestion that Greeks might improve their relationships between men and women by a spot of imitation. Other people might copy Greeks. He notes that Persians, for example, have borrowed the habit of men having sex with younger boys. Greece itself, however, had nothing to improve upon.

Finally, there is the obvious fascination with sex and violence. Hardly a repressed society, Greece nevertheless discouraged promiscuity; from this context it was perhaps not surprising that a man would gullibly accept tales of lecherous strangers. Certainly, this would prove to be a common theme in travelers' accounts: a use of "others" to titillate sexual fancies and/or rouse moral scorn back home (see Chapter 8 on recent Western reactions to Polynesia). Concern with aggressive women mixed an element of reality with some broader fears. As Greeks had contact with nomadic groups, they undoubtedly encountered people who gave wider roles to women than they themselves maintained – including fighting roles. They duly recorded this fact, as in accounts of people from north of the Black Sea, but they also exaggerated, as witness the credulity about the Amazons. The idea of more freewheeling women was intriguing but also frightening, as it contrasted with the careful obedience and domesticity required back home. Here, exaggeration reflected tensions and anxieties, offering a reminder of how any relaxation of patriarchal controls could lead to chaos. Travel, in this regard, generated as many insights about domestic assumptions as it did about foreign ways – but the tendency was to preserve, not to utilize contacts as a source of innovation.

Hellenistic society

The Greek system of patriarchy came under greater challenge when a wider set of exchanges developed, under the great empire established by the Macedonian conqueror, Alexander the Great, from the fourth century onward. By this time the Greek city-states were in decline. The Macedonians conquered Greece and then used Greek soldiers, bureaucrats and scholars to build an empire through the Middle East and Egypt. While the empire quickly degenerated into regional kingdoms, the mixture of Greek and other elements continued for several centuries. Alexander himself married a Persian princess, to symbolize his desire to forge a new cultural fusion in the eastern Mediterranean. The result, Hellenistic society, was unquestionably different from classical Greece, though closely related to it particularly in the cultural realm.

Greek–Persian contact had developed well before Alexander, through trade and war. Herodotus claimed that Persian courtiers had copied the Greek habit of taking boys as lovers – despite the fact that the Persian religion vigorously opposed homosexuality. The mixing of peoples in the eastern Mediterranean, North Africa and southeastern Europe juxtaposed a number of gender patterns, and mutual influence was inevitable. The problem is that, as with Herodotus' claims concerning Persia, adequate evidence is often hard to find.

The most dramatic cultural confrontation that Alexander triggered brought Greeks into contact with Indians, in a northwestern pocket of the subcontinent then called Bactria. For about two centuries, Greeks ruled this Indian kingdom, and possibilities of mutual imitation grew accordingly. From Greece, Bactrians borrowed artistic styles, painting pictures of Buddha in Mediterranean togas and hair-dos, in a pattern that lasted in the region for about a hundred years. Indian mathematicians exchanged with Greek scientists, to mutual benefit – though it was a sign of the great gulf between the cultures and the fragility of the exchange that the Indian numbering system, far superior to the Greek, was not taken over. A number of Greek leaders in Bactria converted to Buddhism. Some Buddhist missionaries seem to have been sent to the Middle East, and historians have speculated that they brought new emphases on ethics and spirituality that would influence later religious and philosophical developments. Specifics, however, are hard to pin down. And, on relations between men and women, it is not clear that the Greek–Indian encounter had any serious impact at all. Possibly the details seemed too different to merge; possibly, as with Herodotus, Greeks were so confident in their own ways that the example of another set of gender relations, more sensual and spiritual than their own, would seem irrelevant or repellent. The contact was, in any event, short-lived; probably it requires more sweeping but also more enduring exchange to affect such personal values as men's and women's mutual relationships. Certainly the lack of clear result here contrasts with the kind of exchange that developed a few centuries later, between India and China (Chapter 3).

Within the more standard range of Greek outreach, the Middle East and Egypt, the situation was different. Hellenistic conditions for women were in several important respects better than those that had prevailed in Greece, and cultural interchange had something to do with the contrast. Women played a greater political role, maneuvering with princes and sometimes ruling in their own right. Laws eased, allowing more women to acquire property on their own and to run businesses. Women participated more actively in cultural life, and several notable writers emerged. Correspondingly, materials written about women became somewhat more favorable, though without going so far as to suggest equality. Finally, artistic representations shifted dramatically, with growing interest in representing the female nude, in contrast to the heavily draped styles that had been characteristic of Greece.

Several developments contributed to these new patterns. Most generally, the shift to autocratic monarchies removed the pressure on the male-headed family, no longer seen as a basis for widespread political participation, but cultural exchange entered in as well. From Macedonia itself came a tradition of politically active royal women, in contrast to the passive role open to the wives of most Greek political leaders. Egypt contributed a different sense of law, in which women could act on their own, without requiring guardians. Perhaps most important was a new wave of religions, called mystery religions, from North Africa and the Middle East, in which highly emotional piety differed from the more ritualistic ceremonies characteristic of Greek religion. In the mystery religions, female goddesses, like the Egyptian Isis, could play a central role. Emphasis on creativity highlighted the female principle; Isis became the most important deity in her cult, with a host of functions including presiding over the cycles of birth and rebirth in nature.

The spread of Isis worship, from Egypt to Greece and, later, to Rome, is a tantalizing example of gender-relevant contact in the Mediterranean world. The goddess had acquired tremendous status in Egyptian worship. She embodied images both of power and of motherhood. Many Greeks added Isis to their worship: she seemed a more cosmopolitan figure than their own gods and goddesses, so helped extend their religion as they traveled to different parts of the Mediterranean. She could help explain matters that the Greek religion left vague: for example, the origins of civilization. There is no question that the worship of Isis provided real spiritual satisfaction to many Greeks and Romans – one Roman wrote of how she "affected his soul and filled it with happiness". At the same time, many Greek and Roman worshippers assimilated Isis to familiar goddesses – for example, to the goddess associated with creation and fertility. It is not clear that the addition of Isis, though a very real change in religious terms, affected actual gender standards in Greece and Rome at all. Isis also aroused a good bit of opposition from religious conservatives who disliked Egyptian influence. Overall, cultural contacts of this sort were a vital part of the classical Mediterranean world, but their gender impact remains obscure.

None of these results of cultural contact should be exaggerated. Conditions in Greece changed less than elsewhere. For example, a Greek woman living in Egypt might avoid a guardian, but her counterparts back home maintained the old system. Further, change particularly affected the upper classes; it is not clear that gender relations in the lower classes shifted greatly. Indeed, an increased incidence of female infanticide – killing girl babies as a means of population control – suggested that some of the new esteem for women might have been quite superficial. Certainly there was no systematic re-evaluation of women's attributes and roles, of the sort the Buddhism would prompt (though with admittedly limited results) in China later on.

Patterns of cultural diversity persisted in the Roman era, the last phase of classical civilization in the Mediterranean world. Initially a city-state, Roman impulses toward women seem at first to have been quite harsh: we have seen that under early Roman law, for example, a husband could kill his wife for adultery. But the gradual improvement in law, combined with the Roman encounter with moderating Hellenistic influences, produced a somewhat milder system by the second century BCE as the Roman republic matured and expanded. Roman intellectuals did copy Greek writers in diatribes about women's inferiority and their demeaning sexual appetites, but they also copied the Hellenistic impulse to honor good women, including those who, as loyal wives and mothers, could contribute to the state. Roman religion, though very similar to Greek, devoted more attention to goddesses, hailing Venus for example as the "guiding power of the universe". Hellenistic influence, coming from Rome's trade and conquests in the eastern Mediterranean, also helped create legal rights for women to own property and some protections from unsubstantiated accusations by husbands. It also helped to generate some literature that took open delight in sensuality, as in the love poems of Ovid.

Influences from Greece and the eastern Mediterranean also provided upper-class Roman women with new models of ornamentation and luxury. In the early Roman republic, plain living had been highly valued, for men and women alike. After successful conquest and resultant contact, however, jewels, imported silks and other adornments caught on in a big way. This gave an additional dimension to women's lives, though it may have distracted them from other possible goals and so actually helped confirm patriarchal inequality. Some Roman men disapproved of the frivolity, while others supported women on the grounds that they had so little else in their lives. At one point dispute over the imported beauty standards spilled over into politics. The Oppian law had been passed, during a series of bitter wars, limiting the amount of gold and colorful clothing a woman could wear. In 195 BCE, the Roman Senate debated repeal. Women lined the streets, urging a restoration of luxury now that the republic was thriving again. Politicians complained, on the grounds that women should not presume to have a political voice but should stay at home and remain modest. Others, however, defended the women: "We have proud ears indeed if, while masters do not scorn the appeals of slaves, we are angry when honorable women ask something of us." They noted that men liked fancy clothes, and women should at least share this right. "Women cannot partake of magistracies, priesthoods, triumphs, badges of office, gifts, or spoils of war: elegance, finery and beautiful clothes are women's badges, in these they find joy and take pride, this our forebears called the women's world." The law was repealed, though the terms used in favor of repeal simultaneously recalled the limits of men's opinions of women.

Rome remained firmly patriarchal, and on the whole its approach toward women was tougher than that of the Hellenistic states. Strong emphasis on family, returning in the early days of the Empire, brought reassertions of male authority, for example over adultery. Later Roman literature began to condemn assertive women, in imitation of Greek themes. The fact was that, as in Greece, political considerations dominated the treatment of women, at least in the upper classes and as expressed in law. Contacts with diverse cultures had only limited, often transitory, impact in this situation. Furthermore, there was no clear alternative system that would have held men and women to a different set of standards. Even the Hellenistic centuries, although they had permitted greater gender contacts than in classical Greece, had not developed a model that was distinctive or powerful enough to reshape Roman patriarchy.

Mediterranean contacts also had implications for masculinity itself. Many Roman traditionalists worried about Greek influence and its possible subversion of military, manly virtues. Greek culture, with its emphasis on art and scholarship, could seem soft. The Greek practice of homosexuality undoubtedly spread to Rome, though Romans practiced it less widely and amid greater disapproval by traditionalist critics.

The classical period in the Mediterranean and the Middle East generated a host of cultural contacts for peoples in western Asia, southern Europe and northern Africa. The results, in terms of relationships between men and women, are not always well documented. It seems that some contacts had in fact few results: the parties involved were sufficiently confident of their own values, or sufficiently convinced that the alternatives were too strange and bizarre, with the result that both sides left laws and images essentially untouched. Other contacts did influence patterns to a degree, particularly in the third and second centuries BCE when the Hellenistic kingdoms prevailed. Rome participated in this exchange to some extent, but ultimately seemed to pull away in favor of renewed emphasis on women's submissiveness. The examples from this period in Mediterranean history are complex, but largely suggest considerable immunity for assumptions about gender relations and roles, even amid substantial cultural diversity.

Further reading

Two books by Sarah Pomeroy provide vital insights: *Goddesses, Whores, Wives, and Slaves: Women in Classical Antiquity* (New York: Schocken Books, 1975; with new preface, 1995; London: Pimlico, 1994) and *Women in Hellenistic Egypt: From Alexander to Cleopatra* (New York: Schocken Books, 1984). See also Mary Lefkowitz and Maureen Fant (eds), *Women in Greece and Rome* (Toronto: Samuel-Stevens, 1977); Roger Just, *Women in Athenian Law and Life* (London/New York: Routledge, 1989). A readable version of Herodotus, *The Histories,* is translated by Robin Waterfield, with introduction and notes by Carolyn Dewald (Oxford/New York: Oxford University Press, 1998). See also Thomas Hubbard, *Homosexuality in Greece and Rome: A Sourcebook* Berkeley, (Calif.: University of California Press, 2003) and Friedrich Solmsen, *Isis among the Greeks and Romans* (Cambrige, Mass.: Harvard University Press, 1979).

Chapter 3

Buddhism and Chinese women

The spread of Buddhism to China, from the late classical period until the ninth century CE, forms the first elaborate contact between two gender systems for which we have reasonably full records. The case is interesting also because Buddhist and Chinese ideas about women, while not totally opposed in that both systems assumed female inferiority, differed markedly. Indeed, Buddhist writers had to make some adjustments in their statements about women, simply to fit Chinese assumptions, but Buddhism did indeed have an impact. Unlike the earlier contact between Greeks and Indians, the spread of Buddhism to China involved substantial conversions to the alien religious system, while religion, in turn, almost inevitably affected ideas about gender. The result in the long run, however, did not change the strict Chinese version of patriarchy very much, so that, in this sense, we are still dealing with a somewhat hesitant case of contact. The interchange did, however, affect the lives of many women individually for some centuries. Along with the adjustments in Buddhism – an obvious example of syncretism as a feature of complex cultural exchange – this influence makes the story of Chinese Buddhism an interesting if fairly unique case of male–female relationships amid contact.

The story obviously differs from the impact of the diverse cultures of the Mediterranean and the Middle East, discussed in the previous chapter. For one thing, records are clearer: Chinese observers, including women themselves, paid more attention to the impact of Buddhism on women's lives. Furthermore, Buddhism was a more systematic spiritual statement than had existed during the centuries of Hellenism, and this probably had more significant results than the scattered currents examined in Chapter 2. The difference, in other words, was real, not just a matter of available evidence. But, finally, there were also similarities: even Buddhism's capacity to change a well-entrenched patriarchal system was limited, and other factors might outweigh its influence in shaping change.

The Chinese system of patriarchy, unusually rigorous in principle, was well established by the early centuries CE, as discussed in Chapter 1. Recommendations to women-urged subservience. Wives were supposed to obey not only their husband but also his parents. They could be divorced if they disobeyed, if they could not have children (and sons were particularly esteemed), even if they talked too much. Many upper-class men took additional wives or concubines, and the behavior code insisted that women should not be jealous. Responsibilities for women focused on the household — weaving and domestic work. The ideal system was closely tied to larger Confucian beliefs about hierarchy and the duties of inferiors.

Uniform rigor should not be exaggerated. The Chinese system could be most fully realized in upper-class families, where women's productive labor was not needed (though even here, household duties were considerable and respected). Individual women, by personality, might impose themselves more than the ideals suggested; and even more women, by using informal influence on husbands and particularly sons, might gain real power. Men were not supposed to abuse women, for Confucianism placed obligations on superiors as well — though constraints were not always effective in practice. Still, the pattern of dominance ran through many aspects of Chinese culture and family practice alike.

Buddhism offered a different, though complex, picture. The religion had started in India during the sixth century BCE (Buddha lived 563–483 BCE), as a partial rebellion against the religious system that ultimately became Hinduism. Distaste for the Hindu emphasis on inequality was a key motivation for Buddhism; and, while this was particularly directed against the caste system, it had implications for gender relations as well. Everyone, in the Buddhist view, regardless of social station, participated in the divine essence, which implied some ultimate spiritual equality.

Like other major religions, to be sure, Buddhism was highly ambivalent where women were concerned, reflecting its operation within a patriarchal framework. Women could be represented as evil, particularly because of their potential for seducing men and leading them, through lust, from the paths of virtue. One Buddhist story told of an evil god who sent three women (Lust, Aversion and Craving) to tempt the Buddha. It concluded;

Women can ruin
The precepts of purity.
They can also ignore
Honor and virtue.

Causing one to go to hell
They prevent rebirth in heaven.
Why should the wise
Delight in them?

But women could be holy as well, in contrast to Hinduism which tended to argue that reincarnation as a man was an essential precondition for a woman's spiritual advancement (though Buddhism retained an element of this belief as well). One Buddhist sutra, or holy verse, described a woman named Ananda, a "goddess of the Ganges", "endowed with knowledge and practice". At a later time, Buddha would change her sex from female to male and allow her to realize "Supreme, Perfect Enlightenment". Another sutra, written in fact by a Chinese Buddhist but describing a woman in India, told of a king's daughter who, along with other women, meditated on Buddha and gained direct enlightenment as a result. Here, it is emphasized that enlightenment is "neither male nor female", because the human body is not involved. The Princess speaks wisely of her commitment to Buddhist virtue, and her wise words guide a host of Buddhist saints (called bodhisattvas). In reward, Buddha promised her Buddhahood: "Her Buddha world will be called radiance."

Many women bodhisattvas were worshipped as sources of holiness and earthly healing. Statues of some were common in India by the fifth century CE, a fact which was noted by Chinese pilgrims eager to learn about the religion. (Some of the women were depicted also as men, maintaining this tension in Buddhist belief.) Holy women might be held up as patronesses not only of female activities – like the desire to have children – but also of male realms, such as seafaring. More practically, Buddhist sects often set up convents for women, analogous to the monasteries for holy men, where lives might be devoted to prayer and contemplation.

Clearly, in principle, contact between Buddhism and Chinese patriarchy could produce some interesting tensions, however cushioned by a shared belief in male superiority. Buddhism might contest Confucian assertions of systematic male dominance by noting women's spiritual potential and their capacity for ultimate advancement toward the holy state of nirvana. Buddhism might also qualify the Chinese assumption that marriage and domestic duties were alone appropriate for a woman, through the opportunity for an independent, holy life. Buddhism suggested a host of problems for the reigning Confucian view of the world, but the implications for gender figured prominently. What would happen when the two systems interacted?

The test began to develop around the fourth century CE. As it had developed in India, Buddhism was at once a tolerant religion, willing to embrace various cultural settings, and a missionary faith. Several Indian emperors had promoted Buddhism to other regions, though Sri Lanka and Southeast Asia, where Indian trade routes were best-established, formed the most obvious target. Buddhist contacts with China began haltingly, mainly through the conversion of nomadic merchants operating from Central Asia, near the great Empire's northern and western borders. By the fourth century, fueled by stories of miracles accomplished by Buddhist holy men, one northern Chinese region was reported to have 10,000 disciples. By this point, not only Chinese merchants trading in India but also religious converts were coming to India explicitly to learn about this faith.

Buddhism in China encountered severe opposition from Confucianists, who disliked what they saw as fanaticism, feared the Buddhist lack of interest in politics as an affront to state authority, and repudiated the monastic movement as an unproductive drain on the economy. Resentment of foreign, "barbarian" ideas entered into this mix, but so did a concern that Buddhism, in its hostility to worldly pleasures including sexuality, disrupted family life. Buddhism advanced nevertheless, winning many converts in south China, including members of the upper class, by the early fifth century. Its progress coincided with the collapse of the great Han dynasty and ensuing political chaos in China (between the third and the sixth centuries CE). Political instability, in a culture that had stressed the central importance of the state and political order, created obvious interest in a religious alternative. Conversions to Buddhism, translations of writings, use of Buddhist themes and styles in Chinese art, generation of Chinese sutras, and the establishment of Buddhist monasteries and convents all proceeded rapidly, particularly from the sixth century onward. About 8 percent of all poems in the Tang dynasty, for example, had an explicitly Buddhist theme. Ironically, when the Chinese imperial system was re-established in the late sixth century, and particularly in the early stages of the Tang dynasty, the government often adopted Buddhism, seeking to benefit from its popularity. Many people blended Buddhism with continued commitments to Daoism (China's earlier religion, not totally unlike Buddhism in a desire for spiritual unity, though without Buddhism's gender implications) and even Confucianism.

While Buddhism had some relationship, for a time, with Chinese politics, its main attraction to Chinese people, at various social levels, was its spirituality, its encouragement to prayer and its promise of ultimate advancement toward unity with the divine essence. Chinese Buddhism encouraged emphasis on holy figures, seen as facilitating advancement for ordinary people. Many Chinese contributed to Buddhism – ranging from funding monasteries to writing or sponsoring a sutra – in response to life's problems, giving thanks for a recovery from illness, for example, or appealing for a future benefit. Many people, including members of the gentry, or upper class, entered monasteries. Chinese Buddhist leaders perpetuated a missionary effort, even converting some nomadic groups who raided the region during the period. For several centuries Buddhism became a thoroughly Chinese product – the only significant cultural borrowing China tolerated from its origins until very recent times.

Here, then, is a massive case of cultural contact between two major civilizations each with its own well-established framework of belief. What was the impact on the Chinese system of patriarchy?

Several connections developed. The first, and in some ways the least surprising, involved an adjustment of Buddhist beliefs and vocabulary where women were concerned, in the interests of reducing potential shock, as well as the real possibility of Confucian resistance. The result was a mixed or syncretic approach to gender. Passages in Indian sutras that offended Confucian morality were simply omitted. Words like "kiss" and "embrace", which in India had indicated gestures of love and respect for a bodhisattva, were dropped off.

Buddhism's high position for women and mothers was also modified in translations. For example, the injunction "husband supports wife" became "husband controls his wife", while "the wife comforts the husband" shifted to "the wife reveres her husband". Many Chinese also sought practical gains from Buddhism that would be in keeping with older goals: thus one female bodhisattva was said to have the power to grant children to any woman who prayed to her, and this kind of prayer became common. Buddhism here could be seen to serve a Confucian-style family.

Nevertheless, syncretic accommodation could not wipe away the fact that, in Buddhism, women could be holy in their own right, which implied both status and spiritual function far different from the Confucian standards. Chinese Buddhism indeed turned out to emphasize examples of holy women, contributing significantly to this aspect of the Buddhist literature. Chinese art, also, frequently portrayed female holy figures. At first, some female saints were given male form, including moustaches, but by the seventh century, during the early Tang dynasty, a very female representation emerged, characteristically slender and clad in white. By 828 there was a statue of the most famous female bodhisattva, Kuan-yin, in every Chinese monastery – 44,000 in all. The saint was particularly responsible for the relief of sorrows, to anyone who invoked her (or sometimes still, his, as the gender reference continued to fluctuate) name.

If women could be holy, what would happen to Chinese family relations? The answer overall was: from a personal standpoint a great deal, but from a structural standpoint very little. Chinese family norms were not redefined; they did not become more similar to those in India, where women's sensuality and cleverness were held in greater esteem. To this extent, the implications of this particular cultural contact were very limited.

Many women, however, found in Buddhism a vital addition to their own lives, which undoubtedly made the Confucian insistence on inferiority and deference more palatable. The opportunity to seek salvation essentially on the same terms as men could be a precious equalizer, without changing surface family relations, while, relatedly, women not happy with life in this world could eagerly pursue that in the next.

For some women, Buddhism provided opportunities for activities outside home or family. Groups of women might join to visit temples. In one temple, a women's club met monthly to study sutras. Some women gained leadership roles in such groups, or as particularly holy figures; in the eleventh century a Miss Ts'ai refused to marry and gained followers from all walks of life who believed her to be an immortal.

More commonly, though, according to biographies (focused mainly, to be sure, on the upper classes), Buddhist women used Buddhism to draw deeper inside themselves, within the home. Many chanted prayers and did Buddhist reading, while fasting occasionally for holiness. A Miss Pien, in the eleventh century, recited Buddhist sutras daily while burning incense. Many put

Buddhist statues in their homes. Men often approved of their wives' piety, particularly if they continued to organize ancestor worship as a domestic ritual (and Buddhism could be quite accommodating here). Many felt that piety helped the family, for example when prayers encouraged a sick person to recover, and might actually make wives more docile. Referring to one Buddhist wife, a biographer noted: "At times of crisis she could be tranquil and satisfied with her fate, not letting outside things agitate her mind." A few couples shared Buddhist interests, but more commonly the husbands were far less involved. A few, as Confucianists, tried to talk their wives out of their enthusiasms, but acceptance was more common – precisely because Buddhism did not rock the family boat in terms of accepted roles and values. Since many women turned to religion later in life, after childbearing, even the Buddhist impulse to "rid herself of worldly desires" might not matter much. (Some husbands even approved of the favorable impact on the family's food budget.) Buddhism could also help with older mothers, keeping them apart from the family business in which they might otherwise interfere. Commenting on one widow who read Buddhist books avidly, a biographer said: "She entrusted family affairs to her children and lived tranquilly without involving herself."

The situation of women who entered Buddhist convents was more complex, for here was an alternative to family life. One story discussed a woman whose shrewish temper made her impossible to live with; a failure as a wife, she finally went to a convent, but the writer made it clear that she realized this was a serious demotion from proper status, not a role model for the young. Many wealthy women entered convents after their husbands died, which was a clear way to reconcile Buddhism with prior devotion to Confucian family values. But some women insisted on convents rather than marriage, which could be far more troubling. Some bitter fights with parents, eager to arrange a match, could ensue, for disloyalty to the father was involved. As one insistent woman noted, "Why must I submit thrice [to father, husband and son), before I am considered a woman of propriety?" – a decidedly non-Confucian sentiment. Some fathers nevertheless consented, often persuaded that a nun-daughter "shall raise her family to glory and bring you blessings and honor". This kind of arrangement was particularly possible in upper-class families where the parents themselves were Buddhists and in the period when the imperial government seemed to be supporting Buddhism. Other arrangements, too, might work: one story told of a daughter who prevailed simply by fasting nearly to death; another told of a woman who prayed that her wedding would not happen, only to be told by a Buddha image that her bridegroom would soon die. "You need only continue your ardent practice [of prayer}" – and sure enough the man died the next day when an ox gored him, and the woman was free to join the convent. Women who explicitly avoided marriage might inspire hundreds of others to join them.

The independence suggested in convent life might carry over into politics. A few women in convents were consulted on important political decisions, their holiness giving them authority; as one account put it: "Thus did [the nun's] power overrule the whole court, and her authority extend both within and without Buddhist circles." The only real Chinese empress, Wu, argued that she should be allowed to serve, against strict patriarchal custom, on the grounds that she was a reincarnation of a previous female saint whom the Buddha himself had promised spiritual rebirth. Backed by Buddhist monks, she usurped the throne in 683, finding in the religion the alternative authority essential to confute Confucian tradition. She held power for over twenty-five years, yielding only when she was ailing.

Political power and life without marriage, even in opposition to family wishes, showed the Buddhist potential in impacting Chinese gender traditions. But, though important in individual lives and in one case in imperial history, these events did not shake basic structures. Indeed, in letting assertive women have their way without challenging marriage as an institution, they may even have provided a safety valve. This added to Buddhism's more common impact, in helping women adjust within the family, often becoming calmer and more subordinate than before Buddhism inspired them. The power of the Confucian tradition, where women were concerned, plus the otherworldly, spiritual focus of Buddhism, allowed this result to predominate. Change occurred; thousands of individuals were affected; but there was no redefinition of systems. The fact that the practice of footbinding began in this very period – where a girl's footbones were broken to prevent anything but a halting walk, held to be the mark of beauty but clearly a further step toward making the women involved purely ornamental – confirms the limitations of Buddhist impact. Buddhism could not, for Chinese women generally, slow the standard tendency in agricultural civilizations to a further deterioration in conditions.

In the ninth century the Tang dynasty turned against Buddhism, attacking many monasteries and persecuting religious leaders. Buddhism did not die, but its influence never recovered. Buddhist elements persisted in Chinese thought and art, but those aspects of the religion that might subvert gender standards were pushed beneath the surface. The number of convents shrank, reducing this option. Individual women could pursue piety within the family still, as some of the examples above suggest, but the larger contact with Buddhism receded.

The attack on Buddhism reflected concern for the religion's failure to emphasize active loyalty to the political system above all. Confucianism returned to unchallenged dominance. Worries about women were not featured in the attack, but more general anxiety about the lack of attachment of Buddhism to the family as a priority was involved. The result, certainly, intensified the limitations of Buddhist influence on relations between men and women in China.

Buddhist interaction with China was distinctive – all cases of contact have their particular features – but it was also subtle. Real change was involved, more than any outside force would bring to gender issues in China until the late nineteenth century. But change can be real without redefining structures, and it can affect many people, over a prolonged period, without turning into a new wave of the future. Weighing what did happen against the potential for more change, and explaining why the results were not more sweeping, provides an obvious spur to historical analysis.

Further reading

A classic study is Arthur Wright, *Buddhism in Chinese History* (Stanford, Calif./London: Stanford University Press/Oxford University Press, 1959); see also Wright, ed. Robert Somers, *Studies in Chinese Buddhism* (New Haven, Conn.: Yale University Press, 1990). See also Kenneth Ch'en, *The Chinese Transformation of Buddhism* (Princeton, NJ: Princeton University Press, 1973). A major source is Shih Pao-ch'ang (ed.), *Lives of the Nuns: Biographies of Chinese Buddhist Nuns,* trans. Kathryn Tsai (Honolulu: University of Hawaii Press, 1994). On women: Diana Paul, *Women in Buddhism. Images of the Feminine in Mahayana Tradition,* 2nd edn (Berkeley, Calif.: University of California Press, 1979); Patricia Ebrey, *The Inner Quarters. Marriage and the Lives of Chinese Women in the Sung Period* (Berkeley, Calif.: University of California Press, 1993).

Chapter 4

Islamic standards outside the heartland

Changes and continuities in India and sub-Saharan Africa

The expansion of Islam, after its origins in the Arabian peninsula around 610, is one of the great culture-contact episodes in world history. The interactions that resulted surpassed the results of the spread of Buddhism, for there was no precedent for this range of religious influence. Islam's strengths as a religion focused attention on prescriptions that would help an individual gain access to heaven, with great attention to the loyalty due to Allah. Islam also spread as a result of successful military conquests, initially by the Arabs, explicit missionary activity and expanding international trade. Within a few centuries, Islam had made major inroads not only throughout the Middle East and North Africa, but also in southern Europe, India, sub-Saharan Africa, Central Asia and Southeast Asia.

Islam as a religion had very definite ideas about the roles of men and women. As with many religions, such as Buddhism, the ideas were complex, almost contradictory. Furthermore, Islam in the Middle East picked up some older practices concerning gender, such as the veiling of women, that were not integral to the religion bur came to seem so – this was in fact a case of syncretism within the Middle East, as we shall see. Complexities of this sort inevitably affected Islam's impact on gender practices outside its home base, particularly in places where it operated as a minority faith.

This chapter looks at two important cases of Islamic influence: India and sub-Saharan Africa. In both cases, Islamic ideas and their Middle Eastern overlays were not picked up entirely; earlier cultures continued to be influential. This led to some criticisms by Islamic travelers, who thought that women's roles in places like Africa seemed inappropriate. Over time, however, Islamic influence worked further changes, leading to a deterioration in women's conditions sometimes more marked than in the Middle East itself.

The Prophet Muhammed, who brought Islam to the Middle East, believed he was improving women's conditions, compared to more traditional Arab forms of patriarchy. His case was strong, bur Islam also confirmed patriarchal relations in many ways and, when blended with practices like veiling and considerable seclusion of women, offered some clearly mixed signals. Many other peoples, though accepting Islam, would continue to prefer their own gender traditions; this is what some of the Arab travelers noted and disliked. In the long run, however, Islam blended with regional versions of patriarchy and rigidified gender relations. Many of the results persist to the present day.

Islam, men and women

The Qu'ran and other central Islamic writings emphasized two vital principles where women were concerned. First, women had souls, and in principle were spiritually equal to men; they could go to heaven. Spiritual equality also allowed some to participate actively in Muslim rituals such as the pilgrimage to Mecca, where they enjoyed greater latitude than their Christian sisters in Europe when engaged in pious travel. Second, they had defined rights, in a religion that was quite legalistic. Women could own property. They had rights to property they brought into a marriage. They could divorce. Muhammed also attacked other invidious inequalities, such as the practice of female infanticide.

Many commentators have argued that Islam offered more voice and protection for women than any of the other major religions. Divorce and property rights were clearly established, and the pilgrimage to Mecca gave many women an opportunity for independent travel. These aspects of Islam, and the debate they engender, retain great importance in the world today.

At the same time, Islam maintained a clearly patriarchal structure. The Koran said: "Men have authority over women because of what God has conferred on the one in preference to the other." Women did not worship alongside men, but separately. Men's family rights were superior to those of women. They could divorce more easily. Punishments for male sexual transgression were often lighter than those for women. If they had the means, men could take up to three wives; the same latitude was not allowed for women. Men had public roles denied to women; the Hadith, a collection of early Muslim traditions and edicts, stated: "The first condition for the *qadi* (judge) is that he must be a man. . . . As for women, they are unsuited to positions of authority." Wives were vowed to the "service of the husband, care of children, and the management of the household". Men were authorized to use violence, if necessary, to keep their women in line. Furthermore, even spiritual equality was conditioned by a deep belief that women were by nature more sinful than men. Using the biblical story of Eve as the first sinner, Muslim doctrine held that hell was disproportionately populated by the female sex. Again from the Hadith: "I had a look into Hell and saw that most of its inhabitants were women." Islamic writings urged that men be kindly to women, avoiding abuse, but these were sincere admonitions introduced to cushion profound inequality.

Obviously, it was possible to see quite diverse messages in Islam where gender was concerned. Even today, feminists dispute Islam: some, holding up Western standards of women's liberation, urge that Islam must change, while others contend that adequate protection for women's rights can be found in the traditional doctrine. It's a question of emphasis.

Islamic complexity was enhanced by Arab adaptation to pre-existing habits in the Middle East. Veiling had spread earlier in the Middle East, including the eastern Roman Empire and also Persia, as a sign of status for the elite. It emphasized the seclusion of women, and their possession by fathers and husbands. Covering the mouth and nose, while clothing the body fully in robes, highlighted the sexual unavailability of respectable women. The custom never spread to rural women who, like women in most agricultural societies, engaged in hard physical labor. Arab Muslims increasingly adopted the veil from the people they conquered; the custom seemed sophisticated and it suited a patriarchal society, perhaps compensating for some of the advantages Islam had conferred on women. As so often happened in agricultural civilizations, syncretism stressed new marks of separateness for women, blending inferiorities initially developed in different cultures. The veiling habit spread so widely that most people, Muslims and non-Muslims alike, today assume it was sanctioned by the Qu'ran, but this is not the case. The Qu'ran urged that women cover their bosoms and jewelry, and that the wives of the Prophet Muhammed cloak their bodies tightly so that they would not be bothered in public, but it did not mention veiling. In fact, Muslims adopted the veiling practice gradually – it spread fully through the urban Middle East and North Africa only by the sixteenth century. It was true, however, that beyond the recommendations of the Qu'ran and the Hadith upper-class Muslim families tended to emphasize the seclusion of women, keeping them at home to minimize their public dealings as a means of supporting controls over sexuality. Precisely because women retained property ownership after marriage, it seemed vital that men regulate their contacts, an ironic result of Islamic rights. Seclusion also followed from Muslim emphasis on women's capacity for sexual enjoyment equal to men's: this view, far different from the idea of female passivity stressed in Christianity, again had complex results in practice. Developments like veiling and seclusion, despite their tenuous relationship to Islam itself, might seem part of a single Muslim cultural package, when the religion began expanding to additional regions.

The spread of Islam

Muhammed, born about 570 CE, had directed his preaching to the Arabs, and Arab conversion to Islam became part of a mission of conquest by this nomadic people through the Middle East and North Africa. The collapse of the Roman Empire had left a welter of small states and various religions in the southeastern Mediterranean, a situation ripe both for a dynamic new faith and for the consolidation of Arab political and military control. Arab armies quickly spread through most of the Middle East, including Persia. Arabs for a time sought to reserve Islam for their people alone, but many others sought access, some adopting Arab language and culture in the process.

Arab military power was enhanced by the position of the Middle East as a

center of trade with Asia, Africa and Europe, and changes within Islam promoted explicit missionary activity. After about 900 a movement called Sufism
took hold, urging spiritual purity and intense piety. The enthusiasm and
example of the holy devotion of Sufi leaders helped persuade many of the truth
of Islam.

The mixture of factors that spurred Islam was not surprising; all world
religions spread through a variety of means and motives. There is, however, a
rough division between cases in which Islam arrived on the heels of military
invasion and those where it reached people through a mixture of contacts with
merchants and missionaries.

India was already dominated by Hinduism, which had largely prevailed over
Buddhism at the end of the classical period. Islam and Hinduism differed in
many ways. Islam insisted on a single God, compared to the more general
Hindu belief in alignment with the divine order and a host of specific divinities.
Islam emphasized spiritual equality more strongly, and rejected the caste
system (though acknowledging inequality in this world). Most Hindus
preferred to ignore Islam, though there was some tolerance, but Islam did
penetrate, through trading contacts and Arab raids on Indian territory. There
was also mutual cultural interaction even when conversion did not result.
Muslims learned about Indian science and mathematics, including the numbering system which passed to the Middle East (where Europeans encountered
it and called it "Arabic"). By the eleventh century, wider Muslim conquests
in India (spearheaded by converted Turks) led to Muslim-run political states
like the Delhi sultanate and some attacks on Hindu religious temples. Sufi
missionaries poured in, and more widespread conversions to Islam resulted,
particularly in the northwest. Hindu leaders reacted by emphasizing more
popular religious ideas and rituals, and there were a few efforts explicitly to
blend the two religions (for example, retaining Hinduism but renouncing the
caste system, in an attempt to keep the lower castes away from the egalitarian
attraction of Islam). Another, still more powerful Muslim wave arrived with
the conquests of the Mughal invaders around 1500, which led to a large
Muslim-run empire that flourished for two centuries. Early Mughal rulers were
tolerant of Hindus, but later emperors attacked the faith, favoring Muslims in
their administration. Through all this varied encounter, over many centuries,
most Indians remained Hindu. The interaction was extensive, though, even
for the majority, and inevitably it involved considerations of gender.

Islam reached Africa below the Sahara in two ways, though only a minority
of Africans converted during the postclassical period. In West Africa, contacts
focused on the growing Sudanic kingdoms, beginning with Ghana. Trade with
Muslim North Africa developed across the Sahara, providing Ghana with tax
revenues and goods, such as horses. The king of Ghana hired Arab Muslims to
keep records, using their experience with writing and bureaucracy. Contacts
also facilitated military raids from the north. The kingdom of Mali, succeeding
Ghana around 1200, regularized interactions. Rulers of Mali used more Muslim

bureaucrats and themselves converted as a gesture of goodwill. One king, Mansa Musa, made a famous pilgrimage to Mecca in 1334–5, dazzling Arabs with his wealth in gold. Sufi missionaries fanned out in Africa, but there was little effort at this point to convert ordinary people. Even Africans who converted kept many of their previous customs, such as belief in the king as divine and rejection of Muslim punishments, like cutting off the hands of thieves, as inhumane. A second strand of Islam spread down the East Africa coast, propelled by Arab traders in the Indian Ocean. From Egypt, traders and missionaries worked directly southward, in the nation now known as Sudan. Farther south, mixed Arab-African cities formed along the coast, blending Arab and African languages and, of course, promoting Islam. Many traders intermarried with elite African women. Conversions to Islam were voluntary, but Islam represented commercial success and high social status, and it did well down the Indian Ocean coast. Finally, beginning in the late eighteenth century, through enhanced missionary activity and outright religious wars, Islam began to spread to a wider populace, a process that has continued to this day. Sub-Saharan Africa today is about 40 percent Muslim, with particular concentrations down from the Sahara, across western and central Africa, and in East Africa.

Two obvious points arise. First, contacts and conversions of the magnitude that affected both India and sub-Saharan Africa inevitably caused reconsiderations of the roles and practices applied to men and women, on the part of Muslims in the regions and non-Muslims alike. Second, the interaction was prolonged, continuing to the present day. Initial results, concerning gender, might change as Islam settled in. A first impulse to hold gender customs apart often changed under more prolonged contact. In the long run, the impact of exposure to Islam has been considerable, altering gender habits even of people who did not formally convert.

The case of India

Early Muslim forays into India had only a mild impact on culture, for the raiders did not stay long enough to leave a mark. There were some reports that Hindus resisted Islam in part because it seemed to emphasize too much seclusion of women, which ran against Indian custom, but there were many motives for resisting a foreign religion. Some people, acquainted with Islam, may have been torn between the social appeal to the lower castes – the promise of fuller spiritual equality – and the implications for a greater distance between men and women.

The ingredients were available, however, for a major clash about women's roles. Would Middle Eastern emphasis on veiling and isolating women predominate over Indian emphasis on affection and sensual delight? Which approach to protecting women would be preferred, the Islamic legalistic emphasis, which Hinduism downplayed where women were concerned while highlighting the power of husbands and fathers, or the Hindu appeal to emotional attachment and admiration?

What components of two complex cultural systems would indeed stand out? Would Islam be seen as a defender of women's spiritual status along with rights (such as property), or would the practical marks of inferiority be taken as the core of this gender framework? How would the familial affection developed in Hinduism be balanced against such features as arranged marriages, dowries to husbands, and even the immolation of widows on the funeral fires of their husbands (the practice of *sati*, just spreading in India during the postclassical period)?

Interaction was complicated, finally, by the fact that both cultural systems were patriarchal, which made it easy to borrow specific elements of the other's practice without great change. Hindus who converted to Islam might well believe that their treatment of women required little alteration, despite the fact that in principle there were major differences in approach.

So what actually happened? Muslims in India, including converts, never adopted some Hindu features such as *sati*. *Sati*, based on the notion that a widow had nothing to live for after her husband died, ran counter to Muslim principles of individual souls and hostility to suicide. The practice was not widespread in India anyway, particularly in some of the regions where Islam was strongest. Mughal emperors in the sixteenth century made some moves toward banning it, though without much effect.

By the same token, Hindus did not widely turn to the kinds of women's dress current in Middle Eastern cities. They did not adopt the same kind of veiling, and they retained a preference for colorful clothing. Nor did Islamic ideas about women's property rights affect Hindu practice, though they did affect Muslim converts, as Muslim-Indian compilations of Islamic law fairly faithfully repeated the provisions of the Hadith.

In other words, despite extensive cultural contact, some of the more extreme symbols of female inferiority did not cross borders, but nor did certain culturally specific measures designed to protect women.

There were, though, several merger points – the predictable symptoms of syncretism – that developed over time. Muslims, both converts and arrivals from the Middle East, frequently picked up Hindu marriage customs. Thus women often returned to their parents' home for the birth of a first child – a Hindu custom – and other Hindu practices surrounded marriage and childbirth. At the same time, converts often retained elements of Hindu customary law, including ideas about provision of dowries from wives' parents to the new husband. Whereas Muslim property law retained wives' ownership of dowries, Hindu tradition gave them to husbands directly. Here, what seemed to be a direct clash in terms of official ideas was elided in practice, to women's disadvantage. Even today, Muslim men on the Indian subcontinent can be as fierce in defense of their dowry rights as their extremist Hindu counterparts. Finally, individual Mughal rulers picked up some of the customs of Hindu princes when it came to the numbers of wives they took, again violating Muslim law. Again, there was some mutual cultural "shopping" when it came to intimate customs as well as ways of extending male advantages.

The biggest result of mutual encounter, however, involved the spread of the *purdah* system among women in the Hindu elite. *Purdah* involved substantial seclusion for women in the home, often behind screens or curtains in separate rooms, so that they would be separate from male society. By the time Islam gained serious influence in India, the idea of veiling women and isolating them in private apartments in the home was gaining ground rapidly in the Middle East, as Arabs adapted to customs they found among Greeks and Persians. This was simply not Indian custom, where women had been allowed to go about more freely. And Indians, including Muslim converts, long avoided the practices. Arab travelers noted, often with some shock, that Indian men and women worked together and that women did not conceal their faces or even all parts of their bodies. In 1415 a Chinese ambassador to Bengal noted that "men and women work in the fields or weave according to the seasons". An Arab observer as late as 1595 commented that women often presented themselves to political leaders and that "the chief public transactions fall to the lot of the women". In other words, even as Muslim communities formed, they long preserved Indian customs about public role and dress, and obviously the Hindu majority did the same.

The Middle Eastern cultural example was powerful, however. It was associated with many rulers in India; it could seem more sophisticated than local culture; and it enhanced male advantage in a society that was already deeply patriarchal. So, slowly, it spread. Muslim Indians began to adopt the veil, though not, usually, the somber clothing of their Middle Eastern sisters. And separation went further still. By the late sixteenth century a Bengali Islamic story of Adam and Eve emphasized division of labor: Adam was the farmer ("agriculture will be your destiny") while Eve learned to cook. Yet Bengali literature for at least another century more commonly emphasized shared tasks. A Muslim peasant in one story around 1700 notes how she and her husband "both used to reap the autumnal paddy . . . then we both sat down to husk the rice... we both sat near the fire and warmed ourselves. . . . How happy we were when after the day's work we retired to rest in our home." Even at this late date, the Middle Eastern version of Islam had not conquered Indian work customs. But the process continued. By the nineteenth and twentieth centuries, men did farm work separately, while women concentrated on post-harvest operations, like winnowing and husking seeds, that could be done within the farmyard.

This change was a striking example of the power of cultural over economic "rationality". For the borrowed system was far costlier, as it limited women's contribution to agricultural production. But, because of the glitter of imported Islam, operating over many centuries, a redefinition of respectable behavior took precedence.

Ultimately, the system of *purdah* spread widely among Hindu elites and among Indian Muslim families generally. The process of change was not only slow but uneven. Ordinary Hindu peasants did not pick up the new emphasis on isolation and gender division of labor. Relatedly, Hinduism in southern India showed less Muslim influence, even among elites, than its counterpart in northern India where Muslim example had been much stronger. But, for those affected, the change was very real. The power of *purdah* was a great inhibition on Hindu as well as Muslim women's political and educational activities as late as the early twentieth century, though under the spur of Indian nationalism it would gradually break down.

Mutual cultural influence took time in the Indian case, but it proved very powerful, affecting Muslim families with regard to law, and some Hindu families with regard to social practice. The common denominator, some informal customs aside, was a selective emphasis on borrowing that would enhance male power over women. Cultural elements, particularly in Islam, that highlighted women's spirituality and rights had less impact, as two cultures interacted extensively if suspiciously on the subcontinent.

Sub-Saharan Africa

Because Islam spread not only slowly but also selectively in sub-Saharan Africa, it is not surprising that its impact on African gender habits was quite limited for many centuries. In the mixed Arab-African cities of the east coast, where the blended Swahili language took hold, African women often enjoyed high status. Many influential women and queens played prominent roles in public affairs in these towns. They helped oversee important events for their kin-groups, they participated in public celebrations like New Year's ceremonies, and they worshipped in mosques with their men. They were even encouraged to become literate and to study Islamic scholarship. Certain evidence suggests that governing authority in some cases was inherited through female members of the ruling kin-groups. In this context, specific Islamic practices, like female property rights and inheritance, might even be extended. One account suggests inheritance rights equal to men's, whereas Islamic law had specified rights to only 50 percent of the male level.

African customs prevailed over Islam in West Africa also, where gender was concerned – again, in a context where only a minority converted. Muslim women did not accept the Middle Eastern dress code or the injunctions toward isolation.

This was an aspect of African society that particularly struck the great Muslim traveler Ibn Battuta (1304–69). A North African, Battuta was accustomed to veiling and segregation, and he simply did not find them, even in sub-Saharan Muslim communities that were otherwise exemplary. "With regard to their women, they are not modest in the presence of men, they do not veil themselves in spite of their perseverance in the prayers. . . . The women there have friends and companions amongst men." Battuta even claimed that the men felt no sexual jealousy ("The condition of these people is strange and their manners outlandish"). Battuta praised one African community for its religious zeal, its meticulous observance of prayers, its insistence that children learn the Qu'ran. But "among the bad things which they do" was the fact that "their serving women, slave women and little daughters appear before people naked, exposing their private parts". Even a sultan's daughters might expose themselves inappropriately.

Battuta was further shocked when an African *qadi* who had taken the pilgrimage to Mecca blithely introduced him to a "female companion". Battuta walked in on the two of them and wanted to leave, but both of them laughed at him, unrestrained by the modesty he thought necessary. In fact, he simply could not understand how Africans who had been in the Middle East and knew how things should be were so nonchalant. One man told him: "'Women's companionship with men in our country is honorable and takes place in a good way: there is no suspicion about it. They are not like the women in your country.' I was astonished at this. Though he invited me many times, I did not respond."

West Africa particularly depended on extensive work by women, including participation in the marketplace selling goods. The Muslim insistence on segregation and cumbersome clothing simply did not catch on. Over time, to be sure, there were greater accommodations, particularly in the regions closest to North Africa such as the modern nation of Sudan. In general, however, this aspect of the Middle Eastern version of Islam and African Islam simply did not mix.

There were some drawbacks to the pattern that resulted. Muslim Arabs bought many slaves from Africa, and the economic versatility and dress patterns of African women made them exceptionally attractive. Even aside from the sexual aspect, unveiled slave women could conduct market operations that respectable free Muslims shunned. Many enslaved African women were held as concubines in the Middle East. Around 1500 an Egyptian satirist, Ibn al Marzuban, ridiculed the resultant Arab preference for "Dark-skinned Peoples". And in Africa itself, particularly East Africa, early patterns of women's status tended to erode with time; after 1600, accounts of significant women's roles in urban public life trail off.

There was one other result of encounter that had especially sweeping consequences. In northeastern Africa (from Egypt south to present-day Kenya), practices of female circumcision — cutting or stitching the labia and clitoris to prevent sexual enjoyment and therefore, presumably, enhance sexual fidelity — had developed before Islam. The practice was viewed as essential to the honor of some male-dominated families. This was not a Muslim innovation, and indeed it did not spread beyond this region. Islam attacked the practice in fact, for it did not coincide with official views of women's rights and sexuality. But in this one African region the practice did spread along with Islam. Muslim views on women's inferiority and confinement seemed to encourage the merger of ideas. Thus most of the people who practiced, and continue to practice, female circumcision and other genital alterations in this region were Muslim, and non-Muslims who adopted the practice did so as part of their conversion to Islam (under pressure from their Muslim neighbors). In this syncretic rendition, many northeastern Africans view genital surgery on women as part of keeping the traditions of their Islamic faith.

Islam in Africa clearly had diverse results. African pressures for greater independence for women had real effects in producing a distinctive version of Islam; this version had little direct influence on Arab thinking – hence the shocked travelers – though its practical results were complex. As in India, change over time heightened the influence of the Middle Eastern model, though never to the extent of producing widespread female isolation or *purdah*. In one region, another version of syncretism gave greater force to a pre-existing patriarchal custom designed to limit women's sexual experiences.

Conclusion

Islam presented a complex model of relationships between men and women. Its most obvious features were not the ones intrinsic to the religion, so much as the Middle Eastern overlay of veiling and segregation. Many contact societies long resisted these features, and some, sincerely Islamic in other respects, never picked them up fully. Over time, however, the pressure to adapt grew, and it could affect people who did not convert to Islam at all, like the Hindus who adopted *purdah*. What is striking, in all the combinations that developed, right through the nineteenth century, was the dominance of the patriarchal angle. The aspects of Islam that emphasized spirituality and rights, though they might affect women in their devotional life, received little attention as part of cultural interaction. Though in different ways in India and in northeastern Africa, the tendency was to adopt cultural blends that would lead to worse results for women than those prevalent either in the original culture or in the Middle East itself.

This same process of assimilation on the basis of rigid patriarchy applied in other cases as well. When Islam first spread to nomadic peoples in Central Asia, such as the Turks, it did not dent nomadic appreciation for women's power and freedom. Turkish women thus continued to participate in tribal councils and occasionally in warfare. (This shocked Ibn Battuta yet again, when he visited this region.) Women tended animals, the tribes' main wealth, and also organized migration patterns. However, as the nomadic Turks moved into the Middle East, they developed settled agriculture and also encountered a fuller dose of Middle Eastern customs, both Islamic and Byzantine, emphasizing veiling and segregation – they quickly complied, at least in the upper classes, producing traditions of veiling and isolation that continue to affect Turkey today.

Only in areas where Islam spread at greatest distance from the Middle East, such as Indonesia (today the nation with the world's largest Muslim population) did veiling and isolation have virtually no impact at all (save for dress on religious occasions). Elsewhere the long-term results of Islamic contact on gender patterns – including those not inherent in Islam itself – are among the most important in world history, in terms of the numbers of people involved and the intimate aspects of life affected.

Islam's impact and complexities apply to aspects of gender beyond conditions of women, of course. Official Islam was rigorous against homosexuality, for example – particularly the Hadith, or compilation of laws, which stipulated severe punishments. But as Islam spread to areas that had been more tolerant of homosexual practices, such as Persia or Spain, some ambiguity might develop. In these regions an important strand of poetry expressed ardent love for same-sex youth, maintaining earlier traditions in the Mediterranean and the Middle East.

The implications of Islam for masculinity could also vary with contact, beyond the basic assertion of male superiority in rights and in religious scholarship. Islam could emphasize military virtues as part of masculinity, and certainly it could encourage jealous defense of family honor. But these aspects were more pronounced in regions such as the Middle East than in areas with somewhat different traditional standards, such as southeast Asia, even as these regions, too, embraced Islam.

Further reading

On Islam itself: Judith Tucker, "Gender and Islamic History", in Michael Adas (ed.), *Islamic and European Expansion: The Forging of a Global Order* (Philadelphia, Pa: Temple University Press, 1993). On India: Richard Eaton, *The Rise of Islam and the Bengal Frontier, 1204–1760* (Berkeley, Calif.: University of California Press, 1993); Zinat Kauser, *Muslim Women in Medieval India* (Patna: Janaki Prakashan, 1992). On Africa: Esther Hicks, *Infibulation: Female Mutilation in Islamic Northeastern Africa*, 2nd edn (New Brunswick: Transaction Publishers, 1996); John Ralph Willis (ed.), *Slaves and Slavery in Muslim Africa*, 2 vols (London/Totowa, NJ: Frank Cass, 1985); Randall L. Pouwels, *Horn and Crescent: Cultural Change and Traditional Islam on the East African Coast, 800–1900* (Cambridge/New York: Cambridge University Press, 1987).

Chapter 5

The Chinese influence

A final case of major cultural contact in the postclassical period radiated from China, during its Tang and Song dynasties (618–1279). Unlike Islam, China did not have missionary values. Its officials were eager to spread cultural integration within their domain, but had little interest beyond. However, China's military power and regional economic influence were great. Under the Tang, outright military expansion brought China into new territories in Central Asia and Tibet, while leading to tributary arrangements with Korea and Vietnam. Other neighbors grew interested in Chinese examples, simply because of its success. Thus a second zone of cultural outreach developed, smaller than that of Islam but very potent within its orbit.

China also, of course, had a well-developed gender system, based on Confucian beliefs and a profound sense of hierarchy. Buddhism had modified this system very slightly, as discussed in Chapter 3, but the later decline of Buddhism reduced even this modest adjustment. Chinese beliefs and practices emphasized the importance of women's deference and domesticity. Of course, variety existed. Peasant women, co-operating actively in the family's work, were not as differentiated from men as those in the upper classes (though it was the upper classes that foreign observers would most likely take as models). During the Tang and particularly Song dynasties, economic growth supported larger cities, and a category of urban women arose with entertainment functions for wealthy men; some of these talented women might attain considerable if informal power. On the other hand, developments during these same dynasties increased the restrictions on larger numbers of women. The practice of footbinding became a physical manifestation of the strict gender hierarchy. In this system, women's feet were severely bound and bent in childhood, often breaking some of the small bones; the result was a small foot, held to be aesthetically pleasing, but also a halting walk that severely limited mobility. Footbinding spread slowly, but inexorably, into the nineteenth century. It started in upper-class families, where the urge to treat women as decorative objects could be most readily indulged. Then it spread in the cities and even to the countryside, at obvious cost to the effectiveness of women's work. Here was a classic case of the tendency for gender inequalities to increase over time within patriarchal societies, as a result of, indeed as a way to use, growing prosperity.

China's growing cultural outreach encountered societies where women's position was initially superior to that in China. The question is, what would happen, in the interplay between traditions that had worked well, and contacts with a clearly superior (in the sense of power and prestige) civilization. No society went to China seeking gender advice. The hope of eager borrowers was information about art, technology or politics. But contact does not respect topical boundaries, and inevitably ideas about gender might circulate as well. This chapter explores two cases: Japan, where a deliberate imitation process began around 600 CE and continued through most of the postclassical period, and then the Mongols, the nomadic herding people who conquered China and its Song dynasty and ruled the country for about a hundred years between the mid-thirteenth and mid-fourteenth centuries (1279–1368).

Japan

Japan had long been isolated from the Asian mainland, aside from periodic waves of migration that populated the islands. Agriculture, the use of iron and some rudimentary regional governments emerged during the classical period. The Shinto religion developed, involving worship of spirits of nature in local shrines, with priest-led ceremonies.

Japanese leaders became aware of Chinese achievements by about 400 CE. Selective imitation began in earnest around 600, with students and envoys traveling to China and reporting on the society's economic and political wonders. In 604 a regional ruler, Prince Shotoku, issued a constitution establishing a centralized government and bureaucracy and urging reverence for Buddhism and the Confucian virtues. Chinese-style architecture and urban planning were introduced, along with Chinese ideographs that provided the first writing form, though ultimately further adaptations to the Japanese language occurred. The Japanese government organized regular exchanges, including annual trading expeditions, and both cultural and technological borrowing increased. Chinese dance, musical and art forms were introduced to the upper classes. Poetic styles were adjusted to the Japanese language; stylized gardening took hold as an artistic expression. For a time, efforts continued to import the Chinese political system, but Japan, regionally divided by islands and mountains in any event, could not sustain this level of centralization, and more feudal forms returned, along with frequent internal wars.

Mongol invasion of China in the thirteenth century, together with the failure of two Mongol expeditions to conquer Japan, reduced the Japanese sense of Chinese superiority, and active contacts diminished by the sixteenth century. However, under the more centralized but still feudal regime of the Tokugawa shogunate, neo-Confucianism gained a new lease of life, becoming the country's principal cultural system. Confucian education spread widely, and a Confucian bureaucracy developed by the seventeenth century to serve the shogunate.

Japan, clearly, was an active if selective imitator, in a process that extended over a considerable period of time. Not all Chinese forms took hold, either because Japan could not assimilate them or because of positive distaste based on prior traditions. At the same time, imitation might suggest different priorities from those of the Chinese themselves. Buddhism, for example, had a more durable impact in Japan than in China. Strong in China at the time of Japanese contact, it was imported with fewer reservations than those that arose under the later Tang dynasty. Even in the Tokugawa period, when Confucianism created a more secular culture, the Buddhist hold continued to be significant.

Here, then, was a complex set of contacts, but one deliberately sought by a culture that admitted its inferiority, for a time at least, while maintaining a separate sense of identity. What were the gender implications?

Like many early agricultural societies, Japan offered considerable flexibility in the cultural and power relationships between men and women, before the contacts with China developed. Because writing did not exist, detailed records are unavailable. Most historians, however, speculate that women shared property rights with men and that descent may have been traced from mothers. Some have even wondered if Japan was an outright matriarchy, with women holding considerable power, though this is unproved. Sharp differences with patriarchal China are clear, and with this the probability that contact would inspire considerable change.

And so it did. China's cultural prestige made attempts to imitate aspects of its gender system almost inevitable, lest Japan seem needlessly unsophisticated. Political imitation brought clear changes in property law, downgrading women's rights by the late seventh century. Family organization and the bases for inheritance shifted to a definite patriarchal model. At the same time, Japan did not become China. Imitation was not taken to the point of copying extremes such as footbinding; and Chinese models, as Japan interpreted them, actually provided some unexpected opportunities for individual women. In one sense, this was a standard case of syncretism, with influence blended with previous customs. But there were some unexpected specific twists, apart from the fact that deterioration in women's position stopped short of Chinese levels.

Two complications were particularly significant. In the first place, Japanese versions of Buddhism provided important spiritual and organizational opportunities for some women. Leaders in the Amidist form of Buddhism stressed personal enlightenment and highlighted women's capacity here, determined that women should have "every opportunity for salvation" open to them. Buddhist clergy worked actively to bring religion to women, even though, with characteristic contradiction, some Buddhist shrines were closed to women lest they bring defilement (probably because they were subject to menstruation, long regarded as a form of pollution). On rare occasions, women achieved high positions in Buddhism, even serving as masters in the Japanese Zen school of the religion, heading networks of convents. Thus Mugai Nyodai, in the thirteenth century, served as director of more than fifteen temples and Zen convents. Born to an aristocratic family, she had been trained by a Chinese Buddhist priest invited to Japan by a regional ruler; Mugai became the priest's successor. This was unusual, to be sure, for Japanese Buddhism had not been so open to women earlier, and the idea of women as impure resurfaced later. But the availability of convent life for some women persisted for several centuries as an alternative to marriage. Buddhist pilgrimages were also important opportunities for women to get out of the home. And male Zen leaders produced some remarkable statements of principle. Thus the Zen leader Dogen:

> When we speak of the wicked there are certainly men among them. When we talk of noble persons, these surely include women. Learning the Law of Buddha and achieving release from illusion have nothing to do with whether one happens to be a man or a woman. . . . What is so sacred about the status of a man? . . . The four elements that make up the human body are the same for a man as for a woman. . . . You should not waste your time in futile discussions of the superiority of one sex over the other.

The second complication to Chinese patriarchal influence was even more unexpected, though it had its own peculiar logic. Because of the prestige of the new Chinese cultural contacts, and in an atmosphere in which male superiority was gaining emphasis, Japanese men claimed the right to guide the infusion of Chinese cultural elements. But this left opportunities in non-Chinese cultural domains, whether new or old, for women. Poetry, for example, was for men, who studied the Chinese language from which women were barred, but women could write prose, and in Japanese (using modifications of Chinese characters, which they devised). As a result, women produced the great literary works of the postclassical period in Japan, including the world's first novel, the *Tale of Genji* (written by Muraskai Shikbu, 978–*c.*1016). Women writers played a greater role than in any other society before modern times. Coming from the upper classes, they had time to study, time enhanced by the new limits placed on contacts between the genders by imported Confucian customs. Their exclusion from Chinese culture surely helped goad them to response, though they did not protest directly. Free to express themselves in their own native language, they composed the classic works of Japanese prose. In some cases, like the *Confessions of Lady Nijo* (written in the fourteenth century) women's literature and Buddhism were entwined, with the author describing life as a nun, fulfilling vows to copy the sutras and traveling to holy sites while also advising the court on matters of dress and decoration.

Even at the political and legal level, where Chinese influence was less condi-tional, Japan maintained its own tone. Laws allowed women to inherit feudal positions. But men's superiority was inscribed as well: thus the Chinese-inspired provision that a husband could divorce his wife for his own convenience. This provision was coupled with the Confucian idea of threefold obedience, to father, husband and son. The position of family master, obviously male, gained growing emphasis.

Furthermore, Chinese influence did not end with the active period of imitation. As with Islam in India, new impacts could occur surprisingly late, as additional assimilation occurred. Thus the rise of Confucian influence under the Tokugawa introduced new constraints on women. Among other things, the Buddhist opportunity for female leadership virtually disappeared, as did any particular literary role. New limits were imposed on women's dress, to keep them humble. A 1683 law prohibited thin silk crepe, embroidery and dappled tie-dye in women's clothing. Other laws became more severe, as a case in 1711 demonstrates. Here, a woman reported her husband's absence and suspected death. It turned out that her father had participated in killing the man. The question arose of whether she had violated Confucian obedience by unwittingly attacking her father. Chinese law codes, cited by the Japanese authorities, noted that "anyone who exposes the crime of his father and mother shall be put to death", while a Japanese code said "anyone who informs on the wrongdoing of his father and mother shall be banished". University authorities, on appeal, cited the "fundamental principles governing human relations", including woman's obligations to father, husband and son. To be sure, fathers should not kill husbands; this, and the woman's ignorance of her father's act, were admitted as attenuating circumstances. Still, while she need not be put to death, the Head of the University opined, "she must still be condemned to become a slave girl" (and she was also jailed for a year beforehand).

Confucianism reigned supreme, not only in new legal inferiorities for women but also in the growing educational gap between the genders as men, but only few women, could take advantage of the proliferation of Confucian and Buddhist schools in the eighteenth and nineteenth centuries. Chinese aesthetic values won attention as well. A Tokugawa novel admiringly describes a woman's ideal beauty: "Her feet could not have had the breadth of eight copper coins, the big toes curled upwards and the soles were translucently delicate." Yet, even with this further assimilation, sufficient remnants of the older, more independent tradition survived to prevent outright footbinding. Syncretism persisted, if increasingly inclined toward the Chinese side of the equation.

The China connection had wider effects on Japanese approaches to gender issues. Despite a brief flirtation with Chinese politics, Japan did not develop the valuation of scholar-bureaucrats that China long boasted. Its definition of masculinity placed greater emphasis on military qualities, though it was a plus if generals could also write poetry. But China's tolerant attitude toward homosexuality definitely affected Japan. Individual Chinese emperors, and many intellectuals, made no secret of homosexual attachments. From the eighth century onward, some Japanese poets and Buddhist religious leaders picked up the same emphasis. Thus a fifteenth-century verse proclaimed: "We passed the night in the same bed. . . . I will celebrate the night's joys of love forever." Indeed, Japan's abundant literature on same-sex love among males surpassed that of China. One historian has compared it to the level of interest in classical Greece.

Thus, during the postclassical period and after, an East Asian gender zone emerged, consistently influenced though not fully determined by Chinese standards. Though less extensive than the Muslim zone, it was also less varied; Chinese values gradually proved more fully persuasive than Middle Eastern ones (in part because there were fewer internal religious complexities to create ambiguities). In both cases, of course, contact helped spread patriarchy to societies in which gender relations had previously been more equal, but the East Asian zone saw patriarchy rest more fully on secular arguments. This difference would prove important in more recent times, when other kinds of contact led to a reconsideration of earlier patterns of inequality.

The Mongol interlude

Chinese influence was less persuasive, however, in the Mongol case. Conditions were quite different here, for Mongols came as conquerors, not as student-imitators. Their gender traditions were probably further removed from those of China than the Japanese had been. (At the least, we know more about what the Mongol contrast was.) The contact period was much shorter, too. Gender interactions were important, nevertheless, but rather in inspiring mutual distaste than in syncretic blending. Contact episodes have diverse potentials, and this was a revealing variant.

We have noted that nomadic herders often downgraded women, praising the military skills and horsemanship of the males. There were exceptions, however, and the Mongols were one. As with several non-agricultural peoples, Mongols esteemed women for a variety of functions. Chieftains and other high leaders might practice polygyny – in part because, with frequent warfare, men were scarce, rather than as an explicit means of demeaning women – but the principal wife of a ruler had special status. Women were important in politics and on occasion in warfare, and they had vital roles in managing the family's flocks and herds. Even before the Mongol conquests of China, visitors noted the importance and independence of Mongol women. Chingiz Khan, the first great conqueror, paid great respect to the opinions of his mother and his chief wife. After the death of a khan, or ruler, his widow frequently served as regent and actively engaged in power struggles over the succession (sometimes losing and facing execution, as a price for a significant role).

The greatest of the Mongol emperors of China, Khubilai, although surrounded by skillful Chinese bureaucrats, maintained the traditions by giving his senior wife Chabi the greatest influence. Chabi in turn displayed great talent, ironically urging greater adaptation to many Chinese ways. Thus she advised the Mongols to respect Chinese agriculture, which was to them a new and inferior system, because she understood its enormous productive potential. She redesigned military uniforms to make them more practical, and managed day-to-day affairs at the court. Her hope was to build a new and lasting dynasty that would rank with the great episodes in Chinese history.

Not surprisingly, though, Chabi had little patience for Chinese treatment of women. She and other Mongol leaders did try to use marriage to cement political alliances in the vast Empire. The result implicitly challenged the great if informal power that the Chinese imperial system gave to the widows of emperors, backed by their families of origin; in the Mongol system, a woman's power resulted from her own talents plus her marriage, not her larger family ties. This was not a durable change, however.

The principal consequence of the Chinese–Mongol contacts was to convince each side that the gender practices of the other were wrong and, in the Chinese view of the Mongols, simply immoral. To Chinese observers, the independence of Mongol women ranked alongside the Mongols' aversion to bathing and their lack of surnames as a sign of barbarism. Contact can increase hostility, rather than generating gender accommodations, and this is an obvious case in point. While the Chinese did not necessarily worsen the status of their own women in reaction, it was true that footbinding continued to spread, while laws during and immediately after the Mongol period reduced the claims of wives and widows to any property rights over the dowries they brought to a marriage. Rulings held that divorced or widowed women could not take their dowries if they returned home or remarried. Reasons for these latter legal revisions are complex, but they included Neo-Confucian scholars' uneasiness about wives' control of property. When the Mongols were finally expelled from China, gender relations reflected no positive trace of their regime, and the Chinese were further convinced of the undesirability of trying to learn much from the outside world, particularly where standards were as deeply ingrained as in matters of family and politics.

Conclusion

The spread of Chinese and Confucian influence significantly influenced gender relations in a large part of Asia, though by no means all people in contact with the Chinese were affected. The contacts demonstrate some of the unpredictable aspects of imitation. The Japanese long respected Chinese superiority, but for a time their borrowing created surprising opportunities for women, both through Buddhism and their role in non-Chinese cultural forms. The obvious differences between Japanese and Mongol reactions reflect different power positions in relation to the Chinese, as well as different traditions concerning women's political role.

Historically, the Japanese reaction was the more important, in showing how contact with Chinese standards helped spread a more rigorous patriarchal system over much of East Asia. Here, comparison with Islamic and Middle Eastern influence in the same time periods, from the seventh century into the seventeenth and eighteenth, is revealing. Specifics differed in important ways, and in neither case was a homogeneous cultural approach forged, but contact did help redefine women's roles and status, leading to greater inferiority and more limited functions for virtually a millennium in huge stretches of the Afro-Eurasian world. While the example of the more patriarchal civilizations was not inevitable, it was very strong. Borrowed gender systems fitted into larger efforts to build states and cultures, and male leaders in the imitative societies were quick to seize on the apparent advantages.

Further reading

On China itself: Patricia Ebrey, *The Inner Quarters. Marriage and the Lives of Chinese Women in the Sung Period* (Berkeley, Calif.: University of California Press, 1993); Ruth S. Watson and Patricia Ebrey (eds), *Marriage and Inequality in Chinese Society* (Berkeley, Calif.: University of California Press, 1991). On the Mongol period: John Fairbank and Edwin Reischauer, *China, Tradition and Transformation* (Boston, Mass.: Houghton Mifflin, 1989); Robert Marshall, *Storm from the East, from Genghis Khan to Khubilai Khan* (Berkeley, Calif.: University of California Press, 1993); David Morgan, *The Mongols* (Oxford/New York: Blackwell, 1986). On Japan: Ryusaku Tsunoda, William de Bary and Donald Keene (eds), *Sources of Japanese Tradition,* I (New York: Columbia University Press, 1964); Conrad Totman, *Early Modern Japan* (Berkeley, Calif.: University of California Press, 1993); David Lu, *Japan, A Documentary History* (Armonk, NY: M. E. Sharpe, 1997); Conrad Schirokauer, *A Brief History of Chinese and Japanese Civilizations,* 2nd edn (San Diego, Calif.: Harcourt Brace Jovanovich, 1989); Kozo Yamamura, *The Cambridge History of Japan, 3, Medieval Japan* (Cambridge/New York: Cambridge University Press, 1990); Jeffrey Mass, *Lordship and Inheritance in Early Medieval Japan* (Stanford, Calif.: Stanford University Press, 1989). See also Louis Crampton, *Homosexuality and Civilization* (Cambridge, Mass.: Harvard University Press, 2003).

Part II

Results of European expansion, 1500–1900

Contacts among major cultures accelerated in the centuries after 1500, often revolving around various forms of expansion and intrusion by Western Europe. These were the centuries of European colonialism and then imperialism. European countries gained vast holdings in the Americas. Slightly later, they also staked out major territories in various parts of Asia, particularly southern and southeastern Asia. Later still, they turned to acquisitions in Africa and Pacific Oceania. Outright conquest, however, was not the only means of European expansion. Europeans played an increasing role in world trade, setting up trading stations literally around the globe. Finally, precisely because of Europe's new successes, leaders in a variety of other societies decided that they wanted to introduce certain internal reforms on the European pattern. Russia was the first to declare what amounted to a program of selective Westernization, but other countries, such as Japan, would launch similar attempts at controlled imitation later on.

All these contacts, obviously, had implications for relationships between men and women and beliefs about gender. Europeans had very decided views about what was right and what was wrong where gender was concerned, and they were not shy about judging others or insisting on change. European expansion was, from the start, accompanied by deliberate attempts at cultural interaction, on European terms. Christian missionaries followed close on the heels of conquerors and merchants. Colonial authorities, private reformers and other groups would also bring messages about gender in the years that followed.

Chapters in this section deal with some of the most important cases of contact, all involving Western Europe or people of European origin interacting with other regional societies. Several points deserve emphasis. First, European expansion was not the only world historical development in these four centuries. A number of societies limited their contacts with Europe; others interacted with more customary trading and exchange partners. We have seen, in Chapters 3 and 4, how Islamic and Chinese influences continued to work themselves out in key parts of Asia and Africa, quite independent of any European role. China provides an obvious example of the complexities of the early modern period, between 1500 and the early nineteenth century. Chinese merchants traded actively and successfully with the outside world, importing much of the silver the Europeans were now taking from South America in return for silks and other manufactured goods. But the Chinese were able to limit their cultural contacts with the West. Christian missionary activity was modest and controlled. Missionaries themselves often criticized aspects of China's gender system. Tolerance for homosexuality drew particular wrath: "the horrible sin to which everyone here is much given, and about which there seems to be no shame or impediment", as one missionary put it. And occasionally Chinese merchants were punished for homosexual practices in the Spanish-controlled Philippines; at one point, two were burned at the stake, which the Chinese found barbaric. But, within China, European views had no impact. The Chinese remained supremely confident in their own gender standards.

It is also true that even where Europeans did gain great influence, as in the Americas, they did not magically transform the nature of international contact. Certainly, Europeans, in dealing with what they often called "native" peoples, were unusually sure of themselves and intolerant of differences. Most of the contacts traced in this section involve largely, though not exclusively, one-way streets, where the main issues are concerned with what regional societies took or did not take from European models, but many of the types of contact were, in broad outline, quite similar to earlier precedent. In particular, Christian missionary activities aligned closely with missionary activities previously conducted by other religions, with some of the same types of implications about male–female relationships. Contradictions within Christianity also affected interactions with previously non-Christian peoples, and these included some of the same tensions between beliefs in spiritual equality and emphasis on male authority that we have seen in Buddhism and Islam. As in the other religions, the results of the tension in Christianity yielded a similar propensity for enhancing patriarchy in practice.

Yet there were some new themes. In the first place, the European reach was unusually vast, even compared to postclassical Islam. Thus, contacts with European gender standards involved a diverse array of regional societies, ranging from hunting and gathering groups to some of the most distinguished civilizations of Asia. By the same token, results varied, primarily because regional precedents varied but also because different groups of Europeans attempted different things. Protestants, for example, were on the whole slower to interfere with local gender arrangements than Catholics were, though once they got going their impact could be fierce.

Further, European standards themselves changed over time. Early contacts, in the sixteenth and seventeenth centuries, revolved heavily around Christianity, with Catholicism particularly important. Christian ideas about appropriate sexuality and male dominance within marriage figured strongly. By the eighteenth and nineteenth centuries, though, the European message became more complicated. Europeans (especially but not exclusively Protestants) launched an unprecedentedly sharp definition of male and female ideals. Men, in this equation, were primarily workers and public figures. Women's responsibilities were primarily domestic (which was of course an old theme), but now embellished by new beliefs about the frailty but moral goodness of the "weaker sex". Arrangements that gave women too much latitude, as workers or as sexual actors, might be criticized on the basis of these standards, but so might arrangements that did not seem to credit women's moral qualities and domestic virtue. Then, by the second half of the nineteenth century, yet a third model began to emerge, in which certain groups of Western women began to be active in demanding new rights, partly on the strength of the moral quality argument, but partly to compensate for inferiorities in work and in public life. These assertions could affect interactions with the wider world. In sum: many international exchanges between 1500 and 1900 had a common component, in that they involved contacts with Europe, but Europe was itself a rapidly changing entity. This complicates judgments about interactions, and it complicated interactions themselves. What, for example, was a missionary effort bringing by the nineteenth century – Christian views of gender, or the newer European ideas about "true" womanhood, or even a suggestion of new women's rights? The answer, sometimes, was all three.

Contact with Europe was also more often accompanied by colonial political and economic status than had been true for the interactions in the classical and postclassical period. European superiority was harder to contest than the Chinese or Muslim had been, brought home as it was through gunships and unequal commercial contracts. Economic changes, moreover, often complicated the results of cultural exchange. Sometimes Christian patriarchalism made changes in men's and women's economic roles easier – in other words, contacts all pushed in the same direction – but sometimes the implications clashed. These complications simply had not been so significant in previous periods. Syncretism and resistance were still possible, but the many features of the growing European world presence did tend to change the rules of the game.

European presence itself became more inescapable by the eighteenth and particularly the nineteenth century. Military superiority increased, and Europeans were able to force their way into societies like Japan and China that had previously remained culturally aloof. With the Industrial Revolution, Europe's economic superiority also became incontestable for a brief but decisive period. Just at a time when Europe's own gender standards were changing, with new emphasis on the distinctions between male and female, European administrators and missionaries gained new opportunities to pontificate on the gender failings of the rest of the world.

To be sure, Europeans, as they wittingly or unwittingly affected gender arrangements in other societies, did not always accomplish what they thought or professed they were accomplishing. This is not surprising, but it must be insisted upon. Europeans usually claimed that they were helping to improve gender relations, and particularly women's conditions – this was particularly true by the eighteenth and nineteenth centuries – but, because of their misunderstanding of gender arrangements in the societies involved, because they were trapped by their own often limited assumptions about men and women, and because their cultural efforts might be contradicted by changes they were generating in economic and political life, their claims were often quite misleading. In recent decades, thanks most notably to feminist scholarship applied to world history, historians have opened new debates about what colonialism or European-dominated trade, supplemented by cultural exchange, actually did to men's and women's lives.

Three final points. Europeans almost never managed to recast regional gender patterns as they hoped. This was partly the result of the contradictions inherent in their own efforts – for instance, they might urge greater importance for women but in the same contact actually undermine their economic independence. It also resulted from the stubborn insistence within regional societies on retaining familiar components and on shaping part of the interaction on their own terms. This, of course, is an absolutely standard feature of culture contact, not new in this period at all. Actual groups mixed and matched, accepting some European features, rejecting others in the best syncretic fashion. The theme of European expansion and arrogant self-righteousness must not obscure this process.

Point two: The interactions involved men as well as women. The chapters in this section deal disproportionately with women because this is the aspect of gender most commented upon, but in fact Europeans often tried to redefine standards for masculinity as well as for femininity. This is obvious, for example, when, by the nineteenth century, Europeans expressed shock at regional differences concerning homosexual behavior. Redefinitions could be more subtle, however. When European arrangements tried to alter traditional expressions in war, or placed local men in positions of unaccustomed economic or political inferiority, they might generate male reactions that attempted to recover cherished identities in new ways. Many Europeans regarded "native" men as childlike, and this view might inspire both male efforts to imitate European respectability and a lashing out against ridicule that could include efforts to assert masculinity in new ways. Not infrequently, this process had an impact on women as well, sometimes supplementing, sometimes complicating changes that Europeans hoped to inspire in this category.

Point three: European imperialism frequently combined earnest attempts to redefine gender relations in the colonies, often under Christian inspiration, with diffuse sexual fantasies about colonial women (and, sometimes, men). Women – slave women, for example, or Asian women – were imagined as highly sensual and erotic. Nineteenth-century European pornography fastened on to images of sexual abandon in the harems of Middle Eastern rulers; by the century's end, postcards of veiled but bare-breasted North Africans were available to excite European and American men. Images of this sort could encourage actual sexual liaisons in the colonies – and also reactions by white women in the same colonies against "native" sensuality. Some historians have argued that the same imagery, at a point when women's rights campaigns threatened masculinity back home, actually encouraged imperialism directly, making it the expression of masculine identity. It is difficult to pin down the results of this final component, but it added important complexity to the gender impact of Western contacts, particularly by the nineteenth century.

Chapters in this section involve extensive sweeps of time, from the onset of new European outreach in the sixteenth century well into the twentieth century. As before, the implications of interaction for male–female relationships frequently took decades, even centuries, to work themselves out. Furthermore, European contact was geographically extensive. We begin with impacts on the Americas, extending into the nineteenth century and with implications even beyond this point. Discussion of India involves the eighteenth and nineteenth centuries, but with spillover into the continuation of European colonialism and the rise of nationalism in the twentieth century. Europe's contacts with Polynesia form an eighteenth- and nineteenth-century topic in Chapter 8, while new types of interaction with Africa began in the nineteenth century but continued through the first half of the twentieth. Finally, Chapter 9 deals with a different kind of interaction with the West, where the societies involved were not seized as colonies but rather launched an independent attempt at selective reform along Western lines. Here, cases of Westernization begin with Russia around 1700, but extend to the late nineteenth and early twentieth centuries.

Most societies in the world remained patriarchal in 1900. But, thanks to contacts, including the results of changes in Europe's own gender formulas, the expressions of patriarchy had often shifted, frequently enhancing inequalities but sometimes modifying at least a few key traditional manifestations.

Further reading

Two historical models discuss the implications of growing European influence in quite different ways, from the sixteenth century into the twentieth century. World economic theory stresses new forms of European political and economic power, and this can be applied to gender: Immanual Wallerstein, *The Modern World System,* vols 1 and 2 (New York/London: Academic Press, 1974, 1980), vol. 3 (San Diego, Calif./London: Academic Press, 1989). Modernization theory stresses efforts to imitate Western models, often in a reform direction. A good recent statement is Alex Inkeles, *One World Emerging? Convergence and Divergence in Industrial Societies* (Boulder, Colo.: Westview Press, 1998). On Europe's changing gender views, see Thomas Laquer, *Making Sex: Body and Gender from the Greeks to Freud* (Cambridge, Mass.: Harvard University Press, 1990).

Chapter 6

Europeans and Native Americans

One of the great episodes of culture contact in world history involved the incursion of Europeans in North and South America from 1492 onward. The outlines of the story are familiar. The discoveries of Columbus led to rapid European conquest, particularly in Latin America and the Caribbean; North America followed a bit more slowly. Virtually all the advantages in the interchange were on the Europeans' side. They had superior technology, with iron weapons and horses as well as guns. They had superior disease immunity; contact with European and African diseases would kill 80 percent or more of the Native American population within two centuries. Europeans quickly set up economic arrangements that would benefit them, seizing land from natives, attempting to use their labor and, where this was insufficient, importing slaves. Native American government structures were quickly undermined, particularly where, as in Central America and the Andes, they had been most elaborate.

Incursions of this sort inevitably shook traditional American cultures – a richly varied assortment. Further, Europeans deliberately sought to convert Native Americans to Christianity. The movement arose first in Catholic areas, under Spanish, Portuguese and French control; Protestant activities were slower to develop, with their impact coming mainly in the nineteenth century. Ultimately, however, the result was a massive assault on existing cultural practices almost everywhere.

Gender was involved early on, both implicitly and explicitly. European domination inevitably affected the status of Native American men, forced into subordinate relationships. This was particularly true where, as in large parts of North America, agricultural economies replaced hunting and gathering patterns. In many cases, a heightened subjugation of women resulted, as men asserted their masculinity in novel ways. The most explicit cultural force was Christianity, whose missionaries were imbued with a firm sense of how men and women ought to relate. Christian views also included strong opinions about sexuality, particularly in the case of nineteenth-century Protestantism, that affected the regulation of relationships between Native American women and men.

Native American cultures were not destroyed. Core elements combined with a Christian overlay, in the characteristic syncretic fashion. Yet change was massive, even where Indian groups were allowed a certain latitude on specified reservations. Gender constituted one of the ways in which European contacts affected Native American life, and often confused it, on the most basic and personal level.

The Indian–European exchange developed over a long period of time, beginning seriously in the sixteenth century in some key areas but generating still-novel contacts well into the nineteenth century. Yet, if only because European superiority in the contact settings remained so consistently dominant, there are some common themes, whether the focus is on sixteenth-century Catholic missionaries or nineteenth-century Protestant Indians in meticulously organized, white-run boarding schools.

Basic patterns

Results of contacts between American Indians and Europeans varied inevitably. In the first place, different tribal cultures involved quite different male–female relations, which in turn would color European views and impacts. In the second place, European models varied, depending on time and place. Indians in Latin America and key parts of Canada were treated to Catholic missionary pressure, which came early. When Protestants in what became the United States began by the later eighteenth century to urge religious conversion, their approach was supplemented by increasing beliefs in the almost sacred domestic role of women – what some have called the "cult of true womanhood".

An important variable divided experiences in North America from those of the great Amerindian civilizations in Central America and the Andes. In North America, contact with Europeans juxtaposed systems that combined hunting and agriculture, where gender divisions were sharp but inequality limited, with the assumptions of European patriarchalism. In the main Latin American cases, contact juxtaposed different patriarchal systems, where inequality was marked even before European arrival. Here, results of contact were also noteworthy, but often more subtle than the obvious deteriorations common in North America.

Despite variety, however, there are some common general threads. First, contact with Europeans usually worsened conditions for Indian women, partly because of Indian male reactions but mostly because Europeans tried to enforce a male-dominant hierarchy. Second, Europeans normally professed great shock at Indian conditions and were often profoundly convinced that they were helping women. Conflicting views of work and of sexuality figured prominently in this confusion, which in turn tended to reinforce the basic trend of deterioration for women. European views of gender were less egalitarian than those of most Indian groups, at least until the later nineteenth century. The views were compounded by pressures to shift to agriculture and away from warfare, which had the unforeseen consequence of turning Indian aggressions inward, often toward women. They were certainly enhanced by the common European failure to grant that any gender arrangement other than their own might work well.

Latin America

Initial Spanish conquest brought obvious challenges to Indians as men and women. Spanish military leaders often faced women as well as men in military opposition. Not infrequently, after a victory, they requested women among other goods as rewards: "You are to deliver women with light skins, corn, chickens, eggs and tortillas," noted one Aztec account. Encounters of this sort might have little direct cultural impact except to drive home to the Indians their inability to hold their own against this invading force. But promptings to convert to Christianity were not far behind. As seemed logical to them, given their own gender assumptions, the Spaniards often initially concentrated on men, assuming that they would lead women into the fold. The strategy often worked. Again, an Aztec account portrays a son who virtually forced his mother to join him in conversion, as she became the first woman in her region to take sacraments. After she told him he must have lost his mind to be so easily persuaded by "that handful of barbarians" he told her that "if she was not his mother, he would answer her by cutting off her head", and then ordered her rooms to be set on fire. It was after this exchange that she complied.

As interaction between Europeans and Indians increased, Christian leaders were rapidly persuaded of a host of immoral sexual practices that particularly involved women. As missionaries saw it, Indians tolerated too much nudity; they engaged in premarital sex, adultery and polygamy. When Christian missions were established, they quickly required full clothing, even in the humid tropics. They often segregated young men and young women, to prevent sexual exchange. They intervened actively in the choice of marriage partners, to try to ensure families that would abide by the new faith. They attacked functional traditional practices such as abortion. In general, as one historian has put it, they worked hard to subvert the normal conduct of Indian family life, in the name of Christian values. The results were mixed. Many Indians withdrew from mission areas or even actively rebelled, precisely because of the sexual regulations. Some managed to hold on to segments of their traditional culture. Even when they remained in the mission compound and accepted Christian marriage, women might engage in extramarital sexuality or lie about the degree of kinship with their husband (an area where Indian traditions allowed matches among close relatives, in contrast to Catholic rules).

In the main, and beyond sexuality itself, missionary efforts sought to reduce roles women had previously played in Indian life in Central and South America alike. In missionaries' eyes, women were childbearers and domestic agents, irrational and often troublesome. They rarely attributed much virtue even to their most faithful female Christian converts, though ironically it was women, including Indian women, who came to be the principal supports of the Latin American church.

A crucial and probably inevitable area of conflict involved women's religious functions. Though the major pre-Columbian American civilizations had been patriarchal, with men the principal religious agents, women often had important artistic and ritual roles in religious ceremonies. They prepared rich cloth and decorations with which statues of the gods were adorned, and they were themselves responsible for household religious practices. These opportunities now largely ceased, though Indians managed to keep some activities and artistic decorations going in secret or to apply some of the traditional touches to Christian worship. Aside from these somewhat concealed remnants, women lost ground, except for the spiritual benefits Catholic worship undoubtedly provided to many. Catholicism demanded that women be subordinate in religious affairs. Women also lost ground when the Spanish state appointed its own bureaucracy, bypassing the native nobility; here, too, colonial authorities could not conceive of women in positions of power, selecting men down to the level of village governors.

The complex results of interaction for gender show clearly in the case of the Mayans, remnants of the great civilization in Guatemala and the Yucatan peninsula. Traditional Mayan society regarded women as distinctly inferior, incapable even of owning property. Sexual behavior was carefully regulated, though not in the same ways as Europeans emphasized. Thus Mayans were shocked by open Spanish lechery and seizure of local women as concubines, while the Spanish complained that Mayan boys and girls shared swimming pools in the nude. As elsewhere, the first results of Spanish conquest, in the sixteenth century, were simply but deeply disorienting: massive death through diseases like smallpox, and the sexual abuse and seizure of many women by the military forces.

When conditions settled, a more complex trade-off emerged, similar in some respects to the results of other cultural exchanges but, on balance, probably unusually bad for women. Mayan women made some gains from the new arrangements. They were told that their souls were as good as men's and given vivid female religious images, such as Mary the mother of Jesus, to be part of their new environment. In contrast to traditional sharp childhood segregation, girls now joined boys, however fleetingly, in whatever religious schooling was available. In some respects, the importance of women's work went up. Mayan women had always been responsible for elaborate weaving; now they were required to make the common cloth that the Spanish required as part of taxation, and thus became even more essential to the family's economic wellbeing.

Their losses, however, were also important. Eager to impose Christian marriage, missionaries worked to break up the large, extended household in which Mayan families had previously joined, viewing them among other things as centers of sexual vice. The result was an increase in women's isolation from each other. Missionaries also worked against a previous practice called bride service, in which a wife continued to live with her parents after marriage but had sex with her husband; traditionally, marriages could be called off if this preliminary period did not work well, and later a woman might marry someone else. From the Christian standpoint the practice was scandalous, and it was quickly curtailed. The result was less marriage flexibility for both men and women and, apparently, an increase of male violence in marriages that did not work out well. And, while work service went up for women, artistic production declined, though attention to making brightly colored clothing for their own festival attire continued despite half-hearted Spanish objections. Finally, some of the gains were more apparent than real: most notably, though schooling might briefly unite boys and girls, it did not cut through earlier patterns of segregation in other aspects of children's lives, or seriously improve women's status in men's eyes.

The result could be the worst of both Mayan and Spanish patriarchal worlds. Despite sincere Christian conversions, religious implications about the equality of souls did not have a deep impact on ideas about gender in Mayan society. At the same time, certain traditional protections and opportunities for women were reduced. This was a cultural merger, a form of syncretism, but one that brought few gains for the women involved.

Spanish occupation affected men as well as women. Defeat in battle and, sometimes, sexual degradation by the European conquerors inevitably affected native American masculinity. In contrast to later European imperialists, however, the Spanish were sometimes at pains to emphasize the masculinity of certain native American men, as demonstrated by their fierceness in war and their own dislike of effeminate behavior. Thus Spanish observers frequently argued that Indian men's bravery in battle highlighted their own virility: only a real man could defeat such masculine stalwarts. The Spanish also noted cases in which native American men looked down on homosexual acts, which confirmed their own views.

At the same time the Spanish did claim to find much effeminacy among native Americans, and much sexual evil as well. As in other cases, given strict Christian hostility to homosexuality, claims of same-sex activity received great attention. As early as 1543, the first bishop of Mexico lashed out against what he saw as widespread native American homosexuality: "nothing fouls or destroys the heart of man as much as the desires and fantasy of carnality". The Spanish (and other Europeans) were particularly puzzled and shocked by a common native American practice of *berdache*, in which boys or men were converted, in dress and in role, to womanhood, doing woman's work and (in some cases) providing sexual service to men as well. While the Spanish were quite capable of using *berdache* for their own purposes, their official view was uniformly hostile. Gradually, European pressure not only reduced the frequency of *berdache*, but also prompted many native American spokespeople to deny that the practice, or indeed even less systematic cross-dressing, had ever existed.

A Canadian case

Though few French settlers actually moved into Canada (the strong French Canadian population would develop through high birth rates), far-flung missionary activity developed quickly. Many missionaries from the new Jesuit order, particularly eager to win converts, followed French explorers and fur trappers. Their reactions to what they thought they saw of Native American gender arrangements were similar to those of Spanish missionaries in Latin America: substantial changes seemed essential if Christian conversion was to have any meaning. The prior patterns against which contact operated, though, were quite different from those in Latin America, for here there was no full-blown patriarchal system prior to European arrival.

Interactions with the Huron Indians and associated tribes, north of the Great Lakes, were fairly typical as they expanded during the seventeenth and eighteenth centuries. In contrast to Mayans and others in Central America, the Hurons mixed migratory agriculture with hunting. Thus their contact with Europeans involved tremendous cultural differences intensified by the common gap between the freer gender relationships in hunting societies and those in settled agricultural civilizations. Needless to say, European spokesmen, confident of the validity of their definitions of male–female roles, did not appreciate the distinction, or even fully understand it.

Like many North American Indian groups, the Hurons organized family relationships around descent from the mother, not the father. Membership in extended family "longhouses" was based on this matrilocal focus, which gave women great power. Because men were gone during the summer months, it was women who really held family life together. Jesuits immediately found this relationship suspect, for in their eyes Huron women had too much freedom. Women also participated heavily in Huron religious and healing rituals, and some women served as shamans, or healers in religion and magic. If a girl was born, there was more celebration than for a boy.

In this context, and in contrast to conversion situations in other historical cases, women were particularly likely to hold back from Christianity, for there was no clear benefit to them. Men were somewhat more open to conversion, but even then they might face strong pressure, even to the point of ostracism from the "grand family", if their wife or mother-in-law disapproved. This female opposition merely intensified missionary concern, for they could not easily arrange for converted men to insist that their wives obey them (which would have been the pattern they would have found logical). Many Huron women believed that Christian baptism would cause great misfortune, and so often insisted that their husbands recant. In one case, according to a French observer, the women "drove him [the husband] from their Cabins, and refused to give him anything to eat; they reproached him with the death of one of his nieces, who had been baptized. He was left without means of support, and was compelled to do what is usually the work of Women." Jesuits, for their part, found the traditionalist women "shrews" and "hellish". It was easy to associate resistant women with the Devil, whom the Jesuits believed was active in the New World: after all, the idea that woman was the original sinner, as Eve, had already developed a powerful influence in European thought. Concern about sexual behavior – for the Jesuits thought women flaunted their sexuality and were unchaste – added to the opposition.

The key to reform, in missionary eyes, was the institution of Christian marriages, in which men, now dominant, could insist that their wives toe the line – by force if necessary. Women were to serve and obey; and, if they failed, violence was justified. Jesuits reported on one Christian husband who "beat his wife who had insolently provoked him". Both parties were reprimanded, but especially the wife "who was more guilty than her husband". Women who were punished by their husbands for disobedience were told that they had sinned, and were prodded to confess as much to the Jesuits. The imposition of Christian marriage also involved new sexual controls over girls as well as wives, against more liberal traditions. A Christian girl might be punished simply for being in a cabin with a man. Gradually, many Huron women were persuaded to keep careful control over their behavior, lest they fall into sin. One girl wept because she had allowed a man to touch her hand, "being greatly afraid that it would prevent her from being a Virgin". Women who left their husbands, which had been a right in traditional Huron society, were beaten and jailed if they were caught, with Huron men joining missionary officials in this punishment.

Huron men, for their part, often welcomed the chance to make women more docile. One convert insisted that his new wife (judged "arrogant") should scream loudly that she would be obedient to him. The French approved: "God has visibly blessed this marriage, and we have never seen a greater change than in this woman, who has now become truly a lamb, and has very deep and affectionate feelings of devotion." Male motives were complex, going well beyond individual power plays. With increasing French colonial control, earlier and often quite brutal forms of aggression, particularly attacks on other tribes that could involve torturing and cannibalizing captives, fell into disapproval. Aggression was turned inward, and women were prime targets. With women held to be inferior, feared as sources of sexual temptation, it was obvious that any deviation from meek submission could be attacked. Jesuits encouraged Huron men to organize village councils to help control women and insist on their conversion; needless to say, there was no female representation.

The result was a massive restructuring of male–female relations. Under Jesuit pressure, many women themselves internalized ideas of their sinfulness, while men became dependent on new forms of inequality in order to feel properly masculine.

Two United States cases

Developments in the United States, where Protestants held the upper hand, added some distinctive ingredients to the common American culture contract patterns. Concerns about women's power and sexuality were similar to the interactions in Latin America and particularly to those in Canada, but missionary activity and other pressures in what became the United States, coming a little later at a time when European gender relations were being redefined, added a new cultural concern about work relationships. On the whole this contributed yet another component to the insistence on change, one that did not work to women's benefit.

Occasionally, contact between Native Americans and Euro-American missionaries seemed to advantage women. In the Sioux tribe, where interactions developed in Iowa in the nineteenth century, women were already held to be inferior. In this context, it was women rather than men who saw benefits in converting to Christianity. After six years of operation, one missionary station among the Sioux had forty church members, of whom only two were men. In traditional religion, men had dominated rituals, with little role for women; women's greater participation in the Christian church, therefore, gave them new outlets without necessarily jeopardizing traditionalist practices. Sioux women also dressed modestly, a custom of which missionaries could approve. Men might go along with all this – in a theme familiar from other contact cases – because Christian schools taught women new and improved methods of homemaking. For no matter what the brand of Protestantism – Quaker, Baptist or Methodist – or for that matter what the tribe, whether Sioux or Shawnee – mission schools taught girls to sew, clean and cook with a vengeance.

Yet there was change here, and it could be troubling. Americans of European origin brought distinctive ideas of the proper work for each sex, and these only intensified with time. Women should concentrate on home, and it was men who should till the fields. Home now meant a settled residence, so women's work in this domain expanded. In Indian tradition, though, setting up a house and farming were considered women's jobs, and a man who cut a tree for a house or guided a plow would be ridiculous and effeminate. In contrast, people of Euro-American origin insisted that men relieve women of the heavy field tasks "altogether unsuited for their sex". Treating women as the purer but weaker sex was, in these terms, a basic "line of discrimination between civilized society and barbarism". A missionary reported the opposite Indian belief: "They have an idea, that to labor in cultivating the earth, is degrading to the character of man, who (they say) was made for war and hunting, and holding councils, and that squaws and hedge-hogs are made to scratch the ground."

Here, then, was a complicated case of contact. Sioux men and women might go along with a basic idea of gender hierarchy, in which women were weaker and in some senses inferior. White Protestant talk of women as bastions of civilization and moral enlightenment might make little sense, even as some female converts found a new means of expression in Christianity, but it might not be seen as harmful given the strong emphasis on domestic roles. But reinforcement of hierarchy ran against the profound alteration of work assignments. Small wonder that Native Americans, particularly men, converted to this European model very slowly and incompletely, despite strong inducements from missionary centers. If they did convert, the result, in the eyes of men and women alike, might long seem confusing.

Native American tribes originally in the South, notably the Cherokee, were different to begin with, for women had much higher status and wider roles. Women did agricultural work while men hunted, but the resultant division of labor brought considerable equality because women were recognized for the importance of their contribution. On the strength of their hard work, women gained a leading role in religious rituals that celebrated harvests. As with the Hurons, furthermore, a person's origins were traced by descent from mothers, and families located around maternal kin. Cherokee women had considerable power and autonomy, and they played an active role in tribal councils. Finally, sexual habits including premarital sex were fairly free, and Indian women usually lacked modesty (by Christian standards) in sexual matters, and joked frequently. In all these characteristics, as one historian has noted, Cherokee women were about as distant from contemporary Protestant standards as any group on the continent.

Then upon the scene, from the eighteenth century onward, entered interaction with missionaries and farmers of European origin. As with the Sioux, but for more limited reasons, women saw some advantages in contact-induced change: it was, for instance, possible to learn more effective methods of farming, and many Cherokee leaders, including men, took pride in their larger ability to assimilate European ways and improve their level of "civilization". Often they believed that only adaptation would allow them to survive in a white-dominated society. Thus there were pressures to adjust from within the community.

Against this was the fact that the potential clashes in views of male–female relationships were massive. Euro-Americans, increasingly imbued with the Cult of True Womanhood, consistently criticized the involvement of women in manual labor; they saw male hunting as a frivolous pastime. "Savage" and "degraded" were two adjectives commonly applied to these aspects of Cherokee culture. Not only missionaries but also government agents eager to stabilize the region, together with white farmers (including George Washington), urged change, associated with what they regarded as standard, male-dominated agriculture. Sexual habits, including widespread polygyny and the revealing clothing worn by women, also came under attack. From 1800 onward a network of white-run schools spread the Euro-American vision of propriety and an appropriate gender division of labor.

Many Cherokees welcomed these further cues. Girls, told firmly that domestic work, not agriculture, was the key to their power in the home, wrote gratefully of lessons that would help them "to make garments which will be useful to us in life" or teach them "how to take care of families so that when we go home we can take care of our mothers [sic] house". Modesty also improved, or so the missionaries reported, as they tried to make sure that boys and girls were never alone together. But Cherokee preference for polygyny and considerable sexual freedom did not quickly pass. While some mission-educated Cherokee families converted fully to the Euro-American model of an agricultural family, with women now playing a subsidiary economic role, many persisted in traditional ways. Nevertheless, at the governance level the tribe changed as it copied European beliefs and in the process found new ways to compensate for other infringements on male authority. New laws gave precedence to fathers, rather than to mothers, as the basis for tracing descent of kin. Women's roles on tribal councils were ended, as only men could now vote. Women also became more isolated from each other, thanks to their declining role among kin and, frequently, their residence on widely separated farms. Yet, for Indian women, any challenge to these new patterns would seem a reversion to savagery; in this sense, they lacked the opportunity to use white values about women as a basis for protest, even as Euro-American women themselves began to engage in feminist agitation on the basis of female purity.

Gender was a battlefield in Euro-American and Indian contact in the United States, and the war continued through the nineteenth and into the twentieth centuries. Government schools and agents, as well as missionaries, continued to press the view that Indian traditions made women slave-like drudges, because of the work they were expected to do and because of freewheeling sexual habits. While some measures did provide relief from abusive practices, or new opportunities for women's expression, on the whole the clash was based on profound misconceptions. Where Euro-American views predominated, women's role in Native American society deteriorated. Where Indians resisted, they were nevertheless forced to modify traditional habits, notably the hunting/agricultural distinction, and their sense of appropriate roles and identities might simply lose any clear-cut definition. Against the power of the Euro-American presence and the self-righteous confidence in its gender model, it was difficult for Native Americans not just to articulate concerns about the erosion of this aspect of tradition, but even to realize clearly what was wrong.

Conclusion

The tremendous power gap between Europeans and Native Americans stands out in most of the interactions that affected gender, as well as the vast distance between the gender traditions involved. Active syncretism was limited, particularly in North America, because Indian groups found it difficult to defend their customs. When women's conditions deteriorated, Indian men might actually support the change, though their own definitions of masculinity became more tenuous as well. Women themselves could serve as agents of change, for example in importing new ideas about home life or sexuality from their stints in schools, but they could not arrest the erosion of opportunities their foremothers had enjoyed in the lives of many tribes. The cultural imbalance, and the resulting inability to effect a vigorous merger of older patterns and new influences, contrasts with other cases involving Europeans, such as the interactions in India discussed in the next chapter, where European superiority was qualified by the size and cohesion of India's communities.

Some American Indians, like individual Cherokee farming families, simply merged with European patterns. On the whole, however, despite the power gap, key Indian groups did not become Europeanized. Rather, they continued to seek a differentiation, even though their own gender traditions were largely destroyed. The result could be confusing to white observers and to Indian communities themselves.

The situation in Latin America was somewhat different. Because Indian civilizations there had been more elaborately developed, and larger populations remained even after the European onslaught, there were more opportunities for syncretism. Patriarchal conditions as well as settled agriculture already existed, as with the Aztecs, which made European forms less foreign, despite huge differences in specifics. Nevertheless, there was substantial movement away from traditional male–female relationships.

Interaction in the Americas tended, to an unusual degree, to be a one-way street. Euro-American men might admire aspects of Native American masculinity, at least in principle – particularly bravery in war – but there was no interest in learning from Indian traditions involving families or women. Native American ways were savage and wrong. Only indirectly, in helping intensify Euro-American insistence on women's daintiness and morality, as a contrast between civilization and the threatening Indian "other", did the contact have potential impact on Euro-Americans themselves. The image of the virtuous, domestic woman started in Europe, but it may have reached more extreme forms in white America as a badge of identity against "savages". Of course there was irony here: individual white women captured by Indians often preferred to stay among them, to the angry horror of the colonists; when white women began in the later nineteenth century to agitate for new rights, such as ownership of property, they were often inadvertently asking for qualities that many Indian women had once had – but lost as a result of the contacts with whites.

Further reading

On North America: Karen Anderson, *Chain Her by One Foot. The Subjugation of Women in Seventeenth-century New France* (London/New York: Routledge, 1991); Robert Berkhofer, *Salvation and the Savage. An Analysis of Protestant Missions and American Indian Response,* 1787–1862 (Lexington, Ky: University of Kentucky Press, 1965); Nancy Shoemaker, *Negotiators of Change: Historical Perspectives on Native American Women* (New York: Routledge, 1995); David W. Adams, *Education for Extinction, American Indians and the Boarding School Experience,* 1875–1928 (Lawrence, Kan.: University of Kansas Press, 1995); Theda Perdue, *Cherokee Women: Gender and Culture Change, 1700–1835* (Lincoln, Nebr.: University of Nebraska Press, 1998).

On Latin America: Inga Clendinnen, *Ambivalent Conquests, Maya and Spaniard in Yucatan, 1517–1570* (Cambridge/New York: Cambridge University Press, 1987); Erick Langer and Robert Jackson (eds), *The New Latin American Mission History* (Lincoln, Nebr.: University of Nebraska Press, 1995); Asunción Lavrin (ed.), *Sexuality and Marriage in Colonial Latin America* (Lincoln, Nebr.: University of Nebraska Press, 1989); Susan Schroeder, Stephanie Wood and Robert Haskett (eds), *Indian Women of Early Mexico* (Norman, Okla.: University of Oklahoma Press, 1997); Richard Trexler, *Sex and Conquest: Gendered Violence, Political Order, and the European Conquest of the Americas* (Ithaca, NY: Cornell University Press, 1995); Merry Wiesner-Hanks, *Christianity and Sexuality in the Early Modern World; Regulating Desire, Reforming Practice* (New York/London: Routledge, 2000).

Chapter 7

Men and women amid British imperialism in India

India was subject to extensive Western, primarily British, influence from the middle of the eighteenth century onward. After the Americas, this was the second great Western-dominated colonial area to emerge. The Indian case, correspondingly, deserves comparison with the Americas. It was in fact quite different: India was an established agricultural civilization able to resist Western example far more successfully than Native Americans, and on the whole the Europeans involved were more hesitant in trying to impose their gender views. Yet there was interaction and resultant change.

Four phases were involved in the Indian–British contrast. Initial British interventions were primarily commercial, seeking goods and markets. The whole operation was run not by the British government, but by the East India Company, government-sanctioned but profit-oriented. Gradually the Company took on the role of colonial government, as a variety of wars with rival European powers (particularly France) and local rebellions required more formal administration. Contacts with Indians beyond commerce were very limited. Though women's economic activities began to be seriously curtailed during this phase, there were few wider, cultural results.

The second phase, beginning around the 1820s, involved much more serious British intervention in Indian life. A number of key laws attacked what the British saw as scandalous defects in the ordinary treatment of women. A larger British presence brought British women to India, who might have some impact, pro or con, as models of behavior.

By the late nineteenth century, even as British rule persisted, Indians began to organize a variety of nationalist movements to resist and reform. These movements would have their own assumptions about men's and women's roles, which could either propel change or confirm continuity. By the twentieth century, leading nationalists embraced a fuller set of women's rights.

Finally, in 1947, India gained independence. The creation of a successful Indian state obviously recast the issue of Western influence, but it did not cause complete rupture. Indians continued to react to signals from the West, though their capacity to pick and choose clearly increased.

This chapter focuses primarily on the first three phases, when interaction was most decisive. By the 1920s, and certainly after 1947, Indian agendas depended less on interchange and more on what Indians themselves had selected from previous experience.

The context

India forms one of the great testing grounds of Western influence and regional reaction in modern world history. This was a complex, well-established civilization with a long tradition of patriarchy in which male dominance and parentally arranged marriage were leavened by praise for women's beauty and sensuality, their cleverness, and their role as mother. Hinduism, the majority religion, confirmed women's spiritual inferiority but also noted their common participation in the process of spiritual advancement; lower than men, they were nevertheless part of the divine community, with the same ultimate goals of fusion with the divine essence.

India's tradition included also considerable experience in dealing with outside influences. New ideas could be received with tolerance, but they rarely drew the majority away from established patterns. No religion had won many Indians from Hinduism and the rituals and beliefs associated with it, and this would remain true of Western attempts to import Christianity, despite isolated pockets of conversion.

British influence in India was not, in the main, religious, despite important missionary activities. By the nineteenth century, British beliefs about gender were mainly secular, involving ideas of what home should be like, what secular education should consist of, and so on. In this sense the British impact on India was quite different from many earlier stories of contact, in which missionary religions had carried the principal messages. The basic clash involved "modern" and Western beliefs about gender standards versus Indian traditions enveloped in Hinduism.

Interaction was simple in one sense. British representatives in India were absolutely convinced of their superiority. While some fell in love with India, there was no large current of Indian influence on British gender standards. As in many cases in the past, this exchange, organized amid great imbalance of economic and military power, was a one-way street.

Nothing else about the interaction was simple, however. There was, for instance, huge variety in the ways Indians might encounter British standards. The vast majority were rural, and their contact with British values was extremely remote. British presence affected them through a few laws and much economic constraint, but the opportunity to envisage a larger alternative culture, where male and female roles were concerned, was not available. For Indians in the cities, however, in the upper castes, and above all in the lower echelons of colonial government service, the story was quite different. These people were in a position to pick up cues about the British version of male–female relations, and some proved eager to do so, at least selectively.

The British themselves were divided. A strong impulse persisted, even after the first phase, to leave gender issues alone. Whether the goal of British imperialism was economic profit or simply political acquisition, it would hardly pay to rock the boat. British rule depended heavily on Indian acquiescence, and tampering with tradition could seem risky. This stance would not preclude unintended consequences, as Indians tried to figure out what made the British tick, but it might limit relevant contact. Most British women in India, as the wives of colonial administrators, were thus carefully tucked away in exclusive compounds, remote from disease and the sights of poverty; correspondingly, few Indians beyond a huge servant group had much to do with them. Even more generally, most British officials themselves harbored patriarchal beliefs. While a few aspects of India's gender patterns might trouble them – it took a special act, for example, to allow traditional Indian art on colonial postage stamps, because by mid-nineteenth-century British standards the scenes were pornographic – the basic idea of male dominance would seem normal and sensible. There might even be a certain envy of the standard male–female gap, in so far as it seemed less contested than was becoming true back home.

For gender values were changing rapidly in Britain itself, and the result inevitably spilled over both into evaluations of reform possibilities in India and into the confusion Indians themselves might encounter when they tried to figure out what the British system was. In Britain, the amount of women's work was declining, particularly in the all-important respectable circles. With industrialization, job opportunities for women shrank. While some women did gain factory jobs, far larger numbers were displaced from many posts in business and in rural manufacturing, while in the middle classes a powerful belief developed that respectable women did not work outside the home. At the same time, however, women's power in the family increased, and their moral stature improved as well. In key respects, and against all earlier precedent, women might now be seen as more moral by nature than men. Certainly, they were held to be capable of greater sexual restraint (though by the same token women who violated this assumption were deeply deplored). Education for women was gaining ground, though arguments persisted over whether women's feebler reason could make full use of it. By the 1870s, other changes were becoming visible. The British birth rate was dropping, as women argued that too many children were bad for them and bad for society. A few hardy women were striking out toward new careers in areas like law and medicine (the same thrust for new, active roles would push many into missionary activity). Legal changes granted women new property rights and some opportunities for divorce. A formal feminist movement arose, insisting on still further gains, including, most feminists agreed by 1900, the right to vote.

How would these various British models interact in India? There was a sanctified domestic model, a new, more assertive model, and a host of way-stations in between. Predictably, explicit steps to intervene in Indian gender relations were most probable when all the major British groups, whether pointing toward domestic bliss or public reform at home, could agree that something had to be done. But there were many other disputed areas for Indian women concerning different aspects of British imperialism – as well as huge consequences – that gender discussions did not clearly embrace.

The economic backdrop

For women, by far the most important result of British intervention in India concerned the loss of work opportunities thanks to policies and industrial competition that disadvantaged Indian production, from the mid eighteenth century well into the twentieth. What was involved frequently operated beneath the surface, but it could deeply distort the more obvious cultural contacts between the two societies.

British businessmen and policymakers quickly realized that Indian manufacturing must be discouraged if the colony was to turn a profit for the imperialists. In the eighteenth century, British laws sought to limit imports of Indian manufactured goods, particularly cotton cloth, so that nascent British industry could gain ground. Cotton cloth, colorful and easily laundered, proved quickly popular in Britain, though in India it was an old industrial sector. Reducing Indian production was a first step in the rapid expansion, and then mechanization, of cotton output in Britain. What the British sought from India, instead of its traditional manufacturing strength, involved expanded agricultural production, particularly of items such as teas and spices, plus a direct market for British industry. As the industrial revolution surged in Britain, from the 1760s onward, this reorientation began to accelerate. By the early 1800s, tens of thousands of Indian manufacturing workers, disproportionately women, were being thrown out of work, their manual methods no rival for the steam-driven British factories.

The result was growing impoverishment for many Indian families and a severe reduction in the economic range available to women. Increasingly, domestic service, begging and, above all, agriculture provided the main recourses for women. Hardships affected men as well, but on the whole they were much more successful in developing alternatives. By the early twentieth century, for example, in Bengal – one of India's main industrial regions – up to 90 percent of all the jobs in modernized industries (textiles, mining, metallurgy) were held by men. Women's relative status, and often their bargaining power within families, was declining.

British officials found it hard to acknowledge these developments. In the first place, they were out for profit, and were hardly likely to reverse the imperialist economic advantage out of humanitarian concern for women. But nineteenth-century British values were hostile to women's employment in any event. While there were many women workers in British industry, middle-class opinion became ever more unfavorable, worrying about the results of work on sexual morality and family life. Regulation of women's work was introduced by the 1850s, and in fact the percentage of women actively employed began to go down. It was easy, in this context, to view the withdrawal of women from the manufacturing labor force in India as a boon. Colonial measures often restricted women's work, limiting participation in mining, for example, in a regulation introduced in 1928. And so the process of reducing women's work opportunities and worsening their economic position relative to men continued, through a mixture of explicit and implicit imperialist policies. In Bengal again, whereas women had constituted about 25 percent of the labor force in manufacturing and sales in the 1880s, it was down to 14 percent in 1931. Traditional opportunities were shrinking (outside of agriculture), while jobs in the growth sectors were almost impossible to come by. Though many men proved highly mobile in search of new jobs, women were often confined to traditional village settings, where work activities became more and more marginal.

In this context, opportunities for male superiority over women clearly increased. Moreover, many Indian men, themselves buffeted by economic change, often resentful of imperialist measures that reduced them to subservient status in government or the military, might look to traditional or novel advantages over women as compensation for the tensions they were experiencing.

Fundamental deteriorations in women's conditions, as a result of British economic and political intrusion, help explain why many results of the more overt cultural contacts proved quite limited. They also explain why women themselves were not particularly active in exploiting reform opportunities, at least until the late nineteenth century: the focus was on adjustment and survival, not on more radical innovation. Yet there were other realms of contact, at first somewhat symbolic but ultimately significant in their own right.

The cultural backdrop

British imperialism in India developed in a familiar cultural pattern of scorn and condescension toward a subject, and very different, people – scorn and condescension cast in highly gendered terms. Indian men were deemed effeminate in British eyes – a common situation with Western imperialism from the Middle East to Indonesia. A British historian in the 1830s constrasted Indian men with the "bold and energetic" Europeans. Indians seemed "languid" and unaggressive, soft in manners and fearful. In short, an ideal subject people, but hardly masculine. Worship of goddesses, as part of the Hindu religion, added to the gender-related charges: this was not a practice manly men would engage in.

The most obvious consequence of this gendered perception was a persistent tendency to underrate the potential for Indian opposition or resistance, and then a shocked overretaliation when resistance occurred. The British were unprepared for such a major rising as the Sepoy rebellion of 1857, because of their confidence in Indian male passivity. When this rising not only occurred, but also led to violence and rape against some British women, the gap between event and perception helped justify an exceptionally brutal retaliation, in which far more Indian civilians, including women and children, were killed.

What the effect of British perceptions were on Indians themselves was harder to fathom. Most Indians, as peasants, were unaware of the rhetoric. For those more aware of British attitudes, the results could encourage silent resentment and would ultimately help fuel nationalism.

The perceptions also had an impact on British attitudes toward Indian women, and here the British approach was even more explicitly self-congratulatory but also led to some direct action. The common wisdom was that Indian women were badly mistreated. (How this related to male effeminacy was not really explored; consistency was not a strong point in gendered imperialism. And of course there was no interest in exploring the relationship of this claim to the actual economic effects of British policy on ordinary Indian women.) Here, ideas could lead to reform efforts.

The reform impulse: British and Indian

It was easy for the British to claim and feel great shock at some of the relationships between men and women they saw in India, based on the standards they thought they knew from home. James Mill, head examiner for the East India Company in the eighteenth century, said it simply: "Nothing can exceed the habitual contempt which the Hindus entertain for their women." A missionary, admittedly trying to raise money from a group of church ladies in his own city of Liverpool, reported: "The condition of Indian women" can be described as "miserable, uneducated, mere animals kept for burden or for slaughter". The poet Robert Southey took up the cause, writing of the custom of *sati* where a widow joins her husband's funeral pyre and burns to death:

> Oh sight of misery!
> You cannot hear her cries, – their sound
> In that wild dissonance is drowned;
> But in her face you see
> The supplication and the agony, –
> See in her swelling throat the desperate strength
> That with vain effort struggles yet for life;
> Her arms contracted now in fruitless strife,
> Now wildly at full length
> Towards the crowd in vain for pity spread:
> They force her on, they bind her to the dead.

Even hardened business officials recoiled at some Indian practices, even if they did not think it made good political or commercial sense to try to interfere.

But gradually, and particularly after the British government began to take a larger role, a few obvious dissonances had to be addressed.

Female infanticide quickly drew shocked comment. A British East India Company official in 1789 learned that female infanticide was a widespread practice even in princely families, as a means of limiting dowry demands and avoiding the shame of permanently unmarried daughters. The resident managed to get a group of princes to agree that "this is a great crime": "we do ourselves acknowledge that, although customary among us, it is highly sinful". The initial agreement had little impact, but British efforts continued sporadically into the nineteenth century, mainly through attempts to persuade. Gradually, by the mid-nineteenth century, the colonial government reported increasing success, as the sex ratio of surviving infants began to even out. While officials continued to disagree about how hard to press, and also about whether Indian family values should be "Westernized" or merely made to conform to more enlightened Hindu principles, there was obvious opportunity for self-congratulation. As one official put it, "we are stemming the torrent of infant blood shed by the hands of unnatural parents".

Sati came next: according to British values, it was criminal to force or even allow a woman to burn herself merely because her husband had died. The practice had begun, not with the earliest phases of Hinduism, but during the postclassical period. It was not very common, so its symbolic importance outstripped its real role in the lives of Indian women. But it did occur, particularly in a few key regions. *Sati* was meant to emphasize the meaningless of life for a woman without a husband, plus of course the low importance, in Hinduism, of life on this earth in any event. The sacrifice was a means of acquiring spiritual merit. It might also help avoid the economic burden of widowhood, always an issue in patriarchal societies. Certainly it provided a dramatic, if in fact atypical, illustration of male dominance in Hindu society.

By the late eighteenth century, British officials began to move against *sati*. (Indeed, Portuguese rulers in their colony of Goa had attacked *sati* as early as 1510, and some Muslim rulers of Indian states had done the same.) Again, their first impulse was to persuade: the practice seemed deeply rooted in Hinduism (more, indeed, than infanticide, which had no religious support). Occasionally officials attempted to argue a widow out of committing herself to the pyre, though they often failed against the widow's resolute wish to join her husband in death. Several reports urged legal action, but the government delayed. Some compromises were ventured, requiring strict regulation of *sati* to make sure that it was entirely voluntary and that no pregnant woman was allowed to die. The government worried about Hindu resistance, possibly rebellion, if a more general measure were attempted, but finally, taking increasing control of colonial administration, it cut through the hesitations, and *sati* was officially banned in 1829. Any assistance would be regarded as homicide. There was little response. Some Indian men petitioned the government against what they viewed as interference with their rights, and occasional *satis* did continue to occur during British rule. Further, it was another few decades before the practice was banned, as a result of British pressure, in some of the states still run by individual princes – the last princely *sati* occurred in 1861 – but there was real change.

Change was enhanced by the participation of Indian reformers in the campaign, despite the fact that Hinduism seemed to sanction the practice. The transition here was potentially more important than the British drive itself. A number of Indian leaders, encountering British ideas, began to be persuaded that change was necessary. Their sense of justice, in gender matters, was open to redefinition, and they felt a certain embarrassment under the bombardment of British attacks on signs of Indian barbarism. Rammohun Roy was the leading Indian reformer of the early nineteenth century, eager to reformulate Hinduism in a number of respects. An intellectual, Rammohun was insistent on the need to defend a separate Indian culture while removing features that seemed to hold India back in Western eyes. Rammohun's first pamphlet against *sati* appeared in 1818, as British officials were debating what policy to adopt and as some Hindu leaders, resisting colonial pressure, were arguing that preserving *sati* was vital to religious independence. Hostile to outright legal restriction, which would counter India's rights, Rammohun argued that *sati* was not in fact supported by Hindu texts. He contended that the practice demeaned women, denying them the "excellent merits that they are entitled to by nature". Rammohun hoped that a campaign of education and persuasion, directed against *sati* but involving larger revisions in ideas about women, would gradually eliminate the practice; he worried about possible reactions to outright prohibition. He shared with the British, however, a belief that certain Indian practices were brutal, though he modified the criticism by contending that pure, original Hinduism did not share this stain. Thus, when the 1829 edict was finally passed, Rammohun joined in the praise. He thanked the British for the prohibition, rejoicing "that the heinous sin of cruelty to females may no longer be committed", adding, in support of his larger agenda, "that the ancient and purest system of Hindu religion should not any longer be set at naught by the Hindus themselves". He vigorously supported the British rejection of the Indian petitions.

The reform trajectory persisted with attacks on aspects of Indian marriage practices, as the British continued to put pressure on Hindu tradition while encouraging Hindu leaders themselves to coordinate and update religious law. Hindu tradition had long prohibited a widow's remarrying, particularly in the upper castes. Again, the intent was to emphasize the tie to a husband and also prevent dispersal of the husband's property. The effect, however, could be devastating, as widows, without significant means of their own, might fall into great poverty, perhaps draining the earnings of their kin. The problem was compounded when a marriage had been arranged for children – a common practice in the upper castes – and the widow in question was not even an adult; here, the prospects for the rest of her life were bleak indeed. British officials, judging by the norms of their own society, looked askance at marriages arranged in childhood, but hesitated to intervene. The question of widows, however, a narrower and more obviously troublesome issue, did draw attention. A law in 1859 legalized the remarriage of widows and legitimized children born of such unions. Property of the dead husband, however, passed back to his own next heirs; the remarried widow had no further claim, though her own property remained intact. This result, ironically, harmed women who had not (because of their low caste or the particular region they lived in) previously come under strict Hindu law – another case in which culture contact could inflict unforeseen damage because of the complexity of the traditions concerned and the limitations of "modern" standards. The new law gave rise to a host of cases brought before British-Indian courts in the succeeding decades, mainly over the property issue. A 1937 law finally revised the edict, by allowing widows some share in the property of the late husband even if they remarried; the more egalitarian laws of independent India, after 1947, equalized property access still more fully.

British reformers clearly intended to clear up what they saw as the most harmful aspects of Indian tradition, as these placed burdens on women when judged by Western standards. Their moves were cautious. Impact was frequently limited and in some cases it actually worsened women's situations, but some traditional Indian practices were reconsidered. Equally important was the stimulus to Indian reformers themselves to think in new ways about gender issues, a current that would be amplified later on.

The reform measures did not, however, involve the voices of women themselves. Neither British nor Indian leaders thought that women were worth consulting; measures should be taken for them, as part of paternal benevolence. We literally do not know, as a result, what women thought of the initial reforms, or how widely they were affected. Culture contact in these decades, cushioned by deteriorating economic conditions in any event, was limited not only by the hesitations of the reformers but also by their own assumptions.

Memsahibs and women's voices

Another form of culture contact developed during the first century or more of British colonial rule: the presence of British women in India. Here, too, results were both limited and ambivalent.

British policy initially discouraged wives from accompanying husbands to India, because the life would be both harsh and boring. Many men married Portuguese or other women. British East India Company policy shifted, though, in the late eighteenth century, to subsidize venturesome British women willing to go to India to see if they could find a husband. By the nineteenth century a noticeable group of British wives resided in India, those in the upper classes being known as memsahibs. Their lives revolved around directing a staff of Indian servants, whose language they almost never spoke. Tolerance for

Indian culture deteriorated as the century wore on, as the British gained greater prosperity and built isolated enclaves in which European habits coexisted with some accommodations to the Indian climate. Daily life concentrated on social rituals, highlighted by dinner parties where the food was an Indianized version of an English dish, cooked by locals in cookhouses where the memsahib never set foot. Life became something of a caricature of the British domestic ideal, with earnest yet rather useless women, focused on the domestic and social setting, shielded from most of the realities of the outside world. Wives of civil service officers were described as dull: "The civil ladies are generally very quiet, rather languid, speaking almost in a whisper, simply dressed, almost always lady-like."

The impact of this European group is unclear, though it has been enthusiastically debated by historians. Indian servants obviously learned a great deal about European women, but they probably found little to their liking. Their dislike could not be expressed as openly as that of the memsahibs about India, but it was surely vigorous.

The situation was not changeless, however. By the later nineteenth century a growing number of lower civil service positions were held by Indians. This could involve some limited, very hesitant socializing with British women and, through this, greater knowledge of European social customs relating to gender. More important still were the shifts on the part of British women themselves. The late nineteenth century saw growing emphasis on activism, even social reform, on the part of women, supplementing the domestic ideal. First a few individual women, then larger groups brought this new range of action to their lives in India. Also, there were growing numbers of other British women, particularly missionaries, not part of the isolated life of the memsahib at all.

Individual British women began to push for change in various aspects of Indian life, ranging from health conditions to marriage. Growing concern for women's rights back home inevitably translated into some attention to gender conditions in the colony. Flora Steele, for example, with her husband in a remote outpost, decided to turn her life outward. She learned the local language, and devoted herself both to providing better information about India to other memsahibs and to encouraging women's education – a strong movement in Western Europe that was now applied to the colony. She started a girls' school and was then appointed inspectress of women's schools in a whole province. Missionaries also sponsored education efforts, beginning with the first school for "native girls" in 1818. By 1901, with some government support, there were 5628 primary schools and 467 secondary schools, handling 44,470 Indian women and also providing training for future teachers.

This kind of initiative increased in the twentieth century, with British, American and other women coming to India to promote women's health as well as education. Women by this point also brought a new lifestyle, interesting themselves in novel fashions, cosmetics and new kinds of dances and parties. Again, by this time, women's efforts were encouraging the training of Indian nurses and midwives in Western medicine. The Lady Hadringe Medical College opened in Delhi in 1916, entirely staffed by Indian women, and in 1922 another medical school for women was established in Madras.

New initiatives often encountered footdragging by the colonial administration as well as opposition from Indian men, including reformers who nevertheless persisted in assuming that women would continue taking a back seat. There was more than male supremacy involved here, for many schools also taught Western eating habits and clothing, while promoting either Christianity or at least religious neutrality. Indian women themselves might object to these aspects of cultural exchange. Furthermore, of India's vast population even the most successful initiatives reached only a handful, disproportionately urban and often upper class.

Paralleling changes in the roles of some Western women in India was a new voice for educated Indian women themselves. In the 1880s, for example, Pandita Ramabai published (in the United States) a scathing critique of women's lives in India, focusing on the upper castes, and criticizing the neglect of British officials as well as Hindu tradition. Spurred by her sister's unhappiness in a childhood-arranged marriage which the Hindu community would not allow her to escape, Ramabai was also influenced by the very different family patterns she saw on her travels to England. Her targets were colonial and Hindu alike. She blasted the limited enforcement of laws against female infanticide, for example, noting that the 1881 census listed 5 million more men than women. She described the thralldom of most marriages, including frequent abuse, claiming that in Hindu law women were classed with animals and slaves. Independent voices of this sort remained rare, but they clearly reflected the impact on some Indian women of new contacts with Western ideas, through education and even travel.

By the early twentieth century, a number of women's journals had developed in India, written either in Hindi or in English, in which a feminist evaluation of Indian marriage customs figured prominently. In one article, for example, a woman wrote:

> A young girl, pure as the waters of Ganga, is married off to a 67-year-old widower who not only has several grown up sons and daughters but is also a grandfather. Such marriages have become customary in society, and it is on the strength of such a practice that men can designate women as discardable, and say that if the old shoe is broken we will wear another, or why wash a ragged garment, why lament a woman.

By this point, educated Indian women were generating a push for innovation on their own, reflecting Western influence but no longer dependent on explicit Western models.

Christian missionary efforts featured a somewhat parallel complexity in their impact on India's gender standards. By the middle of the nineteenth century a handful of upper-caste Indian women were converting to Christianity specifically for its gender message. One wrote, for example, that awareness of Christianity, with its claim of spiritual equality, awakened her to "my own hopeless condition as a woman" within the Hindu tradition. Several women authored powerful statements of their discovery. By the later nineteenth century, some lower-caste conversions occurred for similar reasons. But relationships with European Christian women in India were often bitterly disappointing, for few of them could drop their patronizing racial attitudes just because of a shared religion. Furthermore, the nineteenth-century version of Christianity had its own constraints, for example on freedom of sexual behavior, that many Indian women found demeaning. Here, as with reform efforts more generally, contact with Europeans could bring real change, but not an entirely acceptable alternative model.

Nationalism and reform

The rise of movements for greater national autonomy, and ultimately independence, reflected many of the ambiguities of India's interaction with the West by the late nineteenth century. Early nationalist movements were run by men. They were strongly influenced by Western political ideals – the idea of a nation and national loyalty was itself an import – but did not place a high priority on problems of gender. European nationalism had itself been male-dominated, looking to political and military change but largely assuming a status quo where women were concerned. Indian nationalism also stressed the validity of many aspects of Indian tradition, including Hinduism, which was a further potential limitation on connections with changes in male–female roles and relationships. But nationalists did see that some alterations in Hinduism were needed to create a modern nation, respectable in the eyes of outside observers and capable of forging new levels of unity.

Many nationalist reform movements continued to think of women not as individuals, but as wives and mothers. They urged improvements in women's health and even education, but in order to improve their family service. Many stressed the need for better schools, attacking the colonial regime for failing to provide funding and rigorous standards for women's education (a charge that had considerable merit), but they pushed for largely religious (Hindu) schooling. Some argued for a bit of domestic training as a supplement. The idea was that education would help women relate to educated husbands and improve their talents as mothers – not that education would promote women as individuals or prepare them for new kinds of work. This was a tension that existed in Western debates over women's education as well, but the Indian discussion veered toward a more traditionalist viewpoint:

The character of girls' education should be different from that of boys in many essential respects. . . . The education we give our girls should not unsex them.

With all the sorrow and pain that an educated Hindu feels for the present position of Indian womanhood, he would not have his daughters and sisters go out into the world in search of employment as the girls in Europe do, not to speak of other excesses to which they are all liable by virtue of their conditions of life.

Yet even this halting approach had results. Upper-caste Indians, both male and female, gradually became more accustomed to the idea of education of some type for women. Individual women, operating within the orbit of the nationalist reform movements, were able to establish schools, and some of them were quite successful, training increasing numbers of teachers among other things. A variety of women's organizations and clubs also spun off from the reform movements. The male leaders, too, while maintaining a fairly traditional view of women and their roles, did press for other changes, including limitations on child marriage and better rights for widows – seen as vital to create a healthier family atmosphere for all concerned.

These tentative beginnings blossomed into fuller nationalist embrace of women's educational, political and legal rights as the twentieth century progressed. Gandhi, the inspirational leader from the 1920s onward, actively urged women's support. Thousands of women, including upper-caste (and well-educated), joined demonstrations, gaining political experience for the first time. The non-violent emphasis was crucial in convincing women to venture upon activity outside domestic confinement, as the old system of purdah began to collapse (see Chapter 3). For his part, Gandhi argued that "India's salvation depends on the sacrifices and enlightenment of her women. . . . Man and woman are one, their problems must be one in essence. The soul in both is the same." But again there was a qualification: "The duty of motherhood, which the vast majority of women will always undertake, requires qualities which man need not possess. She is passive, he is active." Gandhi quietly revised Hinduism, as in the explicit equality of souls, and also in his promptings for high-quality education, but he still maintained contact with older traditions.

On independence in 1947, women gained the right to vote, equal legal status as citizens and the ability to serve in elected office at any level. In 1955, the Hindu Marriage Act gave women the right to divorce and raised the minimum marriage age to fifteen for females. Other measures gave female children equal claims with boys in inheriting property. By 1956–7, 40 percent of the eligible women voters were casting ballots, and a handful of women were being elected to national and state parliaments.

Conclusion

The results of culture contact for Indian women were and remain extremely complex. British pressure and example helped open debate about a number of traditional practices. Colonial contacts, and efforts by individual Western women in India, helped spur other changes. British zeal for reform was, however, limited, both by the greater interest in imperial profit and stability and by the long insistence on women's domestic roles. Indian reactions were similarly complex. Association of reforms with the West could generate opposition. Aspects of Indian nationalism were linked to a reassertion of traditional roles and ideals. The whole issue of contact was conditioned by largely unfavorable patterns of economic change, particularly where the masses of rural Indians were concerned.

One consequence of contact was familiar enough: an impulse to syncretism. Few Indian women converted to Christianity; rather, they sought change or continuity within one of the established religions. Many educated, urban women, quite aware of Western values and eager to oppose traditional repression, nevertheless continued to accept certain customs such as arranged marriage. Some even argued that the result was liberating for women, compared to Western requirements of careful grooming and dieting in order to create the appearance that might snare a man. Few Indian women embraced Westernization outright. This is a standard feature of contacts among well-defined cultures, but it was enhanced by the constraints and complexities involved in prolonged interaction with the West.

Finally, change was uneven (as in all societies in the twentieth-century world). India granted many Western-style legal and political rights. But, as Hindu fundamentalism surged in the 1980s, occasional cases of *sati* and female infanticide or neglect of female children re-emerged (though they were against Indian law), while violence over inadequate dowries showed the persistence of a particular evaluation of marriage on the part of an extremist male minority. India's modern amalgam, where gender was concerned, was not yet fully agreed upon. While the nation's tensions between tradition and change were broadly shared with other societies, including Western Europe and the United States, the specifics remained distinctive.

Further reading

The experience of Indian men and women under colonialism has been much debated in recent years, thanks to feminist scholarship and theory and a reaction against the simple equation of British influence with progress: Kumkum Sangari and Sudesh Vaid (eds), *Recasting Women. Essays on Indian Colonial History* (New Delhi: Kali for Women, 1989; New Brunswick, NJ: Rutgers University Press, 1989); Mary Ann Lind, *The Compassionate Memsahibs. Welfare Activities of British Women in India* (New York: Greenwood Press, 1988); Rita Kranidis,

Imperial Objects. Essays on Victorian Women's Emigration and the Unauthorized Imperial Experience (New York: Twayne Publishers, 1998; London: Prentice Hall International, 1998); J. Krishnamurty, *Women in Colonial India. Essays on Survival, Work and the State* (New Delhi/New York: Oxford University Press, 1989). On studies of men and colonialism in India: Anne McClintock, *Imperial Leather: Race, Gender, and Sexuality in the Colonial Contest* (London/New York: Routledge, 1995); Graham Dawson, *Soldier Heroes: British Adventure, Empire, and the Imagining of Masculinities* (London/New York: Routledge, 1994); Mrinalini Sinha, *Colonial Masculinity: The "Manly Englishman" and the "Effeminate Bengali" in the Late Nineteenth Century* (Manchester: Manchester University Press, 1997). See also Ann Laura Stoler, *Carnal Knowledge and Imperial Power: Race and the Intimate in Colonial Rule* (Berkeley, Calif.: University of California Press, 2002); Revathu Krishnawamy, *Effeminism: The Economy of Colonial Desire* (Ann Arbor, Mich.: University of Michigan Press, 1998); and Clare Midgley, ed., *Gender and Imperialism* (Manchester: Manchester University Press, 1998).

Chapter 8

Western influences and regional reactions

Polynesia and Africa

The nineteenth century saw the intensification of Western contacts with the islands of the Pacific, or Oceania, and with sub-Saharan Africa. Parts of the Pacific like Polynesia – with such island clusters as Tahiti and Hawaii – encountered significant Western penetration in the eighteenth century, and then a burst of commercial, missionary and finally colonial activities from the 1820s onward. These areas had long been isolated from other parts of the world, so outside intrusions could be either particularly attractive or disruptive. Western imperialism stepped up in sub-Saharan Africa from the 1850s and 1860s onward. Here, the societies involved had long been in some contact with other parts of the world, but the sheer intensity of Western political, religious and commercial penetration was unprecedented. Both in Polynesia and in Africa, basic adjustments to the interactions with the West – including the United States as well as Western Europe – extended into the first decades of the twentieth century.

Exchanges with Polynesia and Africa had profound implications for gender relations, more profound on the whole than those in India. Different traditions, power positions and Western models all played a role, despite a colonial context which India had shared. Many of the results resembled those that had taken shape much earlier in the Americas, particularly because of the importance of Christian missionary endeavor. As in the Americas also, local people reacted to missionary examples diversely; some, including many women, were strongly attracted, while others resented the interference with traditional gender identities. Western example was itself different by the nineteenth century from that which had been presented to Native Americans. It included stricter sexual codes and a firmer insistence on a proper definition of the family in which men and women had very different roles. The example was also accompanied by much more extensive economic exploitation, for the industrial West was much quicker to penetrate local economies than the commercial West had been in the sixteenth and seventeenth centuries. This development added to the impact of cultural exchange, qualifying results even more than in the Indian case.

One of the chief reasons that patterns in nineteenth- to early twentieth-century Polynesia and Africa differed from those in India in the same period involved the greater missionary inroads. Because most Indians remained attached to Hinduism or Islam, Western interventions, though significant, were clearly constrained. (The same constraints applied to Muslim African regions, which were not drawn to Christian missionary appeals.) It was also in Polynesia and Africa that Western imperialists gave fullest vent to their belief in a civilizing mission – the famous "white man's burden" – to bring enlightenment to backward peoples.

Western missionaries and colonial officials – whose policies, as we shall see, were not the same, especially in Africa – unquestionably thought they were improving the lot of women as part of the benefits Western standards entailed. There were indeed some potentially positive changes, together with indications that local peoples were attracted to certain aspects of the Western model, but recent scholarship, including assessments by women themselves, has emphasized the disruption and deterioration that Western intrusions generated. Long-established traditional systems were torn apart by well-meaning reforms combined with less well-intentioned economic exploitation. The result, inevitably, was not a full Westernization, for local peoples retained important elements of the past and had in addition to react to the disruptive potential. But there was change, plus new divisions, as different groups adjusted in various ways. Among other results, disputes between the genders added to the confusions of decades of contact.

The interactions with external cultural models in Polynesia and Africa affected the history of important regions of the world in very human terms. They extend the larger story of Western impact on gender relationships in modern centuries, with all its complexities. The patterns involve a host of local specifics, like the gender taboos that had applied in Polynesia or the African reliance on extended family relationships. But the patterns also involve components familiar from earlier cases like the Americas and India, beginning with the gap between professed Western intentions and actual results. Like the earlier cases also, the new patterns involve the juxtaposition of external standards with well-developed, often highly traditional, functioning gender systems. Thinking back on the earlier cases should allow some predictions of the main lines of exchange, in advance of the details. What would be most attractive about Western models? What would be most disruptive? Missionaries and imperialists themselves gave little thought to historical subtleties, convinced of their service to unassailable civilized standards, but historical analysts can now do better, informed by prior example.

Polynesia

Key rulers in parts of Polynesia, like King Kamehameha in Hawaii, were impressed with Western standards early on: if nothing else, the clear superiority of Western naval technology made a mark. Interest in Western-style reforms, either to strengthen regional kingdoms or simply to avoid embarrassment in European eyes, began early. At the same time, contrasts between Western gender standards and local traditions were obvious, making relationships between men and women a reform subject almost immediately. It was in this context that, soon after Kamehameha's death, his young son decided to end the traditional taboo, or *kapu,* that prevented men and women from eating together. At a banquet in 1819, he expressly joined the women's table, declaring "The taboos are at an end. . . . The gods are a lie."

Missionaries soon followed, both from Europe and from the United States. They found much to distress them in the conditions of women, aside from the lack of Christianity. Clothing and sexuality were important issues. Most Westerners assumed that Polynesian women were profoundly corrupt, because of traditions of sexual freedom in youth; many believed that early and promiscuous sexual activity was also a sign of women's degradation. It thus seemed important not only for propriety, but also for women themselves, to press for changes in clothing, which would cover bare bodies, and for other shifts, such as curtailment of traditional, provocative dances like the hula. Missionaries also urged an end to the customary reliance on abortion and infanticide as means of birth control. Sexual restraint, in the contemporary Western view, should do the job. Abortion had long been tolerated in the West as well, but by the 1820s and 1830s it was being outlawed in the interests of discouraging excessive sexual activity. Hawaiians resisted many of these changes, but over time gradually accommodated in matters such as clothing styles. Missionaries, and missionary wives, remained suspicious of local ways, but by the 1840s they were reporting improvements.

The introduction of formal education for young women, and even some adults, went more smoothly. Many seemed interested, and missionary teachers soon were commenting on girls who were "anxious to learn" or "delightfully repeating their lessons". Although missionaries were particularly interested in converting men to Christianity, as the proper heads of families, many women took the lead. Here, missionaries seemed to be bringing new outlets for women, despite the fact that traditional polytheistic religions had given significant roles to some female leaders.

Missionaries also urged changes in work roles. They were appalled at the amount of labor women did outside the home, viewing men as idle and women as inadequately focused on the cares of the household. In their view, a proper family involved men providing basic income, with women maintaining a clean home and caring for the children. Agricultural work was "unsuitable to the female sex", "derogatory to the female and inimical to an improvement in morals". Thus, considerable attention was given to promoting female skills such as sewing (which had the added benefit of producing "decent" clothing), while men were employed in the fields. An obvious result was a growing inequality in economic power between men and women, compared to traditional Polynesian standards, which missionaries amplified by insisting that women be deferential to their husbands' authority – as was the current standard in Europe and the United States.

Finally, missionary pressure cut into extended family traditions. The proper family was a nuclear one, and older traditions in which many different adults collaborated in the care of children were vigorously attacked.

The result of the steady campaign for change was a reduction of many of the controls Polynesian women had previously maintained in their lives. It became more difficult to regulate the number of births or of children, given the efforts to curtail traditional methods. Childcare fell more on individual women. Educational gains occurred, but their impact was muted by the restrictions on work opportunities. Above all, the result of contact with insistent Western standards was both confusing and divisive. It was hard to jettison enough traditions to seem fully Western, but it was virtually impossible to maintain traditional habits without modification. The power and self-confidence of Western exemplars could not be shaken, and formal resistance was rare. It was left to hosts of individual men and women to make some sense of the new combinations that seemed possible.

Later, of course, the Western models themselves would change. The advent of tourism from the late nineteenth century onward brought new models of consumerism and sexuality. Now some Western visitors sought to benefit by real or imagined Polynesian interests in sexual enjoyment and enticing dances, and this meant that, in contrast to the initial decades of interaction, some mutual influence was developing. Feminist campaigns would also make a mark, in encouraging interests in new kinds of rights. The process of adjustment continued into the twentieth century.

Patterns of interaction between Western Europe and Polynesia also applied to New Zealand, where the Maori population represented a large Polynesian group. (Polynesian migration to New Zealand, particularly the North Island, had occurred between 1150 and 1450.) As elsewhere, Western contact first developed in the form of scattered trading, with little cultural impact, but colonization speeded up after 1814, with both Catholic and Protestant missionary activity following quickly in its wake.

European impact was accelerated by several familiar factors. Maori social and political structures were severely damaged by European intrusion, including extensive seizures of land. Disease took a huge toll. Maori population had dropped significantly by the 1850s (to 56,000) and would fall further, to 42,000, by 1896. Europeans, including missionaries, offered compelling cultural examples as well as obviously more productive agricultural methods; it was hard to resist entirely. By the 1850s, most Maoris had become at least nominal Christians.

There were some special features. Maori tradition had been polygynous and strongly patriarchal, as elsewhere in Polynesia. Prohibitions against contact, for example in eating, were less fierce. Europeans criticized Maoris for subordinating women, but in fact they did not understand features of the polytheistic religion that imbued women with great power, particularly associated with sexuality. Again, the European impulse was to urge a more Western gender differentiation, with women confined to domestic roles but given great praise for moral behavior. There was yet another distinctive aspect to the New Zealand context: in some parts of the North Island, Maori leadership long remained relatively well organized, capable of substantial (if ultimately futile) rebellions against the English colonial government as late as the 1860s. Government pressure for assimilation became more extensive, and in 1879 the state took over control of Maori education. However, there was some leeway for the preservation of certain customs   for example, extensive male tattooing – and the synergistic mixing of religious traditions with Christianity. Individual Maori women, into the twentieth century, developed claims to prophecy and religious revelation that could give them considerable political voice. European views of Maori family traditions were characteristically harsh, but a desire for peaceful race relations balanced the standard judgmentalism to some degree. Pressure to assimilate nevertheless continued, particularly as some Maoris began to move into the growing cities and as intermarriage increased.

Conditions in New Zealand also encouraged unusually early innovations in some of the laws dealing with male–female relations. As in many Western colonial societies, where women of European origin were long in short supply and where their work in frontier agriculture was exceptionally valuable, movements for gender reform surfaced strongly in the second half of the nineteenth century. New Zealand became the first nation to grant adult women the vote, in 1893, and other laws provided greater equality in work access and in divorce. These developments did not flow directly from the cultural interaction between Europeans and Polynesians, but it fed into the assimilation process during the twentieth century.

Sub-Saharan Africa

Gender issues did not loom as large in Western contacts in Africa from the mid-nineteenth century onward as they had in Polynesia. Great power rivalries, frenzied economic development and attacks on African slavery all seemed more important. European interaction with Africa was also complicated by divisions between Christian missionaries and colonial officials. The missionaries quickly developed an agenda similar to that in Polynesia, in the attempts to inculcate Western-style family ideals in a very different traditional context. Colonial officials, however, were not eager to risk opposition from Africans themselves, for their goal was political stability. They were thus slow to regulate behaviors that missionaries thought clearly needed correction.

While gender conditions varied in different parts of the huge subcontinent south of the Sahara, in general women had maintained various forms of power before colonial contact. They often worked at different tasks in agriculture, and assumed significant responsibilities for marketing goods. Some served as chiefs, since political power was not confined to men; others had religious functions. Women often set up associations and gained informal political voice; a strong tradition of female participation in protest existed. Many groups emphasized matrilineality, or descent from mothers, in their family organization.

Little of this made sense according to contemporary West European standards. Colonial officials and missionaries alike were interested in promoting the work of men, as a source of labor in mines and on commercial agricultural estates and as a basis for new systems of government taxation. Women's traditional work roles seemed burdensome, while also distracting them from appropriate attention to the family. In this spirit, a 1929 regulation in what is now Ghana jailed women traders along with prostitutes. Great pressure was applied to confine women to a smaller number of tasks, usually closely related to the household, while widening the gap between men's and women's economic roles. When commercial pressures also pressed men to leave their families to provide labor for mines or urban industry, the gap widened further. African women became more economically dependent, even as missionaries urged them to be docile homemakers. Numerous programs developed to make women "civilized helpmates" or "purer wives and better mothers".

Women's political rights were also curtailed. British colonial policies attacked local councils on which women sat, while protests in which African women participated, for example against new taxes, were energetically, sometimes brutally repressed. Women should not have political roles, in the colonial view, and careful restrictions served gender reform and protection of public order alike. A number of Western officials commented on African men as "hen-pecked husbands", when their wives maintained customary public functions.

Under the spur of the missionaries, a variety of family traditions were attacked, and gradually some of the attacks passed into colonial regulations. As in Polynesia, the clear goal was promotion of the nuclear family. Arranged marriages, particularly when girls were quite young, were opposed in the name of freedom of choice. French colonial regulations gradually moved against child marriage, while requiring the consent of both parties to any marriage in adulthood. Polygyny was bitterly opposed. Customs that allowed women to return to their paternal family if a marriage dissolved, or that gave a widow in marriage to her late husband's brother, as a means of family solidarity and support, were also attacked, again sometimes by law.

Western example also of course promoted formal education for women, though this was sometimes colored by the desire to teach domestic skills, sewing and the like. Girls' schools opened in various parts of Africa by the early twentieth century, offering emphases such as "a sound moral, literary and industrial education". Many schoolgirls aspired to be teachers or nurses, but by the 1930s a handful ventured further. A Nigerian woman graduated from

Oxford University in 1934, while the first female lawyer began work in Nigeria in 1935.

Education could also spur new kinds of economic activities, despite Western pressure for domesticity, and also novel types of women's organizations. A Women's League was formed in Lagos, Nigeria, in the 1920s, seeking government action on women's education, public health and prostitution.

A great deal of concern focused on sexuality. European racist beliefs tended to emphasize what was seen as excessive African sexuality. Great anxiety developed about having European women settle in Africa, because of the sexual "threat". Some of this concern spilled over into attempts to regulate women's behavior, particularly in the cities. Precisely because of new limitations on their economic activities, some African women did become urban prostitutes, and they were the target of much worried comment. It was in this context that some colonial administrations passed laws against female adultery, leaving male behavior untouched. Many Christian Africans, men and women alike, joined the attempts to regulate sexual behavior, as a matter of religious conviction. Campaigns also developed among urban African men, even more widely. Here, religion and a desire for respectability were supplemented by attempts to reinforce masculine authority over potentially wayward wives and daughters. Many African men deeply felt their economic insecurity and subjection to Western commercial firms, for which they worked in subordinate, often segregated, jobs. Asserting dominance over women was an obvious compensation. In this context, vigorous reform movements might attack not only prostitutes, but also other women who were imitating another set of Western standards by wearing provocative European styles and using cosmetics. Thus a men's group in Southern Rhodesia (now Zimbabwe) attacked women "with painted lips and cheeks" and urged that all women be kept out of bars.

> In the old days girls were protected by their parents until they were well matured, but now-a-days it seems that they are allowed to do exactly as they please. . . . This is not as it should be, what she means is that because she is grown-up she is free from the control of her parents. The lure of town life attracts her and she forthwith becomes immoral.

African reactions to Western gender models varied. Some embraced new opportunities in Christianity and in novel forms of education. Others, obviously, were attracted by consumer standards. Most changes, however, barely compensated for the obvious losses, if they compensated at all. Women sought education, and sometimes new kinds of jobs, in part in reaction to the loss of more traditional economic activities. New associations, sometimes incorporating some of the demands spearheaded by Western feminists, rarely matched the political powers women had wielded before the colonial era. African men, who were also the subject of cultural as well as economic pressure from Western sources, did gain greater economic power within families, including control over property, thanks to the colonial importations of Western laws about individual ownership. On the other hand, some African women began to argue for reforms based on their new, more Western-style roles as homemakers. In Zambia, for example, women began to complain of neglect and assault, using the moral and legal values of the colonial authorities to win improvements in family life, even as their traditional position eroded. Other women publicly insisted on "the responsibility of husbands" to provide proper family support, defining respectability in terms (as a middle-class women's group in South Africa contended in 1913) of "their right to remain at home as housewives". Needless to say, many Africans disagreed over the balance of change and tradition that should define relations between men and women, and many were confused about what standards to apply.

European contact affected African men aside from relationships with women, even aside from economic change. Effeminacy was emphasized less often than with Asia, if only because of the greater racist fears of African male sexuality. But African men were certainly regarded as inferior, even childlike – which was why they were so often referred to as "boy". To this extent, while the European approach to the domestication of African women encouraged new male family power, larger attitudes could undermine masculinity. Not surprisingly, some African men sought to compensate for this new disdain by demonstrating manhood through heavy drinking or abusive treatment of women.

Gender issues inevitably spilled over into the African nationalist movements that began to form in the early decades of the twentieth century. Some nationalists assumed that the cause of the nation would serve to advance both genders, and ringing proclamations were sometimes issued to that effect. Many African women participated extensively in nationalist agitation, assuming that independence from colonial control would lead to improvements in their lot. But it was not always clear how improvements should be defined: would this be a return to older conditions, which were not always clearly remembered, or the advent of rights of a more feminist type? Male nationalists, for whom gender issues were not top priority in any event, might defend traditional gender patterns that some African women now opposed. Thus polygyny might be praised as an expression of traditional African culture and a protection for women in situations where there were not enough men to go around. The great Kenyan nationalist leader Jomo Kenyatta also defended female circumcision (a "mere bodily mutilation"), not because it constrained women's sexuality but because it was an integral part of family and tribal solidarity – essential to institutions which have "enormous educational, social, moral and religious implications". Some nationalist movements finally featured an aggressive masculinity fueled by European condescension. Nationalism, in other words, was unlikely to resolve the pressures on gender roles which Western interference and example had promoted in modern Africa.

Conclusion

Western models, combined with economic pressures, greatly changed gender conditions in Polynesia and Africa, undermining traditions for many people. At the same time, few Polynesians or Africans fully accepted Western norms, and the standards themselves were not fully consistent. Most scholars now believe that women lost more than they gained in the process, particularly in areas such as relative economic power and informal political roles. At the same time, Western standards could also point the way to some remediation, in so far as women learned new uses of education and association and as they gained new perspectives on family practices that might not have been in their best interest. The situation was further complicated by the cultural and economic pressures on men, whose masculinity was often criticized by Western observers and who sought new means of expression of their own.

Further reading

On Polynesia: Patricia Grimshaw, *Paths of Duty. American Missionary Wives in Nineteenth-Century Hawaii* (Honolulu: University of Hawaii Press, 1989); Victoria S. Lockwood, *Tahitian Transformation: Gender and Capitalist Development in a Rural Society* (Boulder, Colo.: Lynne Rienner Publishers, 1993); Alan Moorehead, *The Fatal Impact: The Invasion of the South Pacific, 1767–1840* (New York: Harper & Row, 1987). On New Zealand: Geoffrey Rice (ed.), *The Oxford History of New Zealand* (Auckland/New York: Oxford University Press, 1992); Barbara Griffiths, *Petticoat Pioneers: South Island Women of the Colonial Era* (Wellington: Reed, 1980). On Africa: Elizabeth Isichei, *A History of Christianity in Africa, from Antiquity to the Present* (Grand Rapids, Mich.: Eerdmans, 1995); Ellen Charlton, Jana Evertt and Kathleen Staudt (eds), *Women, the State, and Development* (Albany, NY: State University of New York Press, 1989); Wunyabari Maloba, *Mau Mau and Kenya: An Analysis of a Peasant Revolt* (Bloomington, Ind.: Indiana University Press, 1993); A. D. Roberts (ed.), *The Cambridge History of Africa, 7, 1905–1940* (Cambridge/New York: Cambridge University Press, 1986); Ifi Amadiume, *Male Daughters, Female Husbands. Gender and Sex in an African Society* (London: Zed Books, 1987); Margaret Strobel, *Muslim Women in Mombasa, 1890–1975* (New Haven, Conn.: Yale University Press, 1979). See also John Noyes, *The Mastery of Submission: Inventions of Masochism* (Ithaca, NY: Cornell University Press, 1997).

Chapter 9

Westernization and gender
Beyond the colonial models

This chapter deals with a different – though not totally contrasting – type of contact with the West, one that stretched from the late seventeenth century onward and continues to operate in our own day. Societies not taken as colonies (or, in the case of Egypt and Korea, not yet taken) might undertake changes on their own, seeking to pick selectively from Western models in the interest of maintaining independence. Westernization programs invariably involved gender to some degree, and in certain cases changes in the status of women had considerable priority. The cases of Westernization that began to take shape before 1900 warrant comparison with the instances of colonial impact: did the ability to maintain greater control over the process of change modify some of the downsides of Western impact?

A number of societies that were not directly colonized by Western Europe adopted a host of Western-style reforms during the eighteenth and nineteenth centuries. This chapter looks at the two most important cases of Westernization – Russia and Japan – while also noting two other instances in Egypt and Korea. None of the societies involved focused primarily on gender issues in their reform processes, but their policies inevitably affected male and female roles and often had some unexpected side effects which extended and complicated these results.

The cases of Westernization are varied. Russia began a process of deliberate, but highly selective, imitation of Western Europe under Peter the Great, at the end of the seventeenth century. The initial goals focused on using Western technology and political styles to strengthen the Russian state and military, but there was considerable upper-class cultural imitation as well. Contacts continued and, on the whole, broadened during the later eighteenth and nineteenth centuries. The Russian government occasionally pulled back from Westernization, for example between 1825 and the 1850s, but reformers continued to press, and the amount of travel to and from Russia, mutual cultural exchange, and trading activity increased fairly steadily.

Japan, long in isolation, was thrown open to foreign influence after an American fleet visited Edo bay and pressed for trade rights in 1853. After a confused period involving more extensive American and European pressure and near civil war among factions in the Japanese elite, a more consistent reform process was launched in 1868. During the ensuing Meiji era – taking its name from the label "enlightened one", applied to the new emperor whose bureaucrats guided the reform process – Japan abolished feudalism, set up a limited parliamentary government, began to speed up economic change and early industrialization, launched dramatic new public health programs and instituted a new system of mass education. Visits to Western Europe and the United States and use of Western experts as guides constituted an important part of this process, deliberately designed to make Japan powerful enough to hold off Western interference and, ultimately, to compete with the West itself.

These Westernization programs were, obviously, quite varied. The "West" that was copied depended on the time period. Russian Westernization began when the West's advantages seemed to emphasize science and absolute monarchy, along with extensive trading that Russia in fact was reluctant to copy. Japanese Westernization involved imitating an outright industrial revolution, as well as constitutional monarchy. Westernization also depended heavily on the society doing the copying: Russia's traditional Orthodox Christianity and substantially peasant society represented a very different base from Japan's Confucianism and more active commerce. For Russia, the West was different but not entirely foreign, if only because of shared commitments to Christianity. For Japan, contacts with the West emerged after centuries of great isolation, and the West seemed a society, however powerful, of barbarian strangeness. Distinctions of this sort would significantly affect the impact of imitation on gender. We will see that Japanese and Russian interpretations and uses of what they saw in the West, where gender was concerned, differed enormously.

Other examples of Westernization, though far less extensive than Russia's or Japan's, vividly illustrate the potential variety of response. Egypt's initial Westernization occurred early in the nineteenth century, under Muhammed Ali. Eager to strengthen Egypt's government and economy, after a French occupation in 1798 and amid growing Western economic influence, he focused on power considerations. The government sent male students for technical and military training in Europe. Crash programs sought to expand technical training at home, while spurring agricultural exports and textile factories. In this context, and in a setting in which Islamic principles for women continued to provide certain advantages, for example in property ownership, Westernization efforts did not focus on gender, but indirect consequences were considerable. New economic policies increased pressures on women to work hard. The state directly required women's labor service, for example in canal building, despite the strenuous work concerned; only in the 1850s were these policies eased. Women workers in factories might work alongside men, a noticeable innovation, but in general task segregation continued. Initially, however, new levels of Western contact meant little more than pressures for heightened exploitation.

The first steps of Western reformism in Korea, however, occurring later and with greater input from Christian missionaries from the West, had different implications. Western patterns here, in the context of a previously strict patriarchalism with strong Confucian elements, suggested some reconsideration of women's overall status. Western-inspired reform pressures on the very conservative Yi monarchy in the 1880s led to measures designed to protect women against the worst abuses of arranged marriages, by setting a minimum age of sixteen; new laws also allowed widows to remarry. Reformers issued statements urging respect for women and condemning the "barbarous treatment" of women under Confucianism. While warning against feminist militancy, groups like the 1890s Independence Society pressed for modern educational opportunities and for at least certain kinds of equality. Both foreign Protestant missionaries and a new Korean women's group, Chanyanghoe, established scattered schools for women. A new generation of women writers, often converted to Christianity (Korea became the only Asian setting aside from the Philippines where really extensive conversions occurred), testified to new ideas about women's rights to develop their own personalities; as Yi Kwang-su wrote, attendance at church services with men gave her "the conception that men and women are sons and daughters of God on equal terms". Clearly, as comparisons of the initial Egyptian and Korean experiences suggest, depending on timing and prior context, Western-style reformism could lead toward virtual polar opposites in terms of implications for women. The clearest constant was a pressure for considerable change in light of Western models and the new level of Western power.

For all the distinctions, however, voluntary Westernizations – that is, reform programs based on imitating Western ideas and institutions without outright colonial control – did have some common features. They were always selective. The societies involved wanted to preserve not only independence, but also important cultural traditions. They never wanted to become fully Western. This meant also that a substantial portion of the Westernization programs was concerned with power considerations – strengthening governments, the military and the economy. This emphasis had obvious gender implications, often favoring new masculine assertiveness. At the same time, however, Westernizations usually contained a cultural component, as in new imitations of Western art or popular culture. This reflected a sense of Western superiority that spilled beyond power factors alone. It expressed a desire to avoid embarrassment in Western eyes. Here, implications for relationships between men and women could be quite different, with societies striving to make sure Western observers did not find their treatment of women uncivilized. These factors – selectivity, power emphasis, the embarrassment concern – did not add up tidily, which means that Westernization inevitably produced complex gender results that would not work our smoothly or quickly.

Westernization programs involved profound cultural contacts, with societies seeking to learn more about the West, sending students to the West for learning, inviting Western visitors. How would the results compare with cases of Western colonialism? Did greater voluntarism – the fact that the Western example, however powerful, was invited, rather than imposed by force – reduce or extend the implications for changes in gender relations?

The Russian case

Initial Westernization in Russia provides an unusually clearcut and in many ways distinctive case of the impact of culture contact: conditions of women improved. There are caveats, though: relatively few women were affected, for initial Russian reforms focused on the upper classes alone; and there were a few drawbacks, if rarely noticed by the women involved at the time. Finally, Peter the Great's Westernization program provoked resistance among Russian conservatives, including churchmen, and this could certainly retard the pace of change. Conservatives did not usually focus on gender issues, but their resistance to change included praise for a highly patriarchal tradition. With all this, contact with the West for Russia, up until the twentieth century and to some extent even after the great communist revolution, involved a sense of liberation for many women. This was true even when conditions in Western Europe imposed a host of restrictions on women, by the standards of our own day, and even when, in terms of the West's own traditions, some deteriorations were occurring.

Russia's customs were highly patriarchal. As in most patriarchal societies, differentiation between men and women was greatest in the upper classes. Marriages were arranged by the fathers involved. When a match had been concluded to the father's satisfaction, the bride- and groom-to-be would be introduced. Often, at the wedding itself, the bride's father would symbolically tap his daughter with a whip, before handing the whip to the groom in representation of the transfer of male power. "Should you not behave as you ought to toward your husband, he in my stead will admonish you with this whip." Upper-class women were secluded, confined to parts of the house called the *terem;* when in public, they were often veiled. Great emphasis was placed on virginity before marriage, and then on sexual fidelity. Russian Orthodox Christianity allowed a man, twice in his life, to send an unsatisfactory wife to a convent, where she would become dead to the outside world; the man could then marry again. Women's duties revolved around motherhood and domestic service. To call a man a woman, or *baba,* was a great insult.

Peter the Great's reforms explicitly cut into this pattern. His goals were twofold. First, he hoped to make the aristocracy a more effective source of loyal state bureaucrats. To do this, he wanted to reduce the isolation of individual, hierarchical families, while involving women in new opportunities that would improve their capacity to educate their sons. Second, he wanted to make Russian culture less embarrassingly backward by Western standards, and this meant giving upper-class women chances to participate in public events, like concerts and dances, as they did in Western Europe. To some extent, at least,

Peter, like later Russian reformers, seemed to realize that changing Russia had to involve altering its family structures.

In 1718, Peter ordered that aristocratic women leave the *terem* and participate in cultural and social events in public. He also abolished the custom of arranged marriage. A decree of 1702 ruled that all marriage decisions should be voluntary, that prospective partners should meet at least six weeks before engagement, that each should be free to reject the other, and that the symbolic wedding whip be replaced by a kiss. His Westernization program required changes in the dress styles of both men and women in the upper classes, and women responded far more favorably. They viewed the new styles as opportunities to enjoy the brighter colors and more varied fashions of France, whereas men regarded the requirements of dressing in Western fashion primarily as giving in to tsarist dictates. Aristocratic women, including Peter's own daughters, began to gain opportunities for formal education, learning Western languages among other desirable attainments. As in the West, many upper-class women began to read works of Enlightenment philosophy. While changes in women's conditions were not the main point of Peter's program, most historians agree that the liberating effects were greater in this area than in any other. (Indeed, many other aspects of Peter's reforms worsened conditions, for example for the masses of serfs, placed ever more firmly under landlords' control.) While the increasing emphasis on the responsibility of women to be beautiful was a new constraint, at least according to some feminist analysis, the main limitations on Peter's moves – and they were huge – involved simply their narrow range of impact. Women in the provincial nobility and certainly the vast masses of peasant women saw no real change.

The thrust of Westernization continued, however sporadically, after Peter's death. Catherine the Great embellished his reforms by establishing the Smolnyi Institute for Girls of Noble Birth in 1764, as well as public schools where small numbers of girls of more humble background might obtain an education. Here, again, there were some ironies. Education in Russia gave women (albeit only a minority) opportunities to read Enlightenment works, when the Enlightenment itself, in the Western context, in many ways downgraded women's status in favor of emphases on new freedoms for men At one point, indeed, Catherine's approach urged an end to educational differentiation between men and women, though this was soon scaled back in favor of the notion that "the intent and goal of the rearing of girls should consist most of all in making good homemakers, faithful wives, and caring mothers". But a lingering interest in independent intellectual development persisted – according to one plan, girls should not only be made literate, but should also "have a mind enlightened by varied knowledge useful for civic life". Again, the main limits involved range: of the students who went through school between 1782 and 1800, only 7 percent were girls.

In the early nineteenth century, as Russian policy became more resistant to Westernization in the name of political conservatism, Western example had two major impacts. First, many Russian writers, inspired by Western styles such as Romanticism, began idealizing women. Poets like Pushkin wrote of female beauty and refinement. Many male radicals, aware that real reform had to involve the family, thought that idealization would replace traditional hierarchy. Again, the contemporary Western context suggested the limitations of this approach, which risked a new kind of isolation of women from public life in the name of feminine purity; in the Russian case, however, the association of Western models and liberating change persisted. Second, however, many individual women, aware of Western ideas of liberty, defied conventional limitations, sometimes joining radical movements themselves. Women writers began to condemn the subordination of upperclass wives. In 1807 a noble-woman, Nadezhda Durova, took on men's dress and joined the Russian cavalry, where she served with distinction, later publishing her journals. When the spirit of reform returned to Russian policy, under Alexander II (1855–81), individual women from many social classes began to imitate their Western sisters by seeking education in medicine and law. Articles on the "woman question", by men and women alike, surfaced in the atmosphere generated by the emancipation of the serfs (1861). A male surgeon thus wrote about the need to provide more education for women, partly to make them better wives and mothers, but also to support other functions such as nursing. During the 1870s the government gradually authorized the opening of medical and other courses for women, and finally set up a women's university. A strong feminist movement began to emerge, again looking to Western example at least in general ways. A number of women also began to participate in movements such as anarchism and nihilism. Their service was welcomed by men who, often, sincerely believed in women's freedom but who also realized that women carrying terrorist bombs would be less likely to attract police attention than men. Women themselves served frequently with feminist goals in mind, much like their Western sisters, who, however, had more legal recourses as a means of advancing their cause. By this point, obviously, the impetus for changes in women's conditions was deeply rooted in Russian politics and education, not dependent on Western contact *per se.*

The complexity of the interplay among Western contacts and models, Russian reformism, and a strong traditionalist/conservative impulse showed in debates over legal changes relating to gender and sexuality, at various points in the nineteenth and early twentieth centuries. Western models and reform sentiment pointed at greater separation between religious prescriptions and state law, for example concerning issues of sexual behavior such as adultery; there was a related push to view women's behavior as a matter for individuals rather than for family authority. But the conservative impulse ran strong, which limited change. Furthermore, Western models themselves were often ambivalent or traditionalist, for example concerning homosexuality. Changes did occur, at least on paper, culminating in a major legal reform in 1903. The number of sexual activities regarded as illegal was cut back. Discussions on these issues would continue after the communist revolution, particularly amid the experimental mood of the 1920s, until Stalinism imposed a more family-centered and traditionalist approach.

When revolution finally came to Russia, in 1917, it brought the triumph of Marxist ideology, itself initially a Western product. For Marxists, gender issues were not top priority, but it was assumed that the end of capitalism would liberate women along with bringing a host of other desirable changes. The new Soviet regime, though ultimately quite conservative in family policy, toured signs of women's liberation, including massive educational gains and full, if usually unequal, participation in the labor force. In propaganda at least, and sometimes in fact, revolutionary leaders argued that Russia had now surpassed the West, where women were still more commonly prevented from lifelong work careers. Even this line of argument reflected, in a backhand fashion, the earlier association of Western contact with improvements for women – else it would not have seemed so necessary to boast about a new Russian superiority.

Clearly, for more than two centuries, from Peter the Great onward, increasing contacts with the West helped provide new models and opportunities for women in a highly patriarchal society. Ultimately, and precisely because recurrent imitation of the West stretched over such a long period, the result led to real changes, for example in education and work opportunities, and also concerted agitation for further reform. Western cultural styles, including Marxism, together with educational and family patterns, provided alternatives to Russian conditions and encouraged robust movements for change. Imitation remained selective, even aside from the vital fact that most women were not directly involved in Western-style changes before 1917. There was no large movement to remove women from the labor force, despite the Romantic impulse of idealization. Here, if anything, Western contact worked to differentiate the Russian experience. Before the emancipation of the serfs, Russian landlords increased the rigors of rural work, including labor service on aristocratic estates, to provide the agricultural exports that would help pay for imported Western luxury goods. This work bore on men and women alike. Then, at the end of the nineteenth century, when Russia began to imitate Western industrialization, women's work again seemed vital, as a source of factory labor. In these contexts, the nineteenth-century Western impulse to urge a purely domestic role for respectable women had little echo in Russia. Adding to complexity was the fact that the West continued to suggest stylishness, which might or might not be compatible with the impulse to gain new freedoms. Russian department stores, opening from the 1850s onward in imitation of developments in Western Europe, actively solicited fashion-conscious women, and were condemned by conservatives for precisely this "foreign" slant. Even in the communist period, accusations of Russian women's dowdiness served as critiques of the new society, particularly by foreigners but by some Russian women themselves. The Western model was hardly a single entity.

The Japanese case

Contact with the West in Japan, from the Meiji period onward, shared important features with the Russian case, though it was more concentrated in time. Here, too, traditions dictated great emphasis on patriarchal hierarchy, though the particulars differed. In this context, reformers, including many women, could find in the West important examples of desirable new liberties for women, including the feminist movements that were emerging in precisely these decades in the United States and Western Europe. Because Japan introduced more rapid changes than Russia ventured, at least before 1917, a potential developed for considerable reshuffling of gender roles. Education is a case in point: both Russia and Japan worked for rapid extension of mass education in the later nineteenth century, for girls as well as for boys, but Japan moved much more quickly, which meant that the literacy gap between the genders disappeared more rapidly.

The link between Western contact and gender reform is more complex in the Japanese case, though, for three reasons. First, even more than in Russia, the West might mean style rather than liberty. Japan's experience with the West took shape as the latter was expanding its consumer apparatus, including a host of new products for women, such as cosmetics. Many Western women hesitated between emphasizing lifestyle opportunities – like wearing lipstick and smoking cigarettes – and more narrowly feminist demands, like seeking the vote. Small wonder that many urban Japanese women, interested in the West as a beacon of change, did the same. By the 1920s groups of stylish Japanese women – called "modern girls" – had emerged in the cities, eager to keep up with Western movies, clothes and dance fads and, seemingly, little else.

Second, imitation of the West quickly involved vigorous and eventually successful efforts to introduce Western-style industrialization. As in Russia, this meant great initial reliance on new forms of women's work, which were often both demeaning and demanding. For a time, new work constraints competed seriously with other changes in shaping women's lives, at a time when formal work demands on women in the West were often decreasing. As was so often the case, imitating the West economically might mean differing from it where women were concerned. This complexity emerged in Russia as well, but it had been preceded by a much clearer association of Western example with new intellectual and familial opportunities.

Third, and in the end most important, Japanese contact with the West was hedged virtually from the outset by a clear realization that Western gender conditions were very different from those in Japan and that many Western models were undesirable. Guided by relatively conservative men, including government officials, Japanese Westernization sought to avoid some of the openness for women discerned in the West. More traditional deference and family roles were important parts of an effort to ensure that Japanese identity and political stability would persist amid great change. This was a far more sweeping effort at selectivity where women were concerned than had occurred in Russia. It reflected much greater hesitancy with regard to the Western model. It also reflected the fact that masses of Japanese, and not just an elite minority, were swept up in change from the outset. Russia avoided such explicit defensiveness in part because reforms were so slow and limited. Japan, in contrast, jumped into the reform process feet first, when it finally decided to move, but by the same token actively sought to use gender as a means of offsetting chaos. Traditional approaches toward women, preserved amid great change, not only offered contact with older identities, but also provided Japanese men, swept up in change and often demeaned as somewhat effeminate by officious Western observers, with a chance to find compensation for stress.

Japanese reactions to new Western contacts, from the 1860s onward, combined four components. First was disdain, a sense that this was not an area where imitation would be appropriate at all. Second, however, was imitation, which took several directions. Third, shading off from imitation, was the need to alter the economic uses of women as the basis for initial industrialization. Fourth, most important in the long run, and most complex, was a policy that mixed very selective Western components with Confucian elements, to produce a distinctive and syncretic approach to women that continues to affect Japan to this day.

Disdain was obvious. Pre-contact Japan was a patriarchal society, heavily influenced by Confucianism, as we have seen in Chapter 5. Western gender relations in the nineteenth century seemed both strange and dangerous by Japanese standards. Early visitors to Western Europe and the United States, on the whole eager to advocate Western-style reforms in science, technology and even politics, were appalled by what they saw as the independence and outspokenness of Western women. Women seemed to have the kind of voice in family affairs that should properly be given to elders, in the Japanese view, and this was simply topsy-turvy. The fact that Western women were, if anything, losing in economic power, as their labor-force role was reduced, and were largely excluded from the political process did not register, in comparison to their informal social rights. As in the Russian case, then, the West seemed to represent greater freedoms for women than local tradition had allowed, but with the obvious difference that this seemed, to most relevant officials, largely bad, rather than good. Over time, as Western consumer habits gained influence in Japan, leading to the new interests in women's costumes and public leisure, this judgment would be confirmed, at least among more conservative males. At a time when imitation of the West proceeded rapidly in the power spheres of military and industrial life, gender was a vital point of differentiation which would help Japan remain Japan, while assuring stability and hierarchy amid change.

Yet it was impossible not to imitate. As we have seen, women themselves, as urbanization and industrialization increased, showed interest in some of the consumer features of the West, and this could not be completely prevented. Individual women also gained fresh opportunities from new Western contacts. For example, knowledge of Western patterns opened new vistas for women artists, who had been even less prominent in traditional Japan than in traditional Western Europe. Now, opportunities for individual women to study abroad helped breach this difference. Yamashita Rin, for example, born in 1857, studied in Russia (one of the first women to go abroad, taking the opportunity to serve as babysitter for a traveling Russian diplomat) and contributed important icon paintings to Russian Orthodox churches in Japan. Ragusa Tama married an Italian artist, who had been invited as a visiting instructor by the Japanese government at its new arts academy, and developed a noteworthy career in Western-style art (though in this case her work was long unknown in Japan). Other individual women gained prominence as writers (here renewing an older Japanese tradition) and even as feminist advocates, in close contact with developments in Western feminism.

More systematic imitation emerged as well. Japan committed itself to universal primary school education in 1872; the new Education Code specifically stipulated that "learning is no longer to be considered as belonging to the upper classes, but is to be equally the inheritance of . . . males and females". Abruptly, Japan decided to imitate patterns that had been developing in the West over a much longer period of time, including opportunities for female literacy. The significance of education for women's service in the labor force and for their family duties overrode more traditional hierarchies – though, as we shall see (and as was true in the West at this time), important gender distinctions remained. Widespread primary education was followed by more limited provision of secondary schools for girls (in 1908, there were 159 such schools, compared with over 300 for men), by opening medical schools (1900), a separate women's university (1901) and even limited access to some other universities. Education contributed to the new range of opportunities for individual women; access to the teaching profession expanded (particularly, of course, for service in girls' schools), and from the schools some of the leading feminist writers emerged.

Imitation also applied to sexuality, and here the implications were more ambiguous. Japanese officials were eager to avoid Western criticisms of popular habits that seemed, by current Western standards, uncivilized. In two respects, they moved to introduce dramatic new regulations, at least in principle. Homosexuality had never been a big issue in Japanese culture; and, indeed, tolerance and literary interest were noteworthy. But in 1873, at the height of West-leaning reforms, the government passed a law imposing a 90-day jail sentence on anyone practicing homosexuality. To be sure, this measure was soon relaxed, as Western enthusiasms moderated; the crime was abolished in 1883 and replaced by a vaguer "indecent assault" category, and male–male displays of public affection were once more tolerated. Efforts to impose new family controls over sexuality were more serious. While upper-class sexual codes had long been strict, popular behavior, both urban and rural, was more spontaneous, with considerable sexual activity before marriage. (Interestingly, Shintoism had featured goddesses with a series of sexual partners.) With reform, both traditional upper-class, Confucian morality and the example of Western Victorianism, with its officially strict condemnations of any sexual license, combined to produce a new sexual code, in part to avoid embarrassing Western comments about Japanese morals. Parents were urged to keep their daughters in check.

Along with the odd but very real combination of disdain and imitation, Japanese efforts at industrialization, also modeled on the West, introduced vital changes into the lives of many women. While Japan rook Western style indus-trialization as a goal, its methods inevitably differed. This was a rather poor country, lacking good natural resources, and it needed to amass capital and to earn foreign currency in order to import the materials and machinery it required to get industrial development going. Cheap labor was essential in this process, both for many of the new factories and for workshops devoted to the manufacturing of silk cloth, which quickly became Japan's leading export. In 1909, Japan's factory labor force was 62 percent female, in contrast with 43 percent in France at a comparable industrial stage. (By 1900 itself, 12 percent of the British labor force was female, 27 percent of the French, compared to the Japanese 62 percent.) Most of these women, usually young and unmarried, were imported from distant rural villages, where a father or brother signed them into what often amounted to industrial slavery. They were housed in dormitories under their employer's full control. They worked at least twelve hours a day, while the factories controlled their paychecks ostensibly in their own interest, lest they spend frivolously. Many women workers became ill. Many were unable to form stable family relationships; levels of prostitution and divorce both rose rapidly. These features of early industrial life were exag-gerations of issues Western Europe had faced during its own industrialization – exaggerations that reflected Japan's greater dependence on cheap female labor. The results obviously complicated the larger reactions to the West, often contradicting other impulses such as the regulation of sexuality.

Finally, amid conflicting developments, the Japanese government moved toward its own consensus, which would use Western elements amid misleading hymns to tradition to produce a distinctive amalgam. The key was the growing emphasis on "good wife, wise mother" as the basic framework for women's lives that emerged in the 1880s and 1890s. Women, regardless of social class, should promote family cohesion, practice frugality in order to contribute to the nation's savings for industrial development, and in general make the family the first link in a stable political society. The Meiji Civil Code of 1898 reinforced the authority of the male household head. Wives needed husbands' consent to enter into a legal contract. In divorce, the husband took custody of the children. A wife's adultery (but not a husband's) constituted grounds for divorce and also for criminal prosecution. Fathers' consent was necessary for marriage of women until 25, and of men until 30. Women were resolutely banned from participating in public meetings or joining political organizations; only in 1922 would feminist pressure loosen the ban on meetings, though not membership in organizations. Government publications tirelessly pushed the desirable image of women whose devotion and self-sacrifice allowed their families to survive. The "good wife, wise mother" policy did not preclude working; indeed, some of the idealized women had to take jobs to keep their families afloat. (It was noteworthy, however, that the number of women entrepreneurs declined, as had been the case in early Western industrialization.) Nor did the policy preclude certain kinds of public activities; women were encouraged to form local savings groups or moralization campaigns, and they could help the government during crises such as war.

Obviously, the new policy quickly defined gender differences in education. Secondary schools, particularly, pressed women's special obligations. Materials issued in 1937 urged that "home life occupies, and has occupied throughout the ages, the most important sphere in the life of the Japanese woman. It will do so tomorrow, and for all the days to come." Curricula stressed domestic subjects, but also attainments such as artistic penmanship deemed crucial to femininity. Ethics classes ("rather unpopular among the girls", one woman noted) insisted on loyalty to Emperor, parents and ancestors as the primary moral obligation, and independent thinking was actively discouraged. Rigid manners completed the training. Correspondingly, boys' schools urged a different code, including more academic achievement and the kinds of comradeship relevant to both industrial and military life.

The "good wife, wise mother" policy expressly attacked Western intrusions such as individualistic feminism. It was designed, among other things, to curtail groups such as the 1880s "People's Rights" movement that had attacked both the patriarchal family and the authoritarian state. But it was also a new policy. It extended neo-Confucian principles to all women, not just to the upper class. Gender, indeed, became a more important category than class, and this was novel. The policy gave new importance to women even as it confined their range of activities. It echoed some aspects of mid-nineteenth-century Western beliefs, as in the profound domestic importance of women, but it obviously departed extensively and deliberately from contemporary Western trends, which were moving toward greater legal equality and new political rights. The policy was also accompanied by rapid population growth in Japan, which created new family duties for many women.

The policy did not succeed in pulling all the facets of Japanese gender relationships into a fully coherent whole. Particularly, it did not stop many women from becoming increasingly interested in Western-style consumerism. Nor did it prevent individual feminist writing and agitation. But it did dovetail with the new emphasis on sexual respectability. It did help manage the important new initiatives in education. It obviously encompassed the reaction of disdain for Western ways. The policy, along with further industrial development, also gradually reduced the exploitation of women workers and the family instability this had provoked. The female percentage of the industrial labor force dropped steadily, and by the later twentieth century Japanese women were far less likely to be employed than their sisters in Western Europe and the United States (and also, obviously, in Russia). (Japanese wage differentials for women, compared to male rates, were also steeper.)

The amalgam of reactions to Western contact that emerged in the Meiji era and continued through the 1920s and 1930s was not, of course, fixed in stone. Another round of contacts with the West emerged after 1945, under American occupation. Spurred in part by these contacts, Japanese women won the vote and full legal equality. Sexual restrictions lessened, as sexual behavior once again became a matter more for individuals. The birth rate began to drop. Even with these new developments, however, as well as still further consumerism, a distinctive Japanese' tone remained. Japan was a much more gender-conscious society than the West, at the end of the twentieth century, and men's concerns about their masculinity were higher. Differences in work patterns were echoed within the family, where men and women shared fewer activities than was true in the West.

Conclusion

Reactions to new contacts with Western Europe produced important changes in Japan, just as they had in Russia. Indeed, because the changes quickly applied to most women, rather than to mainly those of the elite, the results in Japan were if anything more substantial, at least up to 1917. In both cases, Western gender patterns (including the implications of women's consumerism) were seen as liberating, though in both cases this reaction was complicated by the more rigorous working conditions imposed on women in the attempts to catch up with the West economically. But the key reactions to the perception of Western liberalism differed dramatically. Russia moved, haltingly, toward a more Western model; until the communist revolution at least, no fully articulated alternative to a Western model emerged, other than sheer traditionalism. Japan, after a brief flirtation with wholesale imitation, did generate an alternative, one that involved change without real Westernization. The approach to gender was not only a microcosm but also a vital ingredient in the larger Japanese program of creating a modern, industrial society that was also definitively Japanese.

On a global level, contacts with expanding Western influence from 1600 to 1900 had occurred in two different settings (three, if societies that managed to ignore much influence, like East Asia until the nineteenth century, are included). The first setting was colonial, with Western impact to some degree forced on the society involved. This produced a host of different results, depending on the time period, but it always tainted the Western models of gender relationships with their association with colonial domination. Many people, including some women, might cling to traditional gender patterns precisely because they seemed to be part of a cherished national identity. The second setting, rarer but extremely important, involved selective Westernization processes occurring as a matter of choice (albeit in a context of growing Western rivalry and interference); Japan and Russia provided the leading examples prior to the mid-twentieth century. Here, too, as these same examples demonstrate, results could be diverse and complex. Furthermore, some of the same themes applied as in the case of colonial societies. Women's work might be more fully exploited as a source of cheap labor (as in Egypt and in early industrial Japan), or commercial pressures might create new inequalities between the work opportunities of men and women (as occurred in India, Africa and Japan). Sensitivity to Western criticisms about "uncivilized" practices emerged in both colonial and Westernization settings as well.

Being able to decide on reforms, rather than have them imposed, did make a difference. Western models of gender relations might appear more straight-forwardly as a liberating force (whether for better or for ill), since they were not tainted by colonialism. The West was seen by Russian, Korean or Japanese reformers in terms of educational rights for women, greater independence within marriage, new consumer opportunities, new opportunities to attend events in public and so on. Some of these elements emerged among reformers in colonial settings like India as well, but they were qualified by greater resentment against Western criticisms and controls and also by colonial policies that sought to keep gender relations stable as a means of preventing unrest. Correspondingly, gender reform in places like Russia and Japan was less associated with nationalism than in the colonial areas; indeed, conservative nationalists might often seem at odds with women's gains. These differences could also color contacts with Western feminist movements later on. Contact with the West could be a force for change in both settings. It could generate complexity and even contradictory trends in both, but certain kinds of change – for example, educational advance – could proceed more rapidly in the non-colonial cases, with more groups of women involved more quickly. This was true even in Japan, where contact with the West produced the explicit attempt to create a distinctive national paradigm for women as part of the process of adaptation.

Further reading

On Korea and Japan: Joyce Gelb and Marian Palley (eds), *Women of Japan and Korea: Continuity and Change* (Philadelphia, Pa: Temple University Press, 1994); Robert Oliver, *A History of the Korean People in Modern Times* (Newark, Del.: University of Delaware Press, 1993; London: Associated University Presses, 1993); Gail Lee Bernstein (ed.), *Recreating Japanese Women, 1600–1945* (Berkeley, Calif.: University of California Press, 1991); Sumiko Iwao, *The Japanese Woman, Traditional Image and Changing Reality* (New York: Free Press,

1993); Kumiko Fujimara-Fanselow and Atsuko Kameda, *Japanese Women: New Feminist Perspectives on the Past, Present and Future* (New York: Feminist Press, 1995). On Egypt: Judith Tucker, *Women in Nineteenth-century Egypt* (Cambridge/New York: Cambridge University Press, 1985); Margot Badran, *Feminists, Islam, and Nation; Gender and the Making of Modern Egypt* (Princeton, NJ: Princeton University Press, 1995). On Russia: Barbara Clements, Barbara Engel and Christine Worobec (eds), *Russia's Women, Accommodation, Resistance, Transformation* (Berkeley, Calif.: University of California Press, 1991); Barbara Engel, *Mothers and Daughters, Women of the Intelligentsia in Nineteenth-century Russia* (Cambridge/New York: Cambridge University Press, 1983); Marc Raeff (ed.), *Catherine the Great, A Profile* (New York: Hill & Wang, 1972); Robert Massie, *Peter the Great, His Life and World* (New York: Knopf, 1980). Laura Engelstein, *The Keys to Happiness: Sex and the Search for Modernity in Fin-de-siècle Russia* (Ithaca, NY: Cornell University Press, 1992).

Part III

The contemporary world

Many familiar types of culture contact persisted in the twentieth and twenty-first centuries, along with many traditional features in gender relations. An interest in Westernization spread to some new societies, such as the modern nation of Turkey, but it had resemblances to earlier Westernization efforts both in general and in its implications for male–female relationships. Western colonial and missionary activities persisted. We have seen that the colonial impact on Africa, which only began in a serious way in the later nineteenth century, gave rise to a number of complex reactions well into the twentieth century, spilling over into the attitudes of nationalist leaders. Christian and Islamic missionary activity accelerated in Africa. A wave of Christian fundamentalism gained ground from the 1970s onward in Latin America and in parts of eastern Europe as well as in the United States, with important though again fairly familiar implications for gender relations. It is vital to remember the hold of past patterns and precedents in dealing with our own age.

The twentieth century opened a new period in world history, though, and this applies to the nature of cultural contacts and to their implications for gender. Overall, the twentieth century featured a decline of the relative power of the West, manifest in the great movement of decolonization and the formation of new nations. New technologies have greatly accelerated the speed of transportation and communication, with even more direct bearing on international cultural contact. The rise of multinational corporations involved world-wide linkages as well. Massive population growth was unprecedented in world history, with huge implications for the lives of men and women, while two world wars demonstrated global connections and the dreadful potential of modern technology.

Culture contacts and their bearing on gender changed in two fundamental ways, though without overturning the important continuities from the past. First, international contacts speeded up, and several new sources were introduced. Second, some vital new elements were introduced into the messages available concerning male and female roles.

More people could learn about gender patterns in other societies – often, very distant societies – than ever before, thanks to increased trade and travel and above all to new media such as film and television. No longer did missionaries and colonial officials bear the only available messages. And while pockets of accidental or deliberate isolation did still exist, the possibility of remaining outside a crisscrossing of cultural connections diminished dramatically.

This was not the only change in contacts. The leadership of Western Europe and the United States in presenting models of cultural alternatives persisted from the previous period, but it was now joined by other sources. The rise of Japan added some ingredients to the international mix, with Japanese television shows, for example, becoming the source of some gender models elsewhere. More important throughout much of the twentieth century was the impact of Russian and then of Chinese Marxism. Here was a secular religion with eager interest in international dissemination, and with pronounced ideas about how traditional gender patterns should change. While Marxism had originated in the West, its twentieth-century international influence stemmed largely from other sources. Many regions – like Africa or the Middle East – were receiving international cultural models from several centers, including the West but not the West alone.

Along with this shift in sources, a variety of immigration routes accelerated the exchange of peoples. Movement from Europe to other parts of the world continued, particularly in the early years of the century. More dramatic was the migration from Asia, the Middle East/North Africa, Africa, and Latin America/Caribbean, which represented an outpouring from regions that were not fully industrialized toward the world's industrial centers. This movement picked up speed in the first half of the century, but intensified after World War II. Here was another source of culture contacts, both for the immigrants themselves and the societies around them, and for people the immigrants might inform back home.

Finally, a variety of essentially international sources of influence arose as well, though here, too, a disproportionate Western contribution persisted. International corporations disseminated culture, selling movies, amusement parks and television shows around the world. The League of Nations and, even more, the United Nations sought a voice over conditions of women. After a tentative beginning in the 1880s, the role of international organizations, both official and non-governmental, in issuing standards for the treatment of women gained ground steadily. By the twenty-first century a substantial body of international law, and even wider norms, sought to change gender relations in many areas. The obvious question was: how much impact would these efforts have, and what degree of homogenization would result from this very new force in world history.

The changes in the sources of international contacts involved technology, geography and organization. They were diverse. Western influence declined in some ways, as other regions provided cultural models, but increased through the disproportionate interest of immigrants in entering Western Europe and the United States and through the new Western-based international corporations that sold culture on a global basis. Overall, while the possibility of remaining free from outside influence dramatically declined, the availability of different sources and models increased.

The second big shift involved the cultural models available, though here, too, there was complexity. Before the twentieth century much of the history of international contacts that affected gender involved the role of religion or of philosophical systems such as Confucianism. Most of these systems, in turn, reflected patriarchal gender structures, though with important differences in particular emphases. This pattern persisted in the twentieth century, as we have seen. Along with the spread of religions, however, three newer models developed. The most explicit was feminism. Feminist movements were variously defined, but they all sought serious modification of patriarchal inequalities, and most tried to overturn patriarchal structures altogether. The addition of feminism to the list of international cultural influences was a vital innovation, though it did not sweep everything before it. Marxism was a second novel influence. Similar to older patterns in being a general ideology with gender implications, it differed from the major religions and from Confucianism in its explicit devotion to unseating existing economic and social arrangements. Finally, consumerist interests, in buying new products, changing fashions frequently and seeking new forms of entertainment, represented a third new cultural force with potential impact on gender. Most of these forces continued into the twenty-first century.

The three new cultural models did not neatly dovetail. Marxists and feminists might agree on the importance of liberating people from the hold of the past, but they did not necessarily agree on how to define liberation or on what priority gender issues should have. Consumerist influences, though seriously challenging traditional habits at least on a superficial level, might or might not prove compatible with feminist strivings. Controversy about what new path to take, in other words, was an important feature of twentieth- and twenty-first-century gender history. This added to the debate about whether any new path should be taken at all, or whether traditional arrangements should be preferred.

And there was a final element as well, not entirely new but reasserting strongly. With Western power declining, with the liberation of almost all former colonies, opportunities to assert real or imagined traditions increased, as part of reclaiming a separate identity. The widespread religious revival – in Hinduism, in Christianity and in Buddhism as well as in Islam – had obvious gender implications, as many religious leaders highlighted a more traditional stance toward male–female relations and female sexual behavior as a deeply held part of their value system. More could be involved as well: new freedoms permitted people in some societies not only to reject Western or international influences, but also to seek new means of redressing earlier insults and changes. Men in former colonies, who had been treated as effeminate or called "boys" by their colonial masters, might seek a more aggressive masculinity in compensation – going beyond tradition in the process. Decolonization movements themselves were telling in this regard. Many movements welcomed women, capable of building up the mass of protests against colonial regimes. But, once these regimes were toppled, most new governments quickly became male-dominated, relegating women to the sidelines and, sometimes, reasserting older, patriarchal laws and restrictions as part of cultural identity.

Forces of this sort were not triumphant globally, any more than international contacts and newly asserted global standards were. The point was that gender emerged as a central contest in the contemporary world, in which contacts and reactions to contacts played a vital role. Debate was almost inescapable.

The chapters that follow trace the new complexities of contact in several ways. One chapter looks at a particularly contested region, the Middle East, in interaction with outside influences. Here is a case study similar to other regional case studies in earlier sections of the book. The other three chapters deal more directly with some of the newer formats of the century, in taking up immigration (which now had widespread repercussions, beyond the experiences of immigrants themselves), feminism and international organizations, Marxism, global consumer culture, and globalization and human rights. In these chapters, individual regions can be singled out, such as China and Africa, while implications of the broader patterns can also be addressed. The final two chapters, in focusing on globalization, raise the obvious question of whether a new level of international intensity, undeniable in some respects, was really capable of revolutionizing gender conditions in a variety of different regions and amid the new potential for local self-assertion and counterattack. The nature of global contacts was changing. Was it producing comparable changes in male–female relationships – and, if not, why?

Chapter 10

Immigration as culture contact

The rates and diverse sources of immigration increased fairly steadily in the twentieth century, providing an important form of contact among cultures which had powerful effects on gender. Differential rates of population growth and economic expansion underlie the phenomenon: despite strong ties at home and, often, severe discrimination in the industrial world, many people seek to move. This chapter looks first at some of the main features of immigrant interaction with the dominant national culture in the United States early in the century, as an example of the larger phenomenon. The patterns display many characteristics familiar from other cases of culture contact: two contrasting views of men's and women's behavior encounter each other, the dominant view seeks major alterations in the patterns of the subordinate culture, and some syncretic compromises usually emerge. Immigration, however, particularly in its usual twentieth-century forms, was culture contact with one vital difference: the immigrant cultures were uprooted from their environment and had as a result fewer defenses against changes in standards. To be sure, immigrant communities usually banded together, and sometimes set up protective formal organizations as well; but, surrounded by the institutions of the majority – from media to schools to government edicts – resistance was harder, and compromises as a result tended to lean farther toward adoption of the standards of the majority.

Immigration was hardly new in the twentieth century. Minority groups had moved into established cultural areas recurrently throughout history, and the pace had greatly accelerated in the nineteenth century. Three features of the later nineteenth and then the twentieth century are noteworthy, nevertheless. First, the numbers increased still further. Turn-of-the-century rates into the United States, Canada, Argentina and elsewhere were unprecedented. There was some slackening in the middle decades of the century, particularly due to depression and war, but then the tide surged forward once again after World War II. Rates of immigration to the United States since the 1960s have been the greatest in the nation's history. By this point also, Western Europe became a key immigrant target. Second, the diversity of sources of immigration increased. More immigration occurred over long distances. Immigration patterns in the nineteenth century – Irish and Germans across the Atlantic, for example – had been demanding enough. Now, however, many more Asians, Africans and Latin Americans participated in the patterns of movement, which widened the range of cultural encounters. Finally, immigration from the late nineteenth century onward more and more involved movement into urban centers and into aggressively national cultures, where immigrants found it difficult to be left alone. Previous immigration experiences had sometimes been cushioned by movement to the countryside (like Germans to the American Midwest), where old habits, including language, could long be protected in relatively isolated rural communities. Even in some pre-modern cities, minority groups might be allowed to form separate enclaves that were regarded some-what suspiciously by the majority, but not actively interfered with. In modern cities, and amid governments eager to make sure that all residents lived up to certain national standards, this capacity to isolate was reduced. Again, the result was a more rapid and sometimes more disorienting kind of cultural contact.

Each immigrant experience has its own qualities, even in the assimilationist twentieth century. The United States examples in this chapter are themselves diverse, depending on majority reactions (more racist when Chinese immi-grants were involved than when Italians were) and, above all, the prior culture and the conditions that surrounded the immigrants themselves. Other impor-tant cases could include movements into Latin America, Canada and Australia; the more recent movements into Europe; and ongoing Asian adjustments, for example in the continued immigration of Chinese into Thailand. Nevertheless, even sampling one national experience adds to an understanding of the widen-ing range of cultural contacts in the twentieth century. Immigrant gender patterns could change quite rapidly. The results could have wider consequences when some of the immigrants returned home either permanently or on visits. In both respects, immigration helped disseminate some dominant models of what men and women were supposed to be like.

American attitudes and interventions

Two features of the cultural interactions involved in modern immigration obviously distinguish them from more conventional cultural contacts, both intensifying the results of immigrants' relative isolation in the host society. First, an array of interventions was possible. In the early twentieth century, immigrants in the United States were required to go to school; and while some separate educational institutions were formed, particularly for Catholics reluctant to accept the dominant Protestant tone of the public schools, most children went to state-sponsored institutions that, in turn, keenly pushed mainstream values. Many urban immigrants also received visits from social workers, eager to straighten out family problems, and they were solicited by neighborhood settlement houses, again bent on assisting integration with the larger society. Advertisements also carried important messages, for example about "modern" forms of cleanliness and women's responsibility to install these forms in the household. Some employers – like Ford Motor Company, with its Americanization program – also sought to regularize immigrant habits, to build a more efficient and stable workforce. In sum, cultural signals were inescapable. They were not all followed, but they certainly became familiar. Obviously, these various contact points were far more extensive than in most cultural interchanges that involved separate, even if unequal, societies.

Second, the contacts quickly became highly personal. American observers developed strong criticisms of the real or imagined habits of immigrant groups. They were not content to comment on the need for education or even behaviors at work. They wanted to strike home, quite literally. There was some variation here. Many social workers and settlement-house officials gained a certain knowledge and sympathy for immigrants' values, and did not think they had to be Americanized entirely. There were tensions in the mainstream values themselves. Most commentators believed that, ideally, women should not work outside the home, at least after marriage. But they also worried about idleness, and so might spend a good bit of time training women in work skills. Warnings about sexual conduct coexisted with advertisements that featured sexual implications, for example in cosmetic use. Still, there were some pervasive issues that particularly informed the various efforts to acculturate immigrants and revise their definitions of gender.

Many of the suspicions native-born Americans harbored about southern European, East European and Asian immigrants focused squarely on gender. Immigrant men were suspect for their work habits, their sexuality and a potential for radicalism. Immigrant women faced a somewhat longer list. They might be seen as unclean. They were often regarded as oversexed, in a society that still believed that women had a special responsibility for sexual restraint. One observer, explaining his claim that many Jewish women were prostitutes, noted that "Since in Europe the feeling regarding sexual immorality is much less pronounced than in the United States, the women presumably in many instances have not the consciousness of degradation from their fallen condition that . . . causes the American girl her keenest suffering". Their motherhood skills were lacking: immigrant women had an irresponsible number of children (their fault along with their husbands) and they did not care for them properly, allowing them among other things to work at an early age.

Attitudes of this sort underwrote sweeping agendas for reform, for the creation of new gender norms suitable for a different kind of family. Not surprisingly, many immigrants did not agree with key goals. Withdrawal of children from the labor force, for example, made no sense in terms of economic survival and longstanding tradition. Protection of established cultures, including religions, added a vital family goal, for which women often felt particularly responsible, that was usually missing from the reformers' list. Immigrants had some possibilities for cultural defense. Their separate neighborhoods and religious centers might be supplemented, as it quickly was for

Jews, for example, by ethnic or religious associations providing a distinct social life. Some groups – Italians headed the list – successfully strove to keep most women working in a family setting, so they would not be unduly exposed to outsiders. Italians differed from Slavic immigrants, for example, in preventing most women from working as servants, where clashing domestic values might result. Women who were married on arrival often held back from assimilation, sticking to their native language and staying at home and in the neighborhood. They might be badly disoriented, even distraught, but their exposure to change was limited. Single women and the daughters of immigrants had fewer defenses. The daughters were more likely to work than their mothers, and their exposure to the English language and new habits was extensive, adding generational clash and guilt to the other factors surrounding the immigrant experience. "So, we have crossed the world for this?" one immigrant woman commented.

Amid pressure and defense, some basic adjustments occurred quickly, reflecting important shifts in values. Birth rates dropped, which led to new beliefs about children and parenting alike. Jewish birth rates moved toward the (falling) national average very quickly, Italian-American rates somewhat more gradually. Even among Italian-Americans, who as Catholics belonged to a church opposed to the use of artificial birth-control devices, the shift was far more rapid than the earlier adoption of new methods by key nineteenth-century immigrant groups such as the Germans. Italians talked of cutting the birth rate by "sleeping the American way", that is, in separate beds or even rooms. Gradually, however, women acquired information about other methods of limitation, including devices such as diaphragms and condoms. The diverse sources of cultural contact had clearly intensified. Ideas about schooling and children's work changed as well, with growing recognition that children should emphasize education, at least through the primary grades, with mothers available to facilitate arrangements at home. Interestingly, immigrant daughters often went to school longer than sons, because there were fewer jobs available for teenaged females, more benefit from an education that might qualify a girl for white-collar work. Ideas about marriage changed. Divorce rates lagged behind those of native-born Americans, but beliefs that marriage should be freely contracted, based on love and safe from domestic violence spread rapidly. Relatedly, immigrant women began marrying later than their mothers had, a reflection of new work patterns but also new expectations about how to launch a marriage.

These changes in personal values did not add up to amalgamation with some featureless national melting pot. Most immigrants retained the religious and ethnic attachments they had brought with them; few converted to Protestantism. Some of the family values urged on them made sense in terms of traditional standards. Historians have studied how immigrants selected consumer products, despite the barrage of nationwide advertising, according to ethnic habits and preferences. Some innovations reflected cultural combinations as well. The Italian spouses who slept in separate rooms often had their same-sex children in bed with them, hardly the reigning native-born American pattern. Marriage most commonly occurred with people of one's own ethnic background, even as the ideas about what marriage entailed shifted. Even in the intense pressures of the immigrant experience, imaginative cultural combinations occurred.

Chinese immigrants

One of the groups subjected to the most intense gender pressure from American culture involved immigrant Chinese women, and through them many men. Chinese immigration to the United States began in the mid-nineteenth century, a result of American labor needs, particularly in the railroad development of the American West, and of Chinese population growth. Most of the immigrants were male. Furthermore, they quickly encountered intense racial prejudice, including working-class fears of competition. Some women arrived as well, though, in arranged marriages and in other imports designed to provide sexual service to the men. Some were sold by their families, others tricked by marriage promises that did not materialize.

Here was ample fodder for cultural conversion efforts. In addition to seeking to ban further immigration – restrictive laws were passed in California in the 1880s – some American reformers sought to rescue the women involved. Efforts began in the 1870s, but intensified in the early decades of the twentieth century. Middle-class Protestants were appalled at what they thought they knew about Chinese patriarchal structures, including of course footbinding. The radical subordination of Chinese women did not conform to prevailing beliefs about women as moral arbiters in the home. In the case of the immigrants themselves, many of whom accepted dubious arrangements because of their own commitment to obedience, Confucian beliefs were obviously compounded by the sex ratio, which led to undeniable sexual exploitation. Many Chinese male immigrants were also goaded by the discrimination they faced in the United States, which demeaned a cherished masculinity. After railroad jobs ended, many had to take up laundry work, traditionally a female endeavor, and the implications were galling. From the American side, sexual exploitation of immigrants – many urban red-light districts formed around Chinese brothels – challenged the continued sexual prudery of mainstream culture, which sought to restrict sexuality to marriage and to limit sexual activity altogether. Some of the resultant shock spilled over to racist attacks on the Chinese in general, but some focused on reform.

Protestant saviors, such as those involved in the Presbyterian Mission Home in San Francisco (1874–1939), tried to provide a dramatic alternative to Chinese tradition and to the special circumstances of the immigrant women. Women who entered the Home were shielded from men. They were vigorously indoctrinated with Christianity, which many accepted, but also with the ideals of the American family: to wit, male domination but also female moral influence based on purity. The organization of the home "on Christian principles" was seen by the reformers as "the first step upwards from heathenism to civilization". Strict work routines were viewed as useful in themselves, and as supports to sexual restraint. Success came in marriages arranged with well-established, and if possible Christian, Chinese-American men. Interestingly, though to the distress of Protestant officials, reform activities extended after marriage as well. Precisely because of the new expectations they had formed, the Chinese wives were eager to report dissatisfaction in marriage, particularly of course in cases of physical abuse. Here, Mission efforts extended to attempts to reform men directly, to wean them from Confucian assumptions of superiority. Poignant cases included women who could not have children: their husbands often sought a concubine or additional wife, according to the more traditional system, but, imbued with the mainstream American family values, the wives involved objected strenuously.

Reformers' efforts were not uniformly successful, even among women themselves. Some who could have entered one of the refuges simply refused. They knew how strict the regimen was, and how foreign to their values, and they opted to continue on their own. Some entered with the intent to manipulate: to find a respite from sexual exploitation but not to yield to a new set of beliefs. One constant in cultural contacts involves diverse reactions. Another insists on the capacity, even of very powerless people, to reshape dominant cultural systems to their own use, without accepting the whole package. Furthermore, even the most fully converted women did not completely enter the American mainstream. Racism impeded this – the insistence on marriage to Chinese men confined most women to particular economic and residential sectors in American society well into the mid-twentieth century. But there was conversion, at least to a degree, and in some cases it was remarkably rapid. A dramatic degree of cultural difference, a special, often agonizing set of problems that left some women particularly open to change, and a self-confident group of American reformers combined to produce a striking case of cultural interchange in the immigrant world.

Contemporary immigration

Rates of immigration, to Western Europe, North America and a few other prosperous centers, soared in the later twentieth and early twenty-first centuries. People from south Asia and the Philippines, from Africa and the Middle East, from Latin America and the Caribbean now formed the dominant migrant groups. Their destinations were far more culturally unfamiliar than had been true for many immigrants earlier in the twentieth century. Some immigrants, furthermore, now had greater opportunities to return home periodically, thanks to air travel. This might confirm the hold of tradition, or create interesting needs to become "bi-cultural", that is, to some degree comfortable with habits both in the new location and back in the old. To take an extreme example: Saudi Arabian women who studied in Europe or the United States might adopt Western dress and drive cars, but then return to a situation where veiling and prohibitions on driving persisted.

As before, gender was deeply affected by the contacts involved in the new round of global immigration. Some groups, reacting to the new environment, sought to tighten gender traditions as a badge of identity and a protection against wider change. Many Indian immigrants, while adapting to European or American education and business styles, pointedly emphasized the importance of arranged marriages, sometimes returning home to accept a spouse their families had selected.

Yet some change was inevitable. In a strikingly novel case, many emigrants from the Philippines were women, taking up jobs as nannies or nurses in the West but also in places like the Persian Gulf states. Traveling without men, they often left husbands and children back home. Their goals were not only economic opportunity, but also the chance to escape abusive family situations which, as faithful Catholics, they could not remedy by divorce.

Latino immigrants to the United States showed familiar signs of change, particularly in the second or third generations, despite a somewhat higher than American standard birth rate and the fabled cultural power of "machismo" and family solidarity. By the 1980s and 1990s this rapidly growing group displayed a predictable mixture of traditionalism and adaptation. Families were likely not only to be larger than average, but also to include relatives besides parents and children; the custom of relying on more extended families continued to prevail. But women became increasingly likely to enter the labor force outside the home. By the 1990s their participation rates were only slightly lower than those of Euro-Americans or "Anglos". Divorce levels increased as well, again nearing the national average. Political differences emerged between men and women similar to national patterns. By the 1990s, for example, Latino women were far more likely than men to seek gun control, the same gender imbalance as among Americans as a whole.

By the twenty-first century, patterns of immigration and adjustment had implications beyond the immigrants themselves. Because immigrants so frequently returned home, at least for visits, their new experiences might have some impact there as well – another, though complicated, contemporary aspect of contact.

Conclusion

The immigrant experience of cultural contact was a vital feature of twentieth-century world history. It deserves comparison with more familiar cases of cultural contact – for example, the more diffuse outside influences on gender practices within China itself, the subject of Chapter 12, obviously contrast with the intense exchange for some of the Chinese-Americans.

The American immigrant experience in the early twentieth century, itself varied, had some special features. Reformer confidence in alternative values would not last forever. By the 1930s, for example, mission homes for Chinese-American women began to decline, in part because middle-class beliefs about sexual restraint were loosening. The moral message became less clear. (Interestingly, Chinese-American-led assimilation efforts increased at the same time, producing among other things regular Chinese-American beauty pageants designed to show connections with mainstream consumerism.) Compared to immigrant situations outside the United States, it may also be true that American zeal to reform cultures was unusually intense. The zeal resulted both from a fear of too much diversity, in a highly immigrant society, and from modestly optimistic beliefs that immigrants are capable of improvement. Other societies may have worried less about assimilation, or believed that immigrants should be permanently segregated on the grounds that their inferiority was irremediable. So the American examples cannot be taken as a general model. Still, the importance of the immigrant experience – for immigrants themselves, for people in the host society and for people from the countries of origin who encountered returning immigrants, or heard from them, or thought about the process – plays a vital role in the changing panorama of cultural contacts in the most recent period of world history.

Further reading

Judy Yung, *Unbound Feet. A Social History of Chinese Women in San Francisco* (Berkeley, Calif.: University of California Press, 1995); Doris Weatherford, *Foreign and Female: Immigrant Women in America, 1840–1930,* 2nd edn (New York: Facts on File, 1995); Kathie Friedman-Kasaba, *Memories of Migration: Gender, Ethnicity, and Work in the Lives of Jewish and Italian Women in New York, 1870–1924* (Albany, NY: State University of New York Press, 1996); Ronald Takaki, *Strangers from a Different Shore: A History of Asian Americans,* 2nd edn (Boston, Mass.: Little, Brown, 1989).

Chapter 11

New international influences

Feminism and Marxism

One of the distinctive features of contacts among societies in the twentieth- and twenty-first centuries involves the emergence of new international institutions and movements that strongly influence relationships between men and women, whether they intend to or not. Some of these institutions have no prior precedent in world history. The attempt to form international government forums – the League of Nations, between the world wars, and then the United Nations after World War II – is a new endeavor. The United Nations, particularly, has attempted to set standards for the treatment of women that must be assessed in a study of cultural and political influences from outside a society on gender conditions within the society.

The emergence of multinational corporations is also essentially novel. Multinational trading companies set some precedent, as did nineteenth-century industrial firms that established branches in different countries, but the true multinational, with production facilities all over the world, is a twentieth-century creation, and it has its own role to play in gender matters. Partially related to the multinational corporations was the development of new linkages in international commercial culture. From the 1920s onward, movies began to be distributed worldwide. Television shows were exchanged widely after the 1950s. International sports events commanded the largest viewing audiences ever assembled in world history. Companies like Disney and Club Med began to set up tourist centers or distribution outlets literally around the world; Mickey Mouse became a global rodent.

Marxism, another largely twentieth-century movement outside Europe, is very definitely a modern ideology, but its role can be compared to that of churches in earlier periods, seeking to spread beliefs beyond a single society on the basis of a vivid conviction of truth. The phenomenon of an international ideological movement, in other words, is less novel in world history, though Marxism, bent on radical but purely secular reform, obviously differs from earlier religious movements (and Marxists are in principle extremely hostile to religions).

Finally, feminism – obviously, expressly devoted to changes in male–female relationships – has emerged as something of an international force, though in most countries it has not achieved the mass organizations periodically created in Western Europe and the United States. Feminism originated in the nineteenth century (though Enlightenment ideas about liberty and equality inspired feminist writings in the late eighteenth century). Early centers included Britain and the United States. Organized feminism reflected new ideas, advances in women's education, and also a realization that men's rights and economic power were outstripping those of women. Many nineteenth-century feminists also utilized the Victorian beliefs in women's special moral power. Feminist issues were varied, but by 1900 they were increasingly coalescing around efforts to obtain the vote and related legal equalities. The vote gained, in Scandinavia, Australia, the United States, Germany and elsewhere, feminism receded somewhat during the middle decades of the twentieth century to re-emerge in the 1960s, urging a new set of demands including fuller equality in the workplace. From the first, Western feminists maintained contacts with each other across national lines. British and American feminists kept close contact in the nineteenth century, for example. Late-twentieth-century American feminism was sparked in part by the influential French writer Simone de Beauvoir and her powerful book *The Second Sex*. By the early twentieth century, feminist commentary was beginning to develop over women's conditions outside the West – in China, for example. Feminist influence also ran high in the international organizations, particularly from the 1970s onward, when they pronounced on gender issues. A real international feminist organization has yet to emerge, but feminist influence can be taken as one of the new contact forms in the twentieth century.

The multinational influences of the twentieth century are varied, with predictably varied results. In this sense, we are still dealing with the kinds of tension and contradiction that have so often emerged in assessing the gender implications of international contacts. The multinational influences also have another feature, which makes them more comparable to other cases of cultural contact than might appear on the surface: the forces are multinational but they derive disproportionately from some of the twentieth century's most powerful societies. There has been relatively little feedback in the other direction, from Africa or the Middle East, for instance, to the gender patterns in industrial nations. Multinational corporations have bases in literally every inhabited continent, and most islands, but their power centers lie in the United States, Western Europe and Japan; thus, they are the latest version of economic power relationships from dominating to dominated societies, and the results on women have similarly familiar overtones. The same holds true for the great cultural distributing outlets. Hollywood became the world's movie capital in the 1920s; by the 1980s popular culture exports ranked second in the American export list (behind aircraft). International popular culture was essentially an American-spiced-with-European product. International Marxism derived initially from Western Europe, then after 1917 from the Soviet Union. Its international professions were sincere, but the sources of influence were not evenly distributed. Feminism obviously had Western roots even at the end of the twentieth century, though important individual feminist voices outside the West, and related diversities, have emerged as well. Finally – and this is the trickiest case – international organizations like the United Nations, though open to quite varied influence, often adopted a surprisingly Western seeming line in gender matters. This aspect needs to be illustrated and explained. The overall point, however, should be clear at the outset. The twentieth-century world saw really unusual, as well as unusually intense, forms of international interaction and influence. Many of these forms, however, continued to embody contacts between particularly powerful societies and other societies more on the influence-receiving end. This characteristic generates the usual complexity in results, in which receiving societies face some unavoidable pressures but also seek to pick and choose and even to resist.

This chapter traces the theme of contacts in the new context of cultural internationalization, particularly during the first two-thirds of the twentieth century. The final chapter will pick up the more recent outcroppings of the theme. This chapter analyzes two cases, primarily involving mixtures of Marxism, feminism and the roles of international organizations. The goal is to look at key international influences as they applied to particular societies, where the idea of new contacts fits the larger history of contact experiences. The cases are varied. China in the twentieth century received influences from international feminism and, of course, Marxism. The history here shows how these influences (plus initially some ongoing missionary impact) helped build a strong set of national forces for change. Africa since decolonization (that is, since the 1960s) is a good test case for the activities of international groups and standards, including the outreach of the United Nations.

One final introductory point: the main international movements considered in this chapter all explicitly and usually sincerely sought to improve women's conditions in places like China and Africa. (We shall turn in the next chapter to other influences, such as international commercial culture, that are less explicitly committed to reform.) Women's issues were not the primary goal for Marxists, but in so far as Marxists discussed gender they thought in terms of removing traditional oppressions. United Nations and, obviously, feminist efforts were expressly devoted to amelioration. Earlier kinds of contacts discussed in this book did not have such an explicit program where issues of gender were concerned, though we have seen that some missionary movements and even some colonial interventions thought in terms of reform. How much does greater explicitness matter? Having good intentions is not the same thing as being effective; and good intentions may be so culture-bound, so dependent on foreign assumptions about what is best for men and women, that they misfire in specific contexts. Here, clearly, are some additional issues to ponder in dealing with this contemporary twist on cultural contact.

Both Marxism and feminism, as international forces, began to take shape in the later nineteenth century, with growing influence during the early decades of the twentieth century itself. Both had strong implications for gender through new forms of international contact, but both featured some limitations as well.

Marx and his followers, urging revolution against capitalist society, saw gender change as a byproduct of a larger effort. They opposed gender inequality: they frequently commented on the injustice of women's subordination within marriage, and they saw practices like prostitution as an outgrowth of the larger evils of exploitative capitalism. The solution, of course, was the replacement of capitalism by an egalitarian society under the banners of proletarian revolution. Gender change was not, in other words, the primary focus of the movement. Marxism could lend itself to some approaches to reform that involved more window-dressing than substance: women might be carefully identified as party leaders but given little real power. But there was no question that Marxists intended to overturn gender inequities along with other kinds of inequality, no question also that their efforts to spread Marxism internationally, seeking a worldwide replacement of capitalism, could have huge impact on gender traditions in many societies.

Feminists, as they began to agitate for new rights toward the middle of the nineteenth century, obviously had changes in gender relations at the core of their agenda. And, at least in principle, they quickly turned toward internationalism. The first international feminist organization emerged, under the leadership of the Swedish Marie Gregg, in 1868. Several international conferences were held during the 1870s, and then in the 1880s three more elaborate international organizations took shape. All urged changes for women in every society, in terms of greater legal equality, property protections, access to education and, soon, the vote. References to a need to remake societies "in the whole civilized world" were common.

The global commitment was sincere, but in fact the organizations were over-whelmingly Western – European and American – and national preoccupations long outstripped any effective internationalism. By the early twentieth century feminist conferences typically included token representation from the Middle East, China, or Africa, but around solidly Western goals and leadership. The most effective international efforts focused not on larger feminist goals, but on specific problems such as international sex trafficking – what was known, and feared, around 1900 as the "white slave trade". While countries like Argentina responded to white slave concerns with new regulations over prostitution, there was little impact on broader patterns of gender relations.

Still, though more vaguely than Marxism, international feminism did provide an interregional framework for the advocacy of change. Small movements within individual countries responded to the Western-dominated effort. By the 1920s, for example, Chinese organizations had formed to advocate women's suffrage, praised by Western leaders as sharing "the same vision which is arousing the women of all the Nations of the Earth". Feminists like

Siao-Mei Djang, in turn, were writing pamphlets for the international movement, again referring to "the problems which are universal to womanhood".
With the formation of the League of Nations in the 1920s, furthermore, an
international body now existed to which women's rights petitions could be
addressed and through which they could gain publicity. A context was
established within which more specific changes could develop.

While both Marxism and international feminism developed extensive
contacts, among countries and between international organizations and
individual countries, two case studies illustrate the new interchange. China
was strongly influenced by international feminism and then communism;
Africa experienced much less communist impact, but was widely affected by
successive waves of international feminism. In both cases contacts began in the
nineteenth century, intensified during the early twentieth century, and then
proceeded (while also creating complexities and resistances) during the most
recent decades.

The case of China: missionaries, feminists and Marxists

China under Confucianism had long ago emerged as a classic patriarchal society.
In principle, Confucianism offered important roles to women, held to be vital
if inferior; and, ideology aside, women's work was very necessary in a largely
agricultural economy. But there was no question that most women were
severely disadvantaged under the Chinese system. We have also seen that
conditions deteriorated over time, particularly with the institution of practices
such as footbinding.

China was relatively slow to adapt to the new kinds of international contacts
forced on the country from the 1830s onward. It had a proud tradition not
only of political independence, only rarely disrupted from the classical period
onward, but also of considerable cultural isolation. It had long contributed to
world trade, but had not depended on it given a diverse internal production
and commercial base. These traditions complicated adjustment to change. New
contacts with Western Europe were introduced by compulsion, as in the first
Opium War of 1839 which led to more open markets. By the late nineteenth
century growing economic interference by European and United States
merchants was combined with seizures of territory, in the form of long leases,
particularly in the regions around port cities. Britain, France, Germany and
Russia all participated in this scramble; and, after its victory in a war with
China in 1894, Japan joined the parade as well. These developments greatly
increased opportunities for foreign contacts, whether desirable or not. Official
policy, though, tried to minimize the need for change, seeking only minor
adjustments in government procedures and military structures. Only in the
1890s did a fuller movement emerge to send students abroad and open the way
to other kinds of change.

It was at this point that international contacts began to affect gender relations. As in Korea and other areas a bit earlier, Western ideas about gender were seen as a liberating challenge. Christian missionaries also played an important role in early adjustments, by criticizing practices such as footbinding and by setting up schools for girls. Protestants, too, sponsored a small but steady stream of Chinese women students in American and European universities. These important developments were familiar enough. What was unusual was the speed with which broader reform pressures, and even a feminist movement, emerged in China, reflecting the pent-up momentum for change within China, the crucial role gender issues played in this larger current, and the fact that Western example by this time included the obvious emergence of a strong and explicit push for women's rights.

Radical intellectuals in the 1890s quickly seized on women's issues as part of the reform package necessary to move China into an effective modern role. Footbinding, an unusually stark and visible differentiation, helps explain this focus. The reform movement's leader, Kang Yuwei, noted how footbinding made China seem backward to Western observers (the embarrassment factor, now escalating in world history): "There is nothing which makes us objects of ridicule as much as footbinding. . . . I look at the Europeans and Americans, so strong and vigorous because their mothers do not bind feet and therefore have strong offspring." Attacks on footbinding proliferated, in newspapers and in petitions to the government. Societies, staffed by intellectuals, worked to persuade peasants to stop the practice; many of them imported Western women's shoes to dramatize their cause. Women's education was a second reform focus, spurred by knowledge of developments in the West and by the missionary schools being established in China itself. Mission schools taught restraint and ladylike conduct, to be sure, but they also attacked the old status and urged women to be ready for active lives, in medicine, in teaching or even simply as wives. Scholarships to schools abroad supplemented this impact. Women's magazines emerged from the new schools, spreading further advocacy of change in gender traditions. From this, a surprisingly explicit feminism emerged, the fruit of Chinese conditions in contact with Western models. Thus an early issue of the *Peking Women's Journal*.

O ye two hundred millions of Chinese, our sisters, listen! In China it is said that man is superior and women inferior; that man is noble and women vile, that men should command and women obey. . . . But we are not under the domination of man. The nature of men and women is the universal sense of heaven. How, then, can one make distinctions and say that the nature of man is of one sort and that of woman another.

Or in the words of Jiu Jin, a Shanghai schoolteacher, in 1907:

Men and women are born equal
Why should we let the men hold sway?

We will rise and save ourselves,
Ridding the nation of all her shame.

Women's groups began to assemble, focusing on all sorts of issues, including the problem of opium smoking. Women also played an active role in emerging revolutionary societies and, to a lesser degree, in the actual events of the revolution of 1911 that overthrew the imperial dynasty – among other things carrying weapons and arranging for shipments of arms from abroad. After the revolution, substantial suffrage campaigns developed, in strong contact with Western models. An American visitor noted that the first question women asked him was "Tell us about the suffragettes in England", while the Chinese Suffragette Society was directly modeled on its English equivalent. Many feminist leaders began to dress in Western styles, or in the styles of Chinese men, both seen as liberating alternatives. To be sure, the size of these movements was limited, with little impact on the rural masses at all. For many women, the spread of foreign-owned factories, exploiting low-paid, sweated labor, was a far more important change than any of the feminism inspired by Western cultural example. The government, moreover, even after the revolution, was not particularly sympathetic.

The trend of feminist agitation continued, however, and the 1920s intensified the use of Western feminist models. Reform articles cited Western examples – the social interaction between men and women, the rise of women in professions such as law and medicine – as an explicit contrast to Confucian inequalities. English feminist articles were often translated in the growing women's press. Reformers began to widen their domain, pressing for example for equality and freedom of choice in the contracting of marriage. Like Western feminists, they also agitated for attacks on prostitution, for improvements in conditions for women factory workers and for liberal divorce laws. Women students began to wear Western clothing and to bob their hair in the latest fashions, while participating actively in political and feminist organizations. Modeled on American patterns, women's clubs emerged in several cities, providing some support for feminists, who faced an uphill battle against entrenched traditions and, often, the views of their own mothers.

Specific campaigns also continued to use Western advocates directly. In 1919, Clare and Hugh Haslewood went to Hong Kong, where Hugh had an appointment in the British colonial administration. There they encountered the practice of *mui tsai*, in which young girls were sold into domestic service by their families. Seeing this as "slavery" (which was not necessarily the case), the Haslewoods roused both international and Chinese reformist sentiment toward abolition of the practice. Considerable debate ensued, and the movement continued into the 1940s when it was overshadowed by the triumph of Chinese communism.

The later 1920s also saw, however, a distinct turning away from purely Western models. The fight for the vote seemed unrealistic or irrelevant in

Chinese conditions, according to many radicals. Christian missionaries now appeared too tame, too devoted to prayer and good works; their relationship even to feminism was suspect. Western observers no longer seemed accurate, and their views often supported Western commercial interests. In this context, and among ongoing difficulties in making headway with the Chinese government, many women's leaders turned to a different foreign model, that of the new Soviet Union. Russian conditions seemed to promise more systematic change, for women as well as for other groups, and this meant that attention should turn away from limited concerns with marriage or voting, toward more sweeping attacks on the socio-economic conditions that kept women dependent.

Marxism, as it had developed in the West and Russia, offered mixed signals where gender was concerned. Many Marxist leaders, eager for the advance of the working class, assumed that the domination of male workers over their wives and daughters was a normal phenomenon; changes in gender balance were simply not part of the agenda. Russian leaders, though championing women's rights in principle, ultimately (by the late 1920s) turned to a conservative approach to family policy. Marxism did stand for change, however, for in principle it was to lead to freedom from oppression for all. Russian leaders talked of the importance of women's rights to work and to the vote, and carefully placed women in visible if often symbolic positions of leadership. Chinese communists, picking up on these cues in their close collaboration with their Russian colleagues, but also using the momentum of the existing woman's movement in China itself, quickly developed their own gender reform goals. The Chinese Communist Party meeting in Moscow in 1928 thus simply resolved, as part of its platform: "Realize the slogan of women's liberation."

There were many reasons for China's communist leaders to pick up on women's issues as the movement formed in the 1920s. Having women as active allies, even participants in military conflict, was a vital practical advantage as the communists struggled to seize power. The theoretical implications of Marxism also provided a powerful spur. But leaders like Mao Zedong were also strongly influenced by their early contacts with Russian leaders. Not only Russian communists but also Russian anarchists who talked of liberating women had a marked impact on visiting Chinese students and leaders in the initial decades of the twentieth century. Small wonder that the Chinese communists made explicit references to the "special oppression" of women, encouraged women's solidarity groups even in the villages, and promised equal legal and material conditions when the party triumphed. Particularly interesting was the effort to encourage women to "speak bitterness" – that is, to articulate their grievances as a gender (rather like what Western feminists would later call "consciousness raising") – as part of arousing ordinary people to the revolutionary struggle.

As with communist movements elsewhere, Chinese communist leaders had some difficulty balancing attention to women's demands with their larger agenda for working-class and peasant liberation. They criticized strictly feminist agitation, divorced from larger revolutionary goals. But, headed by Mao Zedong, communists did insist on the importance of mobilizing women and of working for radical restructuring of gender relations, and they increasingly took over the leadership of China's women's movement. Thus the communists were soon advocating rights to divorce, opposition to child-brides, polygyny and imposed marriages, and women's rights to inheritance. Mao noted that, while all elements of China's masses were dominated by unfair authorities, women were additionally burdened by being "dominated by men". By 1929, and as part of organizing explicit women's groups, the Party urged "the thorough emancipation of women . . . to enable women gradually to attain to the material base required for their emancipation from the bondage of domestic work and to give them the possibility of participating in the social, economic, political and cultural life of the entire society".

Women were actively recruited as Party members and representatives, serving as at least 25 percent of the total in all local organizations. Articles and classes for peasants and workers mixed working-class and women's demands. The latter included explicit attacks on Confucianism, with specific injunctions to "cut the hair short and unbind the feet" and "struggle for the freedom of marriage". Women were urged to take new kinds of jobs outside the home and to participate directly in the wars against the Nationalist government and against Japanese invaders. Popular plays dramatized heroic women who had stood up to oppressive fathers or husbands. In regions under communist control by the 1930s, women's groups pressed individual men to change their ways – for example, to stop using violence against women – with real effect. By 1943 there were over 2 million members of the Party's Women's association.

Then, with the communist victory in 1949, a new constitution proclaimed full equality between women and men. "Women shall enjoy equal rights with men in political, economic, cultural, educational and social life." Active recruitment of women to local leadership committees continued, with membership rising to 48 percent in some cases by the mid-1950s. A 1950 law, based on Marxist doctrines and experiences in the Soviet Union, insisted on free choice of marriage partners, on monogamy and on protection of women's rights. Divorce was possible when both parties wanted it, negotiable if one party resisted. Not only pamphlets but also posters, for the illiterate, spread knowledge of the new law. The expansion of education actively included women, and women were also encouraged to take jobs in factories and other sectors that would get them out of the home (and increase national production as well). Though communist policy changed periodically, birth-control efforts were also supported, and childcare facilities sought to reduce the burdens of motherhood. Here, again, examples from Soviet Russia played a role in the establishment of new programs.

Opposition developed, inevitably. Many men and some older women opposed changes in the structure of marriage. Some older women, for example, argued that beatings of wives were all right so long as performed by mothers-in-law. The Party itself showed signs of hesitation, sometimes opposing women for undue radicalism; its own leadership group included at best only token women. Perhaps most tellingly, when government policy shifted after 1978 to strict limits on the number of children each family could have, there were reports that female infanticide was increasing once again in the countryside, as a means of making sure that the family could have a son. Old ways died hard. It was also true that the new law severely limited reproductive freedom, for both sexes. But the roles available for women, and the possibilities for changes even in family relationships, widened steadily. A mixture of different foreign examples and movements, including feminism and Marxism, had combined to produce a strong internal pressure for substantial change and to associate it with fundamental revolution. Despite intriguing or troubling remnants, China was no longer a bastion of unadulterated patriarchy at the end of the twentieth century.

Africa and the role of international organizations and international law

Sub-Saharan Africa, a vast and varied subcontinent, received two kinds of international contact relevant to gender prior to the national independence movements. First, as we have seen in Chapter 8, missionary activity and, to a lesser degree, some colonial edicts targeted selective aspects of traditional relationships between men and women. Missionaries sought certain changes in African marriage practices, while often promoting new forms of education for women. Colonial officials were typically reluctant to interfere with local customs, where resistance might complicate political stability. But they did tend to install Western-type laws that encouraged private property and that recognized men as heads of household, while also occasionally intervening against practices like female circumcision that seemed particularly immoral by Western standards. The second influence came from the operations of the colonial economy in Africa, as it advanced during the first half of the twentieth century. Recruitment of African labor for the mines and for urban jobs disproportionately singled out men, leaving many women behind in the villages with less economically useful activities than those they had traditionally maintained. Families were often destabilized as well, in a culture that had long prized cohesion. This pattern continued in late twentieth-century Africa.

Western imperialist control was just hitting its full stride in Africa during the early decades of the twentieth century, with its usual baggage of criticizing a variety of local gender practices, continuing a process we have already noted for the nineteenth century. With fuller administrative control, however, and growing levels of Christian missionary activity, additional issues came into play.

Female circumcision, for example, sparked an intriguing interplay from the 1920s onward. European and American missionaries, and some colonial officials, began to attack the practice, using terms like "barbaric" and "mutilating". Politicians back home, including feminist leaders, picked up the charge. Debates in the British parliament called for firm measures against the custom. But there were complexities on all sides. In the first place, many African men treasured the practice as part of their traditional identity. At a time when they had lost control of their economic and political lives, maintaining gender standards seemed unusually essential. Not surprisingly, many nationalist leaders echoed their concerns, sometimes arguing that female circumcision was not only essentially pain-free but also fundamental to the national cause. Many women came to agree. Some maintained a real pride in their ability to endure the operation and a strong belief that circumcision made them real women. Others simply came to accept the practice as a means of protesting against outside interference. For their part, the Europeans were not of one mind. Many colonial administrators wanted to avoid stirring things up; and, back home, various politicians ridiculed the anti-circumcision campaign as a means of attacking feminism more generally. A British conservative, for example, shouted out during one debate: "Women do not count!" Not surprisingly, little change occurred before World War II. Thereafter, as we shall see, the campaign resumed, under international auspices, and some nationalist leaders began to discourage the practice. Even then, evolution, not universal abandonment, was the most general result.

The rise of nationalism during the twentieth century was double-edged where women were concerned. Women participated in nationalist movements, and many hoped that national independence would help lead to gender reform. They joined protest marches, for example, seeking to prod colonial authorities into freeing nationalist leaders from jail. Particularly among educated, urban women, a new level of political consciousness arose. Many nationalist leaders, for their part, had issued pronouncements about ending polygyny and extending voting rights to women. But most nationalist leaders were male. Solidifying new nations after independence was achieved was an awesome task, and could easily supersede attention to women's issues. Indeed, these could appear as a dangerous distraction. Furthermore, African nationalism, like all nationalism, included a strong element of traditionalism, and gender customs could be one of the traditional features some leaders sought to preserve as a badge of national as well as masculine identity.

In the Ivory Coast, for example, a former French colony, a mixture of forces came into play after independence in 1960. The government had issued a constitution guaranteeing equal rights to all citizens regardless of gender. But then in 1964 it established a far more patriarchal family code (though not a traditional one, in that among other things it required monogamy and also vaunted the nuclear, male-dominated family over the customary extended family which had frequently protected wives): the husband was recognized as the undisputed head of household, while widows' property rights were restricted to half the total inheritance. Husbands gained great power over the management of family property, including the wives' work and earnings. Illegitimate children were legally recognized, which constituted an indirect recognition that men could and would be adulterous. In presenting the new law, the Minister of Justice explicitly stated that there was no equality of the sexes where family was concerned. Here was a typically complex postcolonial mixture, combining professions of equality, efforts to shore up elements of Christian family tradition (hence the emphasis on nuclear family and husbands' powers), and some African customs as well.

In sum: by the 1970s, gender relations in Africa offered a host of contra-dictions and complexities. They were no longer traditional but they had not evolved in a consistent direction, either. This was a context in which inter-national pressures, some of which were specifically tailored to Africa, might have unusual potency.

It was, moreover, in the 1970s that international organizations increased their attention to gender issues. There was precedent. French feminists had assembled an international conference in 1919, to influence the post-World War I peace conference, though with few results beyond a reference to women in the new International Labor Organization, an agency of the League of Nations. A variety of international (though initially Western-dominated) women's groups arose, including the Young Women's Christian Association, the International Federation of University Women and the International Federation of Business and Professional Women. American feminists traveled to Latin America in the 1920s to help promote relevant political rights, and the later Pan American Union established an Inter-American Commission on Women. Members of this commission helped insert a phrase "without distinction as to . . . sex" in the United Nations Charter, in the human rights section. Then, in 1947, again with pressure from feminists from the Americas and Europe, including Eleanor Roosevelt, the United Nations established a Commission on the Status of Women. This in turn led to a series of statements, including a "Convention on the Elimination of All Forms of Discrimination Against Women". Commission-enunciated principles included provisions for equality in marriage, property ownership, pay, employment opportunities and education, as well as political and legal rights. Particular attention was devoted to conditions in "developing", that is, non-industrial, areas like Africa.

Then, in 1975, as the new wave of feminism arose in the Western world, the United Nations proclaimed the Decade for the Advancement of Women, and held a first World Conference on women, in Mexico City. Subsequent conferences took place in Denmark, in Kenya (in 1985) and then in China (in 1995). Each conference included delegates from all member nations and reports from each nation on gender conditions, itself a potential spur to change. New international treaties, elaborated by the conferences, re-emphasized the prohibition of discrimination against women in all facets of social, political and economic life, and most nations (including those in Africa) ratified these statements. The 1980 conference also issued strong attacks on domestic violence directed against women. A network of scholars from the developing nations was associated with the 1985 Nairobi conference, while an American feminist, Bella Abzug, later prompted the establishment of a Women's Environment and Development Organization. Other United Nations activities included increasing pressure on the World Health Organization, another agency, to attend to women's health issues including the results of abuse. A major 1994 conference in Egypt, on world population, led to vigorous debates about the need for new levels of birth control, and a recommendation urging greater governmental attention to this issue and, particularly, the promotion of education for women as the most important factor in the social environment in which new levels of birth control could occur.

This growing crescendo of international activity had implications for all parts of the world. Conferences and agencies issued hosts of recommendations; and various governments, including American states such as Pennsylvania, followed up with supportive pronouncements. It was difficult not to seek some association with such widely proclaimed international standards, lest one's region or nation seem backward. Thousands of people attended the conferences themselves, from all parts of the world, and the result could be both informative and galvanizing, as the delegates returned to inform local women's organizations and groups.

African nations were inevitably affected by the emergence of international standards and conference activities. Most of them, like the Ivory Coast, had issued statements of equality in principle upon independence; there was no fully articulated African alternative to the new standards, so it was natural to join in the wave of new adhesions. (In contrast, countries like China, with confidence in a Marxist approach, might be somewhat more skeptical of a need to endorse international resolutions, while the United States, suspicious of international organizations in general, often did not sign relevant treaties.) Impacts showed in three areas: a new if cautious surge of agitation by women's groups, sometimes spurred by the new national pronouncements; a fascinating pattern of legal activity, founded on the international principles; and some signs of a new level of awareness, in part related to the flurry of internationally generated information.

The Ivory Coast provides a clear example of new political activities. By the time of the United Nations declaration of the Decade for Women, the nation's president was promoting his efforts in this area. He proclaimed a Women's Year for 1975, and set up a Ministry of the Feminine Condition and for the Promotion of Women, with a commission appointed to deal with concerns for legal equality, education and employment. Educated women began to press for changes in the 1964 family law. Their particular focus was the injustice of women's lack of control over their earnings. Accordingly, the new commission, by 1983, recommended limitations on the husband's authority and recognition of women's economic autonomy, along with requirements for collaboration in household chores. Elite women worked actively behind the scenes to convince members of the ruling party, and the National Assembly did approve the new laws (amid strong opposition in the name of male dominance and polygyny). Women could now choose jobs on their own, control their wages and personal property, and manage bank accounts in their own names. Many observers believed that changes of this sort would stimulate further political action by women, particularly as education spread more fully; indeed, new women's groups were emerging in the 1990s, taking advantage of new political pluralism, and their existing right to vote, to protest at a wider array of government policies.

Uses of international legal principles stemmed from the adoption, by the Organization of African Unity (OAU), of the African Charter of Human and People's Rights in 1981. One of its provisions recognized "international standards of general application designed for the protection of rights of women", issued by one of the international conferences in 1979. The OAU acknowledged its responsibilities as a regional entity under the United Nations Charter. Its new Charter granted that:

> the state shall ensure the elimination of every discrimination against women and also ensure the protection of rights of the woman and child as stipulated in international declarations and conventions.

Further:

> Given the current advancement on human rights standards, it is simply unacceptable to subject women to subordinate treatment that enslaves them to man. Human rights is about regulated civilized behavior and conduct toward all human beings. . . . In Africa, the subordination of women to men is buttressed by certain traditional practices that cannot remain unaffected by human rights standards.

A series of court cases sought to apply these ringing statements to specific problems. In Tanzania, a woman petitioned the High Court to reverse lower-court rulings that had supported a nephew who challenged her right to sell land she had inherited from her father, on the grounds that, according to traditional tribal law, men alone had the right to sell family land. The Court upheld her plea, with the judge arguing that "females all over Tanzania can at last hold their heads high and claim to be equal to men as far as inheritance . . . is concerned. It is part of the long road to women's liberation. But there is no cause for euphoria as there is much more to do in other spheres." Another case, in Botswana, dealt with a court's ruling that a child born to a Botswana woman and an American man was not a Botswana citizen, because rights derived from the father alone. The woman argued that this notion, however rooted in local tradition, countered the national Constitution's guarantee of rights regardless of gender, which in turn derived from the African Charter. Again, the court ruled in favor of legal equality, one of the judges noting that "now more than ever before, the whole world has realized that discrimination on grounds of sex, like . . . slavery, can no longer be permitted or even tolerated". Other court cases, for example in Uganda, upheld women's claims to a share in family property (often overruling lower courts, which had argued for more traditional definitions) and widows' or daughters' rights to inherit land, even when (as is common in societies that believe it is a bad omen to make a will) there was no specific provision.

Finally, international pronouncements, along with other developments such as frequent male absence and the spread of education, helped persuade many African women that certain kinds of change were essential. East African women interviewed in the 1970s and 1980s frequently talked about the need for schooling and for birth control – "But first, women have to get an education. . . . Girls and boys should be educated the same." Village officials, along with doctors (some sponsored by the United Nations) and other "outsiders", played a growing role in teaching African women about birth control; and, although birth rates remained higher in Africa than in most of the world's regions, they had begun to drop by the 1990s. Goals often remained partly traditional: the same women who stressed the need for education and for women's economic initiatives talked of making sure that the family would support them in old age and of the need to avoid individualism and loneliness. But there was a change in the ways goals were to be realized, at the very least.

Certain international agencies attacked more specific problems, such as female circumcision (cliterodectomy and infibulation) as still widely practiced in northeastern Africa. The World Health Organization (WHO) moved very tentatively in this area despite the considerable mutilation done to many women; officials cited the importance of avoiding disruption to traditions. Some colonial regimes banned the practice officially toward the end of their tenure – as Britain did in Sudan and Kenya in 1946. Some of the more radical nationalist leaders, for example in Egypt and Ethiopia, did the same after independence. The United Nations Social and Economic Council urged WHO action as early as 1958, but its request was rejected on the grounds that "the ritual operations in question arose from a social and cultural context". African women themselves pressed the United Nations; a seminar in 1979 argued that traditional practices adversely affected women's health. Then, in 1982, the WHO moved, urging that

> governments should adopt clear national policies to abolish female circumcision, and to intensify educational programs to inform the public about the harmfulness of female circumcision. In particular women's organizations at the local levels are encouraged to be involved, since without women themselves being aware and committed, no changes are likely.

Specific groups to oppose the practice, often under women's leadership, arose in places like Senegal.

The range of impacts of international principles in Africa is impressive. Of course there are hosts of impediments. Many women, not to mention men, still do not agree with the overturning of traditional practices. Circumcision gained in Mali when women who had emigrated to France, but were blocked from the practice by French law, returned home to have their daughters operated upon. Changes in law do not necessarily reach widespread practice. Women turn to birth control, but often only after the birth of their fourth or fifth child because of an (understandable) desire to make sure, amid widespread disease, that some children will be around – the result, still, is a rapidly growing population. The Organization of African Unity has limited funding for any monitoring activities. Individual nations have often been much more enthusiastic about passing ringing principles than translating them into specific protective laws. Furthermore, the African Charter itself offers a hedge: while endorsing legal equality it also allows states to take into consideration the virtues of their historical tradition and values while endorsing the family as the "natural unit and basis of society" and "the custodian of morals and traditional values recognized by the community". Here is an obvious tension between change and continuity, harbored within nationalism itself. As recently as 1999, a Zimbabwe court overturned a ruling in favor of woman's inheritance of property, arguing that according to "African tradition" only men could own.

Conclusion

China and Africa offer two important cases in which new kinds of international contacts combined with internal pressures to effect significant change. The Chinese case represents the fuller story, because the new contacts have been operating for a full century and because they became intertwined with a fundamental revolutionary process. Even here, however, particularly in the countryside, there are signs of important survivals from more traditional patrlarchy. The African examples are more tentative, because the international feminist pressures are newer and because they interact with nationalist principles in complex fashion. Far more than in China, furthermore, new values war with economic deteriorations, as women's opportunities for productive work are often curtailed. Nevertheless, great change has occurred in both cases, perhaps most importantly in the consciousness of many women themselves, as deeply rooted habits were juxtaposed with a variety of signals from more international movements.

Further reading

Janice Auth (ed.), *To Beijing and Beyond, Pittsburgh and the United Nations Fourth World Conference on Women* (Pittsburgh, Pa: University of Pittsburgh Press,

1998). On China: Elisabeth Croll, *Feminism and Socialism in China* (London/ Boston, Mass.: Routledge & Kegan Paul, 1978); Christina Gilmartin, *Engendering the Chinese Revolution: Radical Women, Communist Politics, and Mass Movements in the 1920s* (Berkeley, Calif.: University of California Press, 1995); Ono Kazuko, *Chinese Women in a Century of Revolution, 1850–1950* (Stanford, Calif.: Stanford University Press, 1989); Arif Dirlike and Maurice Meisner (eds), *Marxism and the Chinese Experience: Issues in Contemporary Chinese Socialism* (Armonk, NY: M. E. Sharpe, 1989); Shirin Rai, Hilary Pilkington and Annie Phizacklea (eds), *Women in the Face of Change: the Soviet Union, Eastern Europe, and China* (London/New York: Routledge, 1992). See also Lise Vogel, *Marxism and the Oppression of Women* (New Brunswick, NJ: Rutgers University Press, 1983). On Africa: Rebecca Cook (ed.), *Human Rights of Women, National and International Perspectives* (Philadelphia, Pa: University of Pennsylvania Press, 1994); Catherine Coquery-Vidrovitch, *African Women, A Modern History* (Boulder, Colo.: Westview Press, 1997); Cora Presley, *Kikuyu Women, the Mau Mau Rebellion, and Social Change in Kenya* (Boulder, Colo.: Westview Press, 1992); Bolanle Awe *et al.* (eds), *Women, Family, State and Economy in Africa* (Chicago, Ill.: University of Chicago Press, 1991); Sue Charlton, *Women in Third World Development* (Boulder, Colo.: Westview Press, 1984).

Chapter 12

Contact and retract

The Middle East in the twentieth century

Of all the societies involved in the growing interaction with outside ideas and images affecting male–female relationships, the Middle East offers one of the most fascinating twentieth-century cases. Gender issues were central to crucial debates about Western and international influence, on the one hand, and Islamic tradition on the other. Complexity was inevitable. Islamic tradition itself was, as we have seen (Chapter 4), a source of debate: it protected many rights for women while also insisting on women's inferiority, and contemporary Muslims continue the argument over which elements predominate. Outside models were not consistent. Close to Europe geographically, and subject to a host of examples and influences, many Middle Eastern areas began to borrow new elements early in the twentieth century. At this point, European influence provided mixed signals, between law codes that stressed women's domesticity and male household leadership, and new currents of feminism, educational opportunity and innovative fashions. Later, for societies that continued to look to European and United States examples, different gender patterns, reflecting changes in work roles and feminism, added new strands. With an ambivalent heritage and amid ambivalent outside standards, it was small wonder that change proceeded fitfully.

As in other areas, Western cultural example was further constrained by economic change. Attempts to imitate Western industrial development, taken with Western commercial inroads within the region, often reduced women's economic range. Men gained disproportionate access to new urban jobs, while the competition of machine-made goods reduced women's activities even in the countryside. In this context, cultural inspiration from the West might fall on infertile soil or even provoke resistance, because of the obvious contradictions with economic realities.

The Middle East came under outside influence in the twentieth century in a situation of unusual political disarray. The once-powerful Ottoman Empire, which had unified much of the region, perished in the aftermath of World War I. A network of small nations resulted, often rivals, rarely able to prevent Western economic and sometimes diplomatic intervention. Here was a setting in which foreign ideas about gender might seem particularly tainted, for they

complicated fragile national identities and were associated with external power
– with what Middle Easterners often felt, with considerable justification, was
a latter-day imperialism.

These factors generated unusually strong and divisive debate about what
changes in gender relationships, if any, should be accepted. The West provided
models that differed from regional tradition, and the West's power was undeniable; it was tempting, depending on the group, to imitate or to resist. In each
country, debates arose about how much to Westernize, or what the alternatives
were to substantial change. By the end of the century, while debates everywhere
continued, results varied widely from place to place. This chapter examines
two cases, Turkey and Iran, in which Western example hit home early but in
which reactions ultimately differed profoundly. Change occurred in both cases,
but it ranged from an insistent secularism to a religious reassertion.

Veiling

From the late nineteenth century onward, new patterns of contact, particularly
with the West, raised complex issues about the practice of veiling throughout
much of the Middle East and among Muslim immigrants to other regions as
well. The practice of veiling was not intrinsic to Islam, and we have seen that
it was not adopted in most of the other regions that adopted the religion. But
it did take wide hold in the Middle East and North Africa, particularly in the
cities, where it unquestionably came to be linked to religious propriety.

Western observers frequently criticized veiling during the nineteenth
century, seeing it as an obvious sign of an unfair treatment of women. The fact
that they knew little about actual gender standards in Islam, and sometimes
were quite hostile to women's rights in their own society, did not dim their
condescension. Thus Lord Cromer, British administrator in Egypt, who
ridiculed feminism back home, saw the veiling and seclusion of women as a
"fatal obstacle" to Egyptian progress. Noise of this sort was sufficiently loud
and embarrassing that a variety of reformers in the region itself picked up the
message: veiling must go.

An extreme Westernizer, Qassim Amin, took up the charge in 1899 with a
book, *Liberation of Women*, arguing that greater freedom for women, including
abolition of veiling, was essential to establishing an "advanced civilization".
In other words, he accepted the Western critique entirely. Amin noted that
Europeans had invented the steam and electrical engines and so "could not fail
to know the means of safeguarding women".

Amin's book set off a storm of protest. Many Egyptian nationalists, as well
as Muslim traditionalists, strongly objected to these kinds of Westernizing
changes: they would not only weaken religious standards but would also
damage national identity. Women themselves, in Egypt and elsewhere, from
the early twentieth century onward, often experienced an agonizing debate
about veiling and other traditional costumes. Some were drawn toward global

consumer standards, which argued for more revealing, Western styles – and certainly no veil or headdress. Others preferred family and community solidarity. Efforts to ban veiling would figure prominently in specific gender reform programs in places like Turkey and Iran, though with mixed results. Attempts to restore obligatory veiling would similarly feature in anti-reform regimes, as in revolutionary Iran and, even more, under the Taliban regime in Afghanistan in the 1990s. Discussion spilled beyond the Middle East. Early in the twenty-first century France banned religious dress from its schools, with immigrant Muslim women the main target and greater homogeneity the goal – and, according to opinion polls, a majority of French Muslims actually agreed, though there were heated protest demonstrations and a strong outcry from the Middle East itself. Most interesting of all, of course, was the continued quiet debate among actual Muslim women who now had a choice in many nations. Some opted for Western dress; many dropped the veil but retained head covering; some, by the early twenty-first century, in places like Egypt, proudly resumed the veil as a sign of resistance to global pressures.

Turkey

Contact with the West helped promote considerable changes in the conditions of Turkish women, though the results were uneven. Change began to occur, in fact, before the emergence of the modern Turkish nation in the 1920s, with Westernizing reforms undertaken by the Ottoman Empire. For example, in 1863 a college for training women teachers opened in Istanbul, followed by the establishment of primary schools for girls. A new Ottoman reform period after 1908 led to further encouragement of women's education, and to the formation of women's associations in certain cities. Women also won new jobs, in factories and offices, particularly during World War I, but government decrees still regulated the skirt lengths permitted to women workers, and a special imperial decree was needed before the veil could be discarded in office hours.

The Turkish part of the Ottoman Empire by this point was crisscrossed by Western contacts. Western businesses operated extensively. Western advisors influenced the military and also higher schools, such as engineering centers. Turkish reformers, though predominantly male, thought in terms of making Turkey more like the West – as a means of preserving independence. When the new Turkish Republic was formed in 1923, this orientation became official policy. The new leader, Kemal Ataturk, was determined to make Turkey respectable in Western eyes, and changes in gender relationships were fundamental here. He made the point clearly in a 1923 speech:

> Our enemies claim that Turkey cannot be considered a civilized nation because she consists of two separate parts: men and women. Can we shut our eyes to one portion of a group, while advancing the other, and still

bring progress to the whole group? The road of progress must be trodden by both sexes together marching arm in arm.

The goals were twofold, neither explicitly directed to women's emancipation for its own sake. First, the embarrassment factor played a great role: Turkey must look more like the West, and this meant attacking Islamic traditions head on. As Atarurk put it, measures like legal equality and reforms in family law were essential as symbols of Turkey's determination "to reach a level of contemporary civilization" – the latter defined by Western standards. Second, changes for women were seen as preconditions for new kinds of economic and political activities because of the vital socializing role played by mothers. In essence, if mothers did not change, their offspring, whether male or female, would not change sufficiently to build a stronger nation. Ataturk again:

> If it is found to be sufficient to have only one of the two sexes that compose a society equipped with the contemporary needs, more than half of that society would remain weak. . . . Therefore, if knowledge and technology are necessary for our society, both our men and women have to acquire them equally.

In this vein, education was made mandatory in 1923 for both sexes; and, though schools in fact spread slowly, women's primary education advanced at only a modest lag behind men's. Another vital arena involved legal and political conditions. In 1926, Ataturk forced a modified version of the Swiss legal code on a reluctant parliament. The new laws assured legal equality to women in theory, while installing monogamy and equal rights to divorce – seen as "principles required for a civilized world". A second set of measures allowed women to vote in municipal elections in 1931, and then to vote and be elected at general elections in 1934 – fourteen years before women gained these rights in places like France and Italy. In 1935, eighteen women deputies entered the parliament. By this time, women's organizations, like the Turkish Women's League, were pushing for reforms of this sort on the model of suffrage organizations in the West. But still it was a handful of male leaders, beginning with Ataturk, who were responsible for changes of which the majority of Turks, women as well as men, undoubtedly disapproved.

Ataturk also attacked the traditions of women's dress, though he worked through persuasion rather than through legal requirements. Laws did force changes in men's dress, designed to make them look more Western, but the question of the veil and the traditional robe (*chador*) for women was too highly charged for such simplistic solutions. The rhetoric was strong:

> In some places I see women who hide their faces and eyes by throwing a piece of fabric, a scarf, or something like that over their heads, and when a man passes by, they turn their backs to him. . . . What is the

meaning and explanation of this behavior? Gentlemen, would the mothers and daughters of a civilized nation assume such an absurd and vulgar pose? This is a situation that ridicules our nation. It has to be corrected immediately.

Many urban Turkish women did increasingly adopt Western dress styles, including cosmetics. The visible divide between traditional and modern Turkish women was one of the hallmarks of the complexities involved in reacting to Western examples.

Reform did more than divide the Turks; it also revealed important ambiguities in the minds of reformers themselves. The Swiss law code that Turkey adopted was one of Europe's most conservative models, insisting on the male role as head of the household. It did introduce important changes into traditional Islamic family law, but it also contained a number of inegalitarian provisions. Thus: "Man is the head of the union of marriage" and "The right and responsibility of deciding the place of residence belongs to the husband". Different penalties for adultery were applied. Men also prevailed in cases of disputes over the guardianship of children. Similarly, where dress codes were involved, Ataturk and his colleagues urged Turkish women to avoid the "promiscuous" dress styles that were gaining ground in the West during the flapper era. They should not reveal too much of their bodies, and should assume "a virtuous attitude". Women were also kept out of public administration in the 1930s, and Ataturk lobbied the feminist organizations not to press their demands too far, in the interests of national unity. Education was another hesitant area. By 1926 there were fifty-four high schools available for men, only fifteen for women. Vocational schools, almost always gender segregated, emphasized home economics and childcare for women, to "train them in managing hygienic, orderly, economical and tasteful homes, allowing them to establish cheerful and happy marriages, and therefore, making them contributors to the social development of the country". While this approach, and the attendant rhetoric, could easily be found in the West in the same period, the impact in the Turkish context was quite vivid. Strong remnants of tradition clearly defined the leading reform approach, while at the same time Western example was sufficiently varied to permit some selection in the approach adopted – as in the choice of the Swiss rather than, say, a Scandinavian legal code.

Yet, for all the hesitations, what some scholars have called a state sponsored revolution did effect real change, making Turkey truly unusual among Islamic countries even at the end of the twentieth century. Atarurk's program of Westernization went noticeably further than Peter the Great's in Russia in altering gender relations, if only because the Western model had itself changed so greatly. Large numbers of Turkish women began to enter fields like medicine and law, and their participation often surpassed that current in Western Europe. Educated urban women retained close economic and cultural ties with their Western counterparts.

The process of change inevitably escalated, because of pressure from women's groups and as a result of simple momentum. By the late 1930s, gender differences in school curricula began to narrow, a precondition for women's growing professional role. By the 1970s, internal forces of reform plus additional contacts with the West and the growth of international feminism prompted further developments. Many Turks spent time as immigrant workers in Western Europe, and while some of them stayed in Europe and many faced great discrimination, there was feedback to Turkish towns and villages from those who returned. Turkey's active participation in NATO brought Western, particularly American, military enclaves, while tourism from the West also greatly increased. The abundance of Western films and fashions spurred interest as well. In this context, new women's groups and publications arose, particularly from the early 1980s onward, advocating a fuller Westernization of gender conditions in Turkey. In 1986, a coalition launched a petition drive to implement the 1985 United Nations Convention on the Elimination of All Forms of Discrimination Against Women, which Turkey had signed but largely ignored. A new journal, *Feminist,* emerged in 1987, attacking forms of patriarchal authority such as domestic abuse and sexual harassment. Agitation did lead to some changes in the legal code, such as the revocation of an article which required women to gain their husbands' permission to work outside the home.

Division persisted. As the Turkish economy changed, many women became more economically dependent on marriage, and the identity provided by Islamic tradition was an important attraction for both genders. A significant Islamic fundamentalist movement arose in the 1990s, briefly gaining political power, and criticism of the secularizing tendencies of reformers, including feminists, was an important part of the platform. But in practice there was no major effort to restore earlier traditions where gender was concerned. Moreover, a significant women's rights movement arose among Muslims, seeking to use relevant Islamic provisions as the basis for greater equality, in hopes of finding a way to construct relationships that were neither Western nor purely traditional. This effort at syncretism was perhaps the clearest sign of the complex impact produced by several generations of interaction with Western models.

Iran

Broadly speaking, Iran developed similar reform impulses to those current in twentieth-century Turkey, based on Western examples, in a context in which, as also in Turkey, Islamic law had long defined basic relationships between men and women. The results, however, were dramatically different. In the revolution of 1978–9, Iranians threw off Western example, as many women joined with men in seeking a different, more traditional, model in the gender arena. The distinction should not be exaggerated: Turks, too, continued a debate between traditional and partially Western versions, while Iranians were not immune to international influence even after the great revolution. Clearly, however, the balance diverged.

Iran entertained some of the same kinds of commercial contacts with the West as the Ottoman Empire had – indeed, the government welcomed foreign investment – but the cultural interaction was less intense. An initial women's school was not established until 1907. A new national constitution in 1906 reconfirmed Islamic principles, legally defining women as dependent wives and daughters within male-headed households. But a new ruler, Reza Shah, began soon after this to dispute religious control, seeking a set of modernizing, secular reforms that gradually would come to include changes in the status of women. In 1937, for example, the Shah issued a decree banning the veil and the all-enveloping *chador* gown; women had to appear in public in Western-style clothes. Schools, including the new University of Tehran, were opened to women. As in Turkey, women, in their capacity as mothers, were seen as vital to the process of modernization. As in Turkey also, however, change was uneven, both because of widespread resistance and because male reformers themselves hesitated before the most dramatic Western models. Thus a new law code, in 1932, did little to change Islamic family laws, only raising the age of marriage for girls to fifteen. A new criminal code, in 1940, went further, abolishing the old Islamic rule that one male witness was equivalent to two female, but the code also gave men the right to murder adulterous wives, while women had no equivalent latitude.

By the 1960s, after the United States helped put down an Islamic government unfriendly to Western interests, the reform current expanded. Western contacts now included active military collaboration, as part of the network of alliances the United States sponsored in the Cold War, and much more extensive Western activities in the oil industry and in economic development. Many Iranian students went abroad. Substantial Western communities developed, often with their own leisure areas, providing dramatic examples of women's freedoms in public and the latest in the fashions of dress (and, on beaches, undress). Imports of consumer products, films and the like extended cultural influences, primarily in the cities. A fledgling women's movement arose, pressing for further change and mounting often significant demonstrations, while the government itself became eager to display its commitment to Western standards. In this atmosphere, women gained the vote in 1963, and quickly moved into positions as judges, deputy ministers and university lecturers. A set of laws enacted between 1967 and 1975 abolished polygyny and reduced the inequality in divorce rights; women seemed poised on the brink of legal equality.

Then came the reaction, deriving from rejection of the reform movement and Western influence in general, with changes in gender relations a key symbol, as well as from explicit anxieties about the erosion of family traditions. Many men joined the reaction, both because of commitments to older values and because economic changes threatened many traditional livelihoods, making it tempting to seek ways of reasserting male authority in compensation. Many women, however, also participated. Western models now became symbols of evil and error. As the ayatollah Khomeini – the leader who would ultimately lead the revolution – put it:

> Women in some western countries have strayed from the natural limits of their unborn selves and gone beyond the social and natural requirement. This has brought suffering and destruction to the women themselves and to society as a whole. . . . In the name of women's liberation, whole generations of children are left uncared for and unprotected. They have become like soulless, mechanical beings devoid of human sensitivities.

A fundamental problem was the nature of the dominant Western models available in 1970s Iran, emphasizing consumerism as they did. Although some urban women eagerly participated in the latest styles, others were dismayed; leaders of the Islamic revival lamented that "woman who ought to be the preserver of the tradition, the family . . . has been brought on the streets. She has been led to wandering, showing herself off; behaving in a loose and unrestrained manner." The whole process emphasized divisions in Iranian society, with mini-skirts, discotheques and luxury hotels juxtaposed with mosques and mud huts. Even more than in Turkey, many Iranian women were facing growing economic hardship, as men monopolized the leading urban jobs; traditional religion offered a solace and an identity that Western-style consumer culture, out of reach in any event, could not promise. Even among educated Muslims, a growing criticism of what was called Westoxification – that is, falling under a toxic cultural influence from the West – mounted. Western-inspired gender reforms were equated with imperialist economic influences, and assailed on the same basis. The Western model was also attacked as leading to divorce, to the poverty of many single women, and to directionless children – it no longer seemed clearly emancipatory. Attacks on the pro-Western but autocratic regime of the Shah involved explicit invocations of more traditional norms; the women involved in the protests pointedly wore *chadors*.

When the revolution came, it was virtually inevitable that Western modes were attacked by law. Women were forced to resume the veil and *chador* (with seventy-nine lashes as immediate punishment for refusal), and their roles in public and at work were greatly restricted. Mothers of young children were not allowed fulltime jobs. Legal rights were eroded, as in the re-establishment of the male rights to polygyny and to divorce at will. Opportunities in education also receded.

Still, however, complexity remained, particularly as the revolutionary mood calmed. International influences hardly ended. In 1989, a radio poll about role models produced a response selecting Oshin, an activist heroine of a Japanese television serial popular in Iran. Western example still counted as well. Zahra

Mustafavi, daughter of Khomeini, deliberately imitated feminist organization in founding a new Association of Muslim Women in 1989, and sponsoring international women's conferences. A surge of Islamic-based agitation for clearer and fuller rights arose at the same time, contesting the conservative, patriarchal interpretations of family law. As in Turkey, debate has not been closed.

Gender and terrorism

As the Iranian revolution suggests, gender played an important role in the revival of Islamic fundamentalism in the later twentieth century. Not only Iranian revolutionaries, but also the reactionary Taliban regime in Afghanistan, were at pains to emphasize women's subordination. In the Taliban's case – and it is important to note that Iranian leaders found the Taliban crude and excessive; this was not a typical regime even in terms of conservative Islam – this included not only insistence on veiling and seclusion, but also extreme penalties for sexual infidelity and even the closing of schools for girls.

Many observers argued that elements of the conservative movement in Islam involved far more than an attempt to revive older gender relationships, and were a more radical attempt to assert masculinity in the face of Western colonial attempts to portray non-Westerners as effeminate and subordinate. Fierce insistence on women's inferiority was part of this process. Terrorism might be another.

A host of factors helped explain the surge of terrorism in the later twentieth and early twenty-first centuries, including resentment against American and Israeli policies and widespread unemployment among many urban men in the Middle East. Masculine assertion may well have played a role. Leading terrorists were uniformly male, becoming "deadly heroes" in the minds of many Middle Eastern groups. Mohammed Atta, probably the leader of the 9/11 airplane attacks against New York and the Pentagon, left a will specifically requesting that no women be allowed to attend his funeral. Women entered terrorist imagery only as virgins waiting to welcome martyrs into paradise; this was a male domain, in which men were seeking to remedy slights against their masculinity as well as attacking any idea of gender reform in their societies. Gender, in other words, helped fuel a new kind of contact, in retaliation for earlier, Western-dominated influences.

Most Middle Eastern Muslims opposed terrorism. Many accepted gradual change in gender relations. The same years that saw terrorists represent a heightened version of masculinity saw women become the majority of university students in places like Iran (55 percent) and the United Arab Emirates (52 percent by 2005). Western influences, and those of international organizations, played a role in these changes. American-style universities, for example, were eagerly sought by a number of Middle Eastern regimes, and they provided new educational opportunities for women including, in some cases, co-educational classes. Gender and contact formed parts of a complex pattern of change and resistance in this vital region.

Conclusion

Western cultural models were fundamental both to major changes in gender relations in the Middle East – in education, law and dress – and to major statements of resistance. Amid pervasive and often bitter dispute, different regions took distinctive paths. Reform predominated in Turkey because it started earlier than in Iran – in the nineteenth rather than the twentieth century – because it was sponsored by extremely effective leadership, including the active role taken by Ataturk himself, and because Turkey's independence, once established, was not seriously threatened, which reduced the need to associate Westernization with imperialism. Conditions in Iran also reflected the dominance of a more conservative (Shiite) Muslim majority, and the consumerist excesses of Western visitors and some urban Iranian women by the 1960s and 1970s. In Turkey, Western models long had more to do with law and education than with personal behaviors, which were not opened to such drastic change.

Different parts of the Muslim Middle East and North Africa fell in different places on the reform-resistance spectrum. Saudi Arabia was a conservative Muslim bastion opened up, after World War II, to growing Western influence. Western business and military and diplomatic connections multiplied. Many Saudi women traveled abroad. The government became committed to some Western-inspired changes, such as new access to education, but nothing like Westernization had occurred by the end of the century. Women who drove cars when out of the country were not permitted to take the wheel in Saudi Arabia itself. Muslim family law predominated, with dramatic punishments for acts like adultery. Egypt, where reform influences began much earlier (see Chapter 9), opted for a more clearly mixed model, with Western influence affecting legal rights and also opportunities for change in dress and work. Everywhere, however, debate predominated. Egypt, like Turkey, saw a vociferous Muslim revival, protesting change. Saudi Arabia faced recurrent pressures to open up to greater change. While hints of an explicitly Muslim, but not fully traditionalist, model emerged in several places, the conflict about how to handle Western patterns – whether to embrace or to reject – showed no signs of settlement.

Further reading

Nikki Keddie and Beth Baron (eds), *Women in Middle Eastern History: Shifting Boundaries in Sex and Gender* (New Haven, Conn.: Yale University Press, 1991); Nira Yuval-Davis and Floya Antlias (eds), *Woman – Nation – State* (New York: St Martin's Press, 1989); Martin Marty and R. S. Appleby (eds), *Fundamentalisms and Society, Reclaiming the Sciences, the Family, and Education*

(Chicago, Ill.: University of Chicago Press, 1993); Valentine Moghadam (ed.), *Gender and National Identity: Women and Politics in Muslim Societies* (London: Zed Books, 1994; Karachi: Oxford University Press, 1994); Fatma Mugu Gocek and Shiva Balaghi (eds), *Reconstructing Gender in the Middle East: Tradition, Identity and Power* (New York: Columbia University Press, 1994); Elizabeth Warnock Fernea (ed.), *Women and the Family in the Middle East, New Voices of Change* (Austin, Tex.: University of Texas Press, 1985). See also Edward Said, *Orientalism* (New York: Vintage, 1979).

Chapter 13

Global consumer culture
The question of impact

One of the important new cultural influences of the twentieth century, growing with every decade, involves the dissemination of consumer culture. Products spread literally around the world. Films and television shows are imported from major centers – from the United States above all, but also from Japan and a few other industrial giants. Tourists fan out from the same industrial centers, seeking the sun and exotic locales, and they provide live models of current sophistication. Many of these developments have implications for gender. At the very least, movies and tourists provide dramatic contrasts in style and appearance to many regional traditions.

Here, then, is a new kind of culture contact, different from the more familiar influences such as religion or even a secular ideology like Marxism. Because the phenomenon is new and because the results are diffuse, the impact of international consumer culture has not been extensively studied. What we do know, furthermore, suggests very contradictory possibilities. In some cases, exposure to international consumerism quickly generates dramatic changes in gender behaviors. In others, the same exposure has almost no impact at all. More conventional patterns of contact, of course, have often had diverse results, so in one sense this range of reactions is just an extreme case of a common outcome, but it is striking nevertheless. Here is a topic in search of a conclusion.

Questions begin in the generating societies themselves. Obviously, the richest and most technologically sophisticated regions stand at the center of the international consumer culture. They produce the most widely exported movies. They provide the pleasure-hungry tourists. But it is not always clear how much impact international consumer styles have even on the societies that produce them. Millions of people watch the same television shows in countries like the United States or Germany, but they do not all pick up the same signals. Some watch as simple escapism, not assuming that the show offers any cues for real life; others rush to imitate the latest Hollywood hairstyle, but with no interest in copying the sex habits flaunted in the same movies or, at least, no realistic hope of doing so – recent studies demonstrate conclusively that the sexual behavior of Americans, on average, is much more conservative than could be imagined from watching television shows like "Friends" or "Melrose Place" – and a few think that the imagery portrayed in movies should be the framework for their lives. Finally, it is not clear that movies and shows really challenge basic gender patterns very fundamentally. To be sure, specific styles and body images differ from real-life averages, but movies do not on the whole urge major upheavals in gender relations. Rather, it can be argued that they merely exaggerate the implications of rather conventional patterns. Thus Western culture has long insisted that one of the roles of women is to be attractive: movies merely up the ante. The culture has long praised men for aggressive behavior: movies merely give aggression an unusual array of weapons and special effects. The deviations from gender patterns that already exist, in other words, are in many ways quite superficial.

Many of these issues apply also to the impact of international consumer culture on societies sometimes described as more "traditional". Certainly, it is not surprising that the range of impacts is at least as great as in the industrial powerhouses, from a lack of application to real life to an eager quest to imitate. This does not mean that international consumer influences do not worry traditionalists. We have seen, in looking at the Middle East, how Islamic leaders attack Western clothing styles and Hollywood films for their disruptive potential. Marxist leaders, too, have often opposed consumerism for luring men and women away from their common purpose in building a socialist society. Thus, in the 1970s, Russian premier Nikita Krushchev, visiting a Hollywood set amid scantily clad chorus girls, blasted the Hollywood emphasis on sexuality. These reactions are, in fact, part of the complex picture, when international fashions provoke explicit efforts to restate traditional or alternative gender values.

There are of course many forms of international consumerism. From the United States, blue jeans once spread as an emblem of rugged masculinity, and they were adopted into avant-garde male wardrobes from Moscow to Tokyo. Then jeans declined as a specific masculine symbol, as women began wearing them as well. More generally, Western clothing styles have won wide interest around the world, and gender imagery has changed accordingly. Western companies have often portrayed cigarette smoking as a sophisticated masculine activity, associated with hard work or sexual prowess. Correspondingly, societies where smoking remains common, as in many parts of East Asia, exhibit strong gender differences in smoking behavior. Many link smoking with masculinity – a link supported by gender-specific advertising by international companies, while also insisting that smoking is unfeminine. Whether this has much fundamental effect in defining male–female relationships is another question, part of the larger issues raised by consumerist trends. This chapter begins with two areas of new contact: tourism and movies/television.

Tourism

The facts are striking. From the late nineteenth century onward, but with especial intensity after the return of industrial prosperity after World War II, tens of millions of tourists have poured into the resorts and hotels of the world every year. Huge complexes have developed in places like the Caribbean and the islands of the Pacific, to receive Americans, Europeans and Japanese looking for fun. Tens of thousands of workers, drawn from peasant backgrounds, serve these exotic strangers. What, if anything, do they learn?

Some results are quite direct. Large numbers of women in some tourist areas are drawn into the sex trade. From the 1970s onward, male travelers constituted 70 percent of the international visitors to Thailand, and many of them were and are primarily interested in sex tours. The pattern began with servicemen on leave from the Vietnam war, and then extended to organized tours from Japan and Korea. Large numbers of Thai women have been drawn into this trade, with consequences ranging from disease to new habits of drinking. Even where sex is less explicit, exposure to tourism can change the recreational patterns of local women involved. Greek women who come from rural backgrounds but get caught up in the tourist trade on the Aegean islands drink more freely than their sisters back home, and gain a wider range of leisure interests. They also adopt more urban styles of dress and body care (for example, in shaving legs and underarms, a fashion compulsion that began in some parts of the West early in the twentieth century).

Similar results can apply to men. In Jamaica, some men specialize in entertaining women travelers, some of whom are visiting on "romance tours" from the United States or Europe. These men adopt distinctive dress and hairstyles – partly Western, partly stereotypically local, like the "Rasta" (Rastafarian) dreadlocks and red-green-gold designs that presumably mark an African heritage and a commitment to reggae music. Hustling white women involves "going foreign", and the men who do this separate themselves from the rest of Jamaican society.

Tourism can alter gender relationships by providing new earning opportunities for women. In Bali, many women make craft souvenirs for the tourist trade, and improve their economic position in the process. Here and in many societies, women often run some of the smaller hotels and bed-and-breakfast spots, again improving their earnings. In the Philippines, a number of women are able to remain single because of job opportunities in the resort areas. Some of these opportunities are linked to the sex trade (in operations often owned by American, British or Australian expatriates), but others involve work as maids, singers and receptionists.

On the whole, however, tourism does not seem to alter local gender patterns dramatically, despite the presentation of different modes of gender interaction and considerable economic impact. Even for those people who see the tourists daily, foreigners often seem exotic and irrelevant, not real models for behavior.

Preserving more traditional gender patterns may in fact be an antidote to the subordinate status local men and women have to accept in dealing with the strangers. Tourists themselves often seek isolation. They look for resorts that will keep them away from extensive involvement with local conditions. The Belgian-based Club Med chain, founded in the 1950s, specializes in setting up European-style compounds, serviced by locals but with scant daily interaction with neighboring towns and villages; even the meals are European, except for one weekly night of local fare. An approach of this sort obviously minimizes effective cultural contact.

Finally, tourism typically reinforces gendered economic roles in the locality rather than disrupting them. Women are seen as people who serve, who do some traditional handicrafts and who provide sexual access for men. There is no revolution in work roles or even imagery involved. Work in the tourist industry does not, usually, alter household tasks. Hotel maids come home to families in which they are expected to do most of the household chores (along with their daughters or sisters). Common patterns of female subordination, in societies ranging from Bali to Panama to the Philippines, have not been fundamentally recast by the tourist explosion.

Movies and shows

Widely exported films and television series, and more recently video games, obviously reach a far larger number of people than tourism does. While rural areas may have limited exposure, and while governments in some societies regulate imports strictly, access to Western and Japanese products spread exponentially during the twentieth century. Hollywood became the international movie capital of the world as early as the 1920s, setting up branch distribution outlets not only in Europe but also in Egypt, South Africa, Latin America and Japan. It was after World War II that movies and television shows became the second-largest export for the United States. Hundreds of millions of people could watch particularly popular international staples such as the television show "Baywatch". It was through television, also, that organized sports, most of which had also originated in the West, won mass audiences. Over a billion people watch World Cup soccer finals, the largest and most international spectatorship the world has ever known.

Exposure to spectator imports can have dramatic effects. Television first became available in the Fiji Islands in the Pacific in 1995. Local shows were limited, for the costs of production were too high. As a result, the one TV channel showed largely American, British and Australian fare. Top-rated shows included "Melrose Place", "ER" and "Xena, Warrior Princess". Young women, exposed regularly to Western-style body imagery, quickly contrasted what they were seeing with the plumper body styles conventional in their own society, and many of them decided that it was the Western stars who provided the more relevant role models. As a result, in a culture that traditionally promoted eating well (and looking it), and that viewed weight loss with great concern, a large number of women began to resort to drastic measures to become thin. Within three years, a 500 percent increase in bulimia occurred, with girls in their late teens vomiting in order to lose weight.

Global beauty standards spread widely, thanks to shared media. In 2001 a Peace Corps worker, in a village in eastern Russia that had never before seen a live American and that had no internet access, found that the grade-school boys she was teaching agreed on who was the most beautiful woman in the world: the pop singer Britney Spears. In the same year (by coincidence) an American anthropologist studying prostitutes in Madagascar found out why they chose the cosmetics and hair coloring they preferred: they were seeking assistance in looking more like Britney Spears. Opportunities to take gender cues from the same international media standards had no precedent in world history.

Contact with international sports can have some impact as well, though general results are harder to measure. Growing attention to women's sports occurred, particularly after World War II, as a result of widely publicized competitions in the Olympic Games. Some women in the West increased their interest in athletics in conjunction with the new wave of feminism that surfaced in the 1970s. Communist countries enthusiastically promoted women's sports as part of their national athletic effort. The result could provide women elsewhere with new sources of inspiration. Thus a number of successful women runners emerged in North Africa, despite the opposition of Muslim fundamentalists to this kind of public activity.

In general, though, current evaluations suggest that the impact of growing exposure to international media on gender relations has been surprisingly modest. A few new opportunities have opened for individuals, through awareness of patterns elsewhere – as in athletics. Interest in new fashions, including body shape, has spread even more widely, though there is no uniformity in the result and some people continue to separate the styles they see from what they seek for themselves. But the fundamentals have rarely altered.

A 1994 study of the media in Uganda, in East Africa, shows a common pattern. The television and radio services are both government-owned. They combine national news services with many imported features, particularly on television. Government sponsorship has prompted the formation of a "Women's Desk" as part of the television service; the Ugandan government became aware of the need to do more for women in part as a result of the United Nations' Women's Decade. But the Desk does not have its own production facilities, and it commands only 2 percent of the broadcast time. Overall, media representations of women lag behind the changes that are actually occurring in Ugandan society. Thus women are rarely portrayed as working outside the home, and assertive women are depicted as insubordinate upstarts. Most of the imported television shows and films largely support these impressions. Women are shown as sexual creatures, men as natural and legitimate sexual predators. Women who achieve out of the ordinary usually seem to use sex, rather than any other capacity, to get ahead. As a United Nations unit reported, commenting on locally produced and imported shows alike, women are usually portrayed as dependent (spouses, mothers and sex objects) and are "rarely shown as rational, active or decisive members of society".

Several factors are involved in the surprisingly superficial impact of media exposure in so-called traditional societies. First, many people everywhere distinguish between entertainment and real life. In some cases, the different behaviors one sees as a spectator may actually help make ordinary constraints more palatable, rather than raising questions about the constraints. Many cultures have often featured stories about heroic individual women, without promoting female assertiveness in ordinary situations. Women may take pleasure from the stories that help them cope with the confinements of daily life. The new media seem dramatically different, because of their international quality and technological sophistication, but they may nevertheless reproduce familiar results. When people are watching clearly foreign fare, with actors and situations that are obviously different from their daily reality, the capacity to separate what one likes to watch, and how one wants to behave, may increase still further.

Again, the international media themselves are hardly bastions of fundamental innovation in gender matters. It is revealing that some of the most dramatic changes the media do promote, such as shifts in young women's eating habits, involve not new assertions of power, but a redefinition of what it takes to be beautiful and sexually appealing. It is easy to conclude, from the shows most widely watched around the world, that patriarchy should still reign: men decide things, women strive to please them. This effect is enhanced by the selectivity of the imports. American or European shows that depict women in new work situations and that dramatize women as decision-makers are not, in the main, the shows that receive the widest international play. Small wonder that it is style, more than substance, that is most open to alteration.

Buying things

The wider reaches of consumerism, particularly the process of coveting and acquiring new goods that are not essential to life, have long had gender implications. Even before modern times, Middle Eastern women in the wealthier classes might acquire fashions and jewelry that they could enjoy in the privacy of their homes and that would constitute a form of savings in an otherwise male-dominated society. When modern consumerism began to take hold in Western Europe, it often had gender overtones. Both men and women participated, but they sought different kinds of goods, using consumerism to help distinguish the sexes, and they may have attached different meanings to the process. English women in the late eighteenth century were thus more likely than men to leave specific consumer items to particular relatives in their wills, apparently believing that the items had emotional meaning. In societies where women remain subordinate, consumerism may be an outlet for self-expression and a certain degree of independence – beyond what men experience.

Certainly modern consumerism, from its Western origins onward, has emphasized the importance of female appearance and, often, sexuality, using consumer items to define new criteria of gender.

Global consumerism, as consumer opportunities expanded in the twentieth century and as international corporations sought wide markets for their goods and advertisements, picked up many of these emphases. People were urged to buy things that would make them more masculine or feminine and enhance their sexuality. The spread of Western-style cosmetics and fashions created new ways to define womanhood, and they clearly drew wide interest in many parts of the world. Urban Africans, for example, were eager to identify where fashions came from – New York, Paris, or Milan – as early as the 1950s. A classic consumer story told of a young African man who took his girlfriend with him to buy a shirt, only to find her pressing him (successfully) to buy a blouse and two pairs of nylons instead.

Specific consumer goods might provide new ways to identify gender. In many places, at least for several decades, cars and motorscooters were male preserves, with femininity associated with passenger status.

At the same time, certain forms of consumerism might erode gender – and this could be another form of change. Men and women ate as equals in the global fastfood chains, and this had not always been the case (at least for respectable women) in traditional restaurants. Blue jeans at first identified men, but later women might pick up the habit as well. More generally, a global youth culture emerged in which males and females both participated; age group became more important than gender in certain forms of consumerism.

Whether providing new markers or expressions, or subverting distinctions, consumerism's impact on gender standards inevitably drew resistance and protest. Many traditionalists were simply not interested in consumerism, finding meaning instead in more customary gender identities. Religious leaders often condemned consumerism outright. The leader of the 1979 revolution in Iran, the Ayatollah Khomeini, often railed against foreign-inspired consumerism, arguing that it was the equivalent of "women going naked in the streets". Consumerists, in his view, were filled with "lechery, treachery, music and dancing, and a thousand other varieties of corruption". "It is a veritable flood of forbidden consumption that sweeps past us, right before our eyes." The Iranian regime quickly moved to restore traditional women's dress as an antidote, though by the early twenty-first century consumerism, including fashion interests, was picking up again among Iranian youth.

As with other kinds of contacts earlier in world history, consumerism also provoked efforts at compromise or syncretism. From the mid-1990s onward, beauty contests for women gained ground in India (as in many other parts of the world). This initially American innovation of the 1920s began to attract wide interest through contests like "Miss World", and when an Indian woman won the contest in the final decade of the twentieth century the practice spread like wildfire. Cities and schools could have scores of contests annually. Of course this prompted Hindu traditionalists to condemn the whole process as demeaning to women and a distraction from spiritual values. But some leaders sought to acknowledge the inevitable while shoring up tradition at the same time. In the southern state of Kerala, beauty contests were sponsored in which part of the scoring depended on knowledge of the regional language and culture. Some problems emerged, admittedly, with this particular effort. The girls interested in modern consumerism and beauty pageants rarely knew much about Keralan culture, while those more expert did not find beauty contests very appealing. The complicated relationship among gender, global consumerism, and traditional cultural identity was still being worked out, here and in many parts of the world.

Conclusion

The rise of international consumerism is a new phenomenon, and its results to date are tentative at best. This may well change. One of the lessons of a study of culture contact is that first results can be misleading. It often takes considerable time for the deeper impact of exposure to alternatives to sink in, in an area so deeply personal as many aspects of gender are. Hotel maids may be picking up some new signals about how to treat girls, or about how wives can speak to their husbands, that will show up later on, even in subsequent generations (whether for better or for worse). Attempts to copy Western clothing styles and body types, particularly affecting young people in any event, may foreshadow attempts to introduce more fundamental change in subsequent adulthood. For some people, particularly among the young, consumerism was already a deeply meaningful way to suppress gender, or defy traditional gender standards, or both. Consumerism may also, of course, turn out to distract from more fundamental reform efforts, with women more concerned with slimness and clothes than with other issues. It is simply hard to know at this point. International consumerism is a new factor in gender relations. It may ultimately lead to important changes, even to greater homogeneity around some common models. Its results clearly need to be monitored, along with the other factors that shape the relationships between men and women.

Further reading

On the impact of media, the journal *Media, Culture and Society* is an excellent source; it began publication in the 1970s. On tourism: M. Thea Sinclair (ed.), *Gender, Work and Tourism* (London: Routledge, 1997); also the journal, *Annals of Tourism Research,* which also began in the 1970s. For a more general historical view: Theodore von Laue, *The World Revolution of Westernization* (Oxford/New York: Oxford University Press, 1987).

Chapter 14

Globalization and resistance

The second half of the twentieth century saw an unprecedented level of contact among major societies around the world – a phenomenon that, by the 1990s, was being called globalization. Globalization depended on new technologies, like satellite television transmission and ultimately the internet, that sped communication. It depended on a new business organization – the multi-national corporation – that generated more intricate economic relationships among different parts of the world in its quest for markets, and raw materials, but also cheap labor costs and loose environmental regulation. It depended on policy change: the Chinese decision in 1978 to open up to international contacts and markets was a huge step toward globalization, as was Russia's somewhat similar decision in 1985 and the subsequent collapse of European communism.

By 2005 only a few, small societies were isolated from frequent and multi-faceted contact: Myanmar (Burma) and North Korea headed this short list. Of course, openness to contact varied within societies: by 2005 only a third of the world's population had any access to the internet. Upper classes and urbanites were far more affected by contact than were the rural and the poor, and this could generate huge internal clashes over the results of contact as well. Suspicions of contact remained widespread.

A key element of globalization involves consumer exchange, of course. But there were other facets that affected gender. The global economy tended to spread the use of women workers, cheap, available and now sometimes relatively well educated. Massive exploitation could result (for men and women alike): many factories producing for the global economy paid low wages and trapped workers for long hours amid unsafe conditions. On the other hand, many women, working for multinationals, reported that they found pay and treatment better than in local firms; here was, among other things, the basis for some modest indulgence in consumerism. By far the worst problems occurred when global competition led to increased unemployment, particularly among the young. Here, too, there could be gender implications. Young men frequently had higher unemployment rates than young women. Efforts to find compensatory outlets for masculinity, including protest and (in some cases) terrorism could result. But global economic dislocations also encouraged an increasing sex trade, in which women were seized or induced to go to centers in places like Thailand where sexual tourism thrived. The global economy could unsettle established gender standards, but in a variety of ways.

Global rights campaigns

Global political institutions expanded, many with a direct stake in gender reform. The establishment of the United Nations in 1945 intensified themes that international feminism had pushed in earlier decades. The UN Charter and the ensuing Declaration of Human Rights stipulated legal and political equality for women, along with equal pay for equal work. Various conventions in the 1950s and 1960s pushed for "the equal right of men and women in the enjoyment of all civil and political rights". In 1975, carrying the effort further, the UN proclaimed the "International Woman's Year", complete with a major conference in Mexico City that thundered against "sex-based discrimination" and "condemned all the great historic deprivations imposed on women as a group". A spokesperson made the new international goals quite explicit: "to make the social roles of the two sexes, with the notable exception of child-bearing, as nearly interchangeable or equivalent as possible". Subsequent "decades" and "years" of women simply expanded on these themes, with meetings in various parts of the world.

By the 1970s, the number of international women's organizations also soared: 59 new groups were formed between 1940 and 1974, then another thirteen per year between 1976 and 1985. Many were local groups in active contact with umbrella organizations, exchanging information and motivation. We have seen the increased activity in, and international attention to, gender issues in Africa, but Latin America and other areas were also important sites. Both international agencies and nongovernmental organizations also steadily expanded their agendas. By the 1990s rape had been declared a war crime – another first in world history. In 2004 the venerable rights organization Amnesty International declared a campaign against domestic violence, claiming that a third of all women worldwide were subject to unacceptable abuse. Population conferences – a major United Nations effort occurred in Cairo in 1994 – while facing religious objections to birth control and abortion from Catholics, Muslims and the United States government, also pressed to provide greater facilities for women to make their own decisions about birth rates. It was possible to agree that women should have greater access to education, which would provide greater access to alternatives to traditional birth-rate levels.

An American historian, Judith Zinsser, who participated in the 1995 "woman's year" conference in Beijing, made the point clear: international efforts had "made the rhetoric of feminism the common phrasing of national and international speeches and reports. The world community has acknowledged that women live in an inferior condition and that this situation is not acceptable." This was, in truth, an extraordinary innovation in the long history of international contacts relating to gender.

Results of global standards

The problem, of course, lay in interpreting significance and impact. Many people were largely ignorant of these proclamations, despite the proliferation of local groups. Many – including many women – disagreed with them, preferring traditions and more regional identities. Men and male-dominated governments, as we have seen in Africa, might accept international rhetoric but then undermine it in practice. Waves of regional conflict, as in the Balkans in the 1990s and various parts of Africa between the mid-1990s and the ensuing decade, subjected women to massive violence, including sexual violence, and displacement. Some of this involved retaliations for real or imagined slights to masculinity by previous colonial administrations or the larger forces of global change.

Changes introduced with a reformist intent, like Chinese population policy, might have unexpected gender consequences. China clearly hoped that its policy, though distinctive, would put the country in line with the population stability of the industrial world, making economic growth easier. As many Chinese interpreted the policy, combining innovation and tradition, female infanticide revived, while 90 percent of all orphaned children were girls: the goal was to accept the new policy but maintain the older preference for sons. An unsettling further result, by the early twenty-first century, was a huge numerical gap between young men and young women. It was going to be hard for many young men to find female partners, and this posed its own dangers for gender behavior.

Inconsistencies in globalization also challenged the international consensus on women's rights. It was fine to sign agreements on equal pay for equal work, but many global corporations, and local firms as well, eagerly sought and found women workers whose main charm was exceptionally low salaries. On another front, international pronouncements did not seem to be keeping pace with sex trafficking. The contemporary world of contacts was immensely complicated, and global rights rhetoric was only one ingredient, and not necessarily the most important.

Diversity of resistance

Finally, a significant countercurrent developed, urging regional identities and conventions over international standards or even recommending alternatives. Two related trends emerged.

The first, familiar enough, was the resurgence of religious and other conservatism, often directed explicitly against changes in gender relations such as global consumerism or shared rights. Islamic, Hindu and many Christian fundamentalists all urged a more traditional gender hierarchy and the importance of female modesty, and their voices were growing.

Equally interesting, if less important numerically, was the growing group of women's leaders who objected to international standards because they were too Western and too individualistic. These were people who wanted women to have an active voice in their lives and societies but who did not find the international formulas persuasive. An Indian woman's magazine thus objected to global consumerism on the grounds that it tended to force women to waste time and effort on personal beauty in the hope of finding and keeping men. Far better, in terms of real women's interests, was the Indian custom of arranged marriages, which made the Western appearances game irrelevant. A host of Muslim leaders, eager to defy aspects of the traditional interpretation of Islam (often including veiling) in the interest of fuller women's rights, also resisted the notion that Western feminism provided a desirable option. Reformed Islam itself could be the basis of a more relevant statement of rights; there was no need for outside standards. A Nigerian woman intellectual, Idi Amadiumi, contends that Western feminists assume they monopolize truth, looking down on African alternatives. But Western feminism, she argues, had pulled women out of protective community structures, left them too individually vulnerable – for example, to poverty. The solution is not the international rights wisdom, but a revived African traditionalism that will see men and women alike joined in community, with women regaining a customary public voice that Western colonialism, seeking domesticity for women, had eliminated. Amadiumi claimed that a growing number of Western-educated African women were "preaching the doctrine of cultural revival" not for the sake of traditional identity but because it would provide more opportunities and protections for women than international standards did.

Finally, of course, at the grassroots level, many ordinary women sought to effect compromise, using new standards to a degree but combining them with older goals. Thus a grandmother in Kenya talks of the importance of education for women so they can find for themselves, and also accepts new levels of birth control. But beneath this interestingly cosmopolitan surface she hopes not for individual fulfillment for her granddaughters, but for a revived family cohesion in which different generations of women will take care of each other, regardless of what the men do. International influences have had some effect, here, but more on the means by which goals were to be met than on the purposes themselves. Here is a familiar syncretic result of contact, operating even amid the pressures of globalization.

Conclusion

Clearly, globalization, building on earlier contacts, produced a truly revolutionary context for discussion of gender relations. The novelty was striking, with no precedent in world history. Clearly, also, a variety of gaps remained between rhetoric and reality. Novelty itself spurred resistance and compromise. Globalization remained a contested project overall, and gender focused many of the debates and uncertainties.

Further reading

H. Pietila and J. Vickers, *Making Women Matter: The Role of the United Nations* (New York: Zed Books, 1990); A. Winslow, ed., *Women, Politics and the United Nations* (Westport, Conn.: Greenwood, 1995); D. Zoelle, *Globalizing Concerns for Women's Human Rights: The Failure of the American Model* (New York: Palgrave Macmillan, 2000); D. Sienstra, *Women's Movements and International Organizations* (New York: St. Martin's, 1994); Nadine Berkovitch, *From Motherhood to Citizenship: Women's Rights and International Organizations* (Baltimore, Md: Johns Hopkins, 1999); Peter N. Stearns, *Global Outrage: The Impact of World Opinion on Contemporary History* (London: OneWorld, 2005).

Conclusion

Patterns and trends

A collective look at key cases of international interchange that affected male–female relationships invites three evaluations. All respond to the legitimate question: what happens when one moves from a set of good individual stories to an inquiry about broader patterns? The first evaluation, and it can be brief, involves the range of contacts itself. The second seeks generalizations about the results of contact on gender, and whether any patterns emerge. The third, looking at the historical cases sequentially, asks about any trends of change over time.

Typologies

Using results on men and women as a vantage-point on the nature of cultural interchange drives home key characteristics of interchange itself. World historians increasingly emphasize contact as one of the anchors of their ambitious subject, a means of linking individual societies to broader, sometimes global processes. The gender dimension illustrates how varied contacts can be. They range from casual, limited exchange to the complex results of introducing a new religion into an established cultural system. They can include interaction among relatively equal societies, but also virtual cultural compulsion, as in Western Europe's approach to Native Americans – and various possibilities in between the two extremes. Along with variety, the gender factor consistently suggests complexity; even the most overt cultural compulsion does not generate the expected or desired results.

Contacts also embrace unexpected tie-ins. The spread of Islam included interaction with other Middle Eastern practices such as veiling; Christianity often was linked with unusual Western definitions of family life and domesticity; international consumerism combines glitz and style with messages about women's distinctive obligations to beauty, a blend of seeming freedom and new compulsions. Interaction packages are untidy.

Impacts

What role has cultural exchange played in confirming or changing men's and women's ideals and behaviors? Here, the examination of the kinds of contacts in world history that affected gender relations suggests several general points. The first, admittedly, is simply cautious: each case of contact is distinctive, the consequences often complex and hard to predict. There are no easy "laws of history" in this area. Thus contact may promote better conditions for women in relation to men, or the precise opposite – or, most commonly, some combination effect. Variation depends on the complexity of the outside influences but also on prior customs in the receiving society, which is why no two cases are exactly alike.

Variety shows in patterns of timing. Some contacts seem to affect men's and women's behaviors rather quickly; a case in point may be the impact of Buddhism on China, where women could use Buddhism as an outlet without disturbing fundamental gender relationships. Certainly contacts that involve compulsion, like the European entry to the Americas, can make an effect quickly, but some contacts work out only over prolonged periods, like the impact of Islam on parts of India. There are simply no clear regularities. Will some of the new contacts that developed in the twentieth-century world also vary in the time it takes to determine basic results?

Beliefs and institutions surrounding male–female interactions are extremely important in any society. They often seem part of the society's identity, and of the identity of individuals within it. They often, indeed, seem Absolutely True – based on human nature or divine command – and not open to alternatives. This is why cultural exchange may have relatively little effect, particularly when the two societies in contact are roughly equal, so that borrowing can be quite selective. Thus the views on women that were valued in the Middle East were not widely imported into sub-Saharan west Africa, even when the religion, Islam, was adopted; thus the early exchange between Indian and Greek cultures, after Alexander's contacts, had little result on gender patterns. When exchanges involve greater inequality, with one powerful society impinging on another, efforts to alter male and female roles may nevertheless be strongly resisted, even when other cultural offerings are accepted. This of course is one reason gender arrangements continue to vary even when international contacts grow tighter.

Another society's gender arrangements are hard to understand. The history of cultural contacts is full of examples where well-meaning outsiders simply could not grasp the actual meaning of men's and women's roles when they differed from those they were accustomed to back home. Here is another reason that culture contact produced less change than some intended (or yielded results that no one expected).

Contacts are frequently multifaceted, which complicates overall impact and may nullify or redirect reform efforts. Missionary Christianity usually combined with the economic changes induced by colonial commerce. Both forces might encourage women's domesticity, but Christian educational efforts and economic dislocation did not mesh so easily. International feminism in the twentieth century pushed for new rights, but growing male–female job differentials in some societies may require a more defensive stance. The impact of consumer lures may also counter that of feminism, another twentieth-century tangle of literally global importance.

But contact does produce change in many cases. Pressure from a powerful culture can combine with advantages that groups in the other society see in the alternatives now visible. Complexity results from the common impulse toward syncretism: societies tend to borrow some elements and combine them with homegrown components, thus producing a system that differs both from tradition and from the foreign model. (The new system may, correspondingly, be disapproved both by local conservatives and by foreign observers.) Complexity also results from the common tendency of key groups – perhaps men in particular, as the sex that characteristically enjoys the higher status – to use gender as a way to compensate for problems in other aspects of a cultural exchange. When men feel their economic situation threatened by new foreign trade, or their political power overturned by outside control, they may seek changes in gender relations to give them some new advantage. This is another reason that imported ideas so often have unforeseen consequences and why gains for women flowing from new reform notions may be undercut by deteriorations in other respects.

Using historical cases, in sum, helps us look for examples of syncretism or efforts at compensatory power when a new case of cultural contact is presented. This is more than a classroom result. Societies today and in future will continue to develop new patterns of interaction that may call existing gender arrangements into question. The 1991 Gulf War, for example, brought large numbers of American military women into Saudi Arabia, a crucial American ally in the conflict. The Saudis faced obvious dilemmas about how to please their powerful friend while minimizing impacts of American gender habits on their own women, while Americans also had to decide how to avoid offense, for example in the dress codes or public activities allowed their servicewomen. Precisely because ideas and practices concerning men and women continue to vary widely, even as international contacts increase, the story is ongoing. The history of gender-in-contact does not allow precise forecasts, but it suggests some common analytical issues and possibilities.

Change over time

Have there been trends in the history of gender-in-contact over time in world history? We have seen that some of the key frameworks that help shape the results of exchange have shifted. The rise or spread of the great world religions constituted an important new component in international contacts from the third century CE onward. More recently, while religions continue to affect relationships between men and women, new and more secular value systems, such as consumerism and feminism, have come to play a greater role when different cultures interact.

The period between 1500 and 1900 stands out from what happened either before or since. This was the period when cultural contacts largely supported greater rigor in gender relations, despite attacks on specific symbols of inequality such as *sati*. European standards, when asserted in other societies, had some built-in limitations (for instance, ideas about what appropriate women's work or property rights were, or what sexual respectability meant), and Europeans' insistence on the superiority of their own values often reduced flexibility as well. Compared to earlier international influences, then, Europeans offered some distinctive components. Reactions within other societies also played a role, however, when men sought new authority over women to compensate for insecurities and limitations they experienced as Europe's power widened.

In contrast, results of cultural exchange prior to this period were often varied, seldom overturning earlier patterns but moving in different potential directions. Buddhist impact on China thus for a time created new alternatives, whereas Chinese influence on Japan illustrated another case of a powerful society imposing some of its gender rigidities through contact.

And what of the twentieth century? The imposition of Western values remained powerful, but these values were no longer those of earlier times, particularly as they included more sweeping definitions of women's rights and a standard commitment to women's education. Further, the decline of colonialism increased the power of other societies to point out limitations in the "Western" approach – limitations even in the capacity of Western feminism to define what was good for women elsewhere. International contact, including the role of international organizations concerned with gender issues, was more likely in the twentieth century to be associated with reform than with reinforcements of patriarchy, though evaluation remains complicated. Certainly, the increased pace of international exchange made alternative gender arrangements more visible than ever before, pressing societies to conceal, resist or adapt in new ways. This is a pressure for change that is clearly continuing into the twenty-first century.

Some American sociologists describe what they call a "global culture", emerging over the past 150 years, and setting standards for behavior and policy that are widely accepted across national boundaries. Gender, in this formulation, is a key component. Global cultural norms argue that women and men should share basic educational opportunities and voting rights, and that women should be protected from distinctive forms of abuse like domestic violence and rape. We have seen that modern forms of contact, including the thrust of current Western influence and the impact of the preponderance of international movements, do indeed push in these directions. But, if change accelerates, so do efforts at compromise and outright resistance. Gender can be a locus of counterattack against what are seen as excessive outside controls or pressures to change. These are time-honored features of the contact process as well, and they have certainly not disappeared – indeed, they, too, may expand. The nature of contact has changed, its impact has undeniably intensified, but exchange remains complex and, often, rather unpredictable. And this means that history must continue to inform any realistic analysis.

Index